Collaborative Decision Making

The Pathway to Inclusion

ELLENMORRIS TIEGERMAN-FARBER
Adelphi University

CHRISTINE RADZIEWICZ
*School for Language and
Communication Development*

MERRILL,
an imprint of Prentice Hall
Upper Saddle River, New Jersey ✺ *Columbus, Ohio*

Library of Congress Cataloging-in-Publication Data

Tiegerman-Farber, Ellenmorris.
   Collaborative decision making : the pathway to inclusion /
Ellenmorris Tiegerman-Farber, Christine Radziewicz.
     p. cm.
   Includes bibliographical references and index.
   ISBN 0-13-382086-6
    1. Inclusive education—United States—Decision making.
  2. Mainstreaming in education—United States—Decision making.
  I. Radziewicz, Christine. II. Title.
LC1201.T54 1998
371.9'046—dc21
                                                        97-21687
                                                              CIP

Cover art: Lauren Rosen, age 14, is a former student of the School for Language and Communication
                  Development on Long Island in New York. Her talents were discovered and she won a scholarship
                  award for the "Imagination Celebration" art contest for students from kindergarten through 12th
                  grade. Her work was displayed in the state capitol in Albany . . . she being the youngest winner
                  and only in 1st grade. Lauren has illustrated other educational texts by Dr. Tiegerman-Farber. Her
                  ambitions are to go to France to study art and become a fashion designer and model.

Editor: Ann Castel Davis
Production Editor: Mary M. Irvin
Design Coordinator: Julia Zonneveld Van Hook
Text Designer: Rebecca Bobb
Cover Designer: Tom Mack
Production Manager: Patricia A. Tonneman
Director of Marketing: Kevin Flanagan
Marketing Manager: Suzanne Stanton
Advertising/Marketing Coordinator: Julie Shough

This book was set in Galliard by Carlisle Communications, Inc., and was printed and bound by
Bookpress. The cover was printed by Phoenix Color Corp.

© 1998 by Prentice-Hall, Inc.
A Pearson Education Company
Upper Saddle River, NJ 07458

Photo credits: Tom Watson/Merrill: xvi; Anne Vega/Merrill: 14, 64, 181; Scott Cunningham/
Merrill: 24; Barbara Schwartz/Merrill: 39, 87, 132, 158; Todd Yarrington/Merrill: 114, 211;
Anthony Magnacca/Merrill: 190.

Printed in the United States of America

10 9 8 7 6 5 4 3 2

ISBN: 0-13-382086-6

Prentice-Hall International (UK) Limited,London
Prentice-Hall of Australia Pty. Limited, Sydney
Prentice-Hall Canada Inc., Toronto
Prentice-Hall Hispanoamericana, S.A., Mexico
Prentice-Hall of India Private Limited, New Delhi
Prentice-Hall of Japan, Inc., Tokyo
Pearson Education Asia Pte. Ltd., Singapore
Editora Prentice-Hall do Brasil, Ltda., Rio de Janeiro

P R E F A C E

*J*ust as a developing child may grow in ways we can't predict, a book can develop into something quite different from what an author first envisions. This textbook has been through a transformational process that reflects significant changes in our thinking. Perhaps the best advice that we could share with all of our readers is the fact that inclusion, if it is going to be successfully implemented, requires the combined commitment of all of the stakeholders. If the process of collaboration begins with the understanding that parents and teachers cannot and should not be coerced into a classroom context that does not coincide with their belief system about education, then inclusion has a chance within the public schools.

ORGANIZATION OF THE TEXT

This textbook describes theoretical as well as practical information necessary to begin the process of planning for inclusive classrooms.

Chapters 1 and 2 ("Mainstreaming and Inclusion: A Historical and Legal Overview and Program" and "Placement Issues") describe the historical issues underlying special education policies, procedures, and regulations. It is important to understand the changes in theoretical thinking in order to appreciate the issues underlying educational reform in special education.

Chapter 3 ("The Collaborative Team") discusses the mechanism by which educational stakeholders will make decisions about inclusive classrooms and resources. It is our opinion that only through collaboration can inclusion successfully be achieved. Collaborative decision making is a process that will transform all of the individuals involved. The collaborative process requires a group consensus and mutual respect that must be developed over time. Parents, teachers, and administrators approach the collaborative process as equals, each having something significant to share. The nature of this relationship is dramatically different from anything that presently exists within the public schools. Top-down decision making must be replaced by the collaborative decisions of school-based teams. It is the collaborative relationship that must be established first to ensure that programming will be appropriately implemented.

Chapter 4 ("Collaboration for Inclusion") provides several case study examples of how collaboration can be applied to the development of an inclusive classroom. The special needs of children, parents, teachers, and administrators are discussed intensively to highlight the complexities related to the decision-making process. This chapter also describes the specific modifications that must be made to develop an inclusive classroom for children with and without disabilities.

Chapter 5 ("The Role of the Family in the Collaborative Process") describes the changing role of parents within the educational system. It also discusses the fact that not only parents of children with disabilities, but also parents of children without disabilities must be committed to the inclusive process if schools are going to reorganize classrooms successfully. The time has come for parents to function as equal collaborators in school-based decision making.

Chapter 6 ("Formalizing a Collaborative Model: Questions and Answers") describes how various professionals are engaged in a collaborative process to create inclusive classrooms at the School for Language and Communication Development. This chapter provides an insight into the thoughts and feelings of parents and teachers in various educational settings about the barriers that interfere with effective collaboration. Finally, a survey completed by 56 school districts presents some of the barrier issues that must be addressed in order for inclusion to be successfully achieved.

For us, this has been an extraordinary process of learning and development. Although many of our ideas have changed in the process of writing this textbook, one central idea has not changed—collaboration is the key to successful inclusion. Departments of education nationwide beware: the degree to which departments mandate inclusive assignments without a collaborative process is the degree to which the system will fail. We have also learned that part of the transformational process includes bureaucratic thinking; this may in fact be the most significant barrier to the success of this mission.

ACKNOWLEDGMENTS

In beginning the Acknowledgments section, before we each separately identify individuals in our lives who have supported us through this time-consuming creative process, we both acknowledge Ann Davis (Senior Editor of Special Education) at Merrill/Prentice Hall. In working with you over the years, Ann, we both recognize your extraordinary talents in the field of education. We would also like to acknowledge that you have a natural ability—a talent to work with highly stressed academicians and challenge their creativities to stay focused and to complete a very intricate tapestry—one that captures the essence of our professional thinking and philosophy— a textbook. Wherever you go, Ann, take us with you.

Over the past several years, my personal and professional lessons have been experienced most profoundly with those that I love. To my husband, Joseph Farber, there are no words to express my deep love and devotion. You remain the very center and core of who I am.

To my children, you have taught me a great deal about myself as a mother, a parent, and a teacher. I thank my children, Jonathan, Jeremy, Andrew, Douglas, Dana, and

Leslie—from you I have learned more than any course or textbook could possibly teach. The most important lesson that I have learned from all of you is that life is most fulfilled within the framework of a family. We teach that to each other and we teach that to ourselves.

My deepest appreciation goes to the Honorable Dean G. Skelos, Deputy Majority Leader, New York State Senate, 9th District. As a legislator and staunch supporter of preschool special education, you represent a symbol in government—at its best—at its final hour of achievement. It is important for you to know that everything that I have written over the years and worked towards at the School for Language and Communication Development reflects the work that you have done in the New York State Legislature. Without your support and commitment to children and families in New York State, there would not be a School for Language and Communication Development. Your vision of education in New York State has enabled thousands of preschool children to achieve their potential in life. There are not enough words in this book to thank you for all that you have done for the children and families at SLCD. Truly, you are a shining symbol as a legislator. Finally, in all of these years, you have never once lost your patience with me and for that I am especially grateful.

My love, devotion, and respect go to Dr. Stephen Cavallo, Dr. Helene Mermelstein, Mrs. Andrea Rieger, Mrs. Rosemarie King, Mrs. Marie Dalli, Ms. Joanne King, and Mr. Andrew Plastrik for being the support, the heart, and the soul of the SLCD mission. To Florence Lieberman—you are the best executive secretary.

To the parents of SLCD— education is the cornerstone of life. You are the first teacher and primary advocate for your children. You must never be silent and you must always advocate excellence.

To the professionals at SLCD, I give you the spirit and the future of education. I hope that your experiences at SLCD will remain as a cornerstone in your personal and professional lives. In being here together at SLCD, we have created an extraordinary vision of education. We will share this vision and this experience wherever we go in our lives.

To SLCD's Board of Directors—Paul Rosen, Joseph Gnesin, Mark Weinstein, Toya Davis, Bonnye Kaufman, and Mario Fischetti—with all the perspiration and frustration, there is great inspiration. Thank you for your strength, suggestions and support.

To the reviewers of the manuscript—I thank you for your insights and thoughtful suggestions: Mark P. Mostert, Moorhead State University; and Diane T. Woodrum, West Virginia University.

To my parents, Morris and Rita Jacobs: I give you another book—in return for all those books that you gave me—those I read, and these I write. My love and gratitude for all of your years of giving—to me.

Finally, to my colleague Dr. Christine Radziewicz, I express my admiration and my deepest friendship. We have been together as colleagues for 14 years and there has never been a harsh word between us. In writing this book together, we share our vision for education and our mission for excellence with all of our colleagues in the field. If this were a movie, I would suggest a number of "sequels."

Dr. Ellenmorris Tiegerman-Farber

No creative work is achieved without support and inspiration from many people at both the professional and personal levels. This book reflects the influence of all the children, parents, and educational teams at the School for Language and Communication Development. You are my models; you are the future of special education. I thank you. I am also grateful to my friends and colleagues. First, I would like to thank Dr. Tiegerman-Farber; you are tireless, loving, and forever dedicated to the children. Next, very special thanks to Rosemarie King; you are the sparkle and energy of the School for Language and Communication Development. A special understanding of collaboration has been an outgrowth of our conversations. I also want to acknowledge Marie Dalli and Andrew Plastrik. Your support enabled me to devote the time required on an endeavor such as this, and you have worked hard to develop the collaborative teaming model at SLCD. My thanks go to Dr. Helene Mermelstein as well. You have enabled me to consider collaboration from a psychological perspective. To Jacqueline Ilardi I send a grateful thank you. You keep me organized, on time, and moving.

I also want to acknowledge my mother, Veronica, and my children, Alisa and Hank. You have patiently endured the time demands that writing places on authors. Lastly, I thank Tom. You have given your time, support, and encouragement without which this book could not have been written.

Dr. Christine Radziewicz

*A*s a New York State senator and a legislator for many years, I have had the opportunity to work closely with issues involving educational policy and reform. The issues discussed in this textbook are reflective of theoretical and educational discussions taking place across the nation involving school reform. I believe that educational policy must reflect the diversity of children and families in various communities. Schools cannot function apart from the children that are served and the complex needs that they present in our society. Schools must be a mirror for excellence, individual achievement, and family values. Educational reform provides us with an extraordinary opportunity to reorganize our schools for the twenty-first century.

This textbook raises many issues about decisions that must be made by parents and teachers as partners in the child achievement process. Education will succeed only if parents and teachers both invest in a mutual belief that the classroom environment will provide significant benefit for child learning. This may not represent a new idea to education but the challenge of inclusion requires that schools formalize a process for decision making so that parents and teachers will contribute to all levels of reorganization. Many of the problems that schools have faced involve the lack of collaborative interaction between the primary stakeholders, parents and teachers. The altruism of inclusion is a mission, but it has a message that must become a reality. There are, of course, pragmatic aspects in all missions, and the solution to inclusion involves the ongoing working relationship between parents and teachers, given the reality of "everyday issues" in inclusive classrooms with typical children *and* children with developmental disabilities. In reforming the schools, we must raise some difficult questions. How will the role of teachers change in inclusive classrooms? How do we ensure that typical children and children with development disabilities will benefit from inclusive classrooms? How will parents and teachers establish collaborative models to develop inclusive classrooms?

Finally, the mission of inclusion must be considered given the individual rights of individuals with disabilities. The continuum of services within P.L. 94-142 ensures that decisions involving the placement of children within the least restrictive environment will be based on the individual needs of the child. As a moral society, we must never lose sight of the individual child. As a moral society, our policies must ensure that programs and services will challenge children to achieve—*all* children.

Inclusion presents the opportunity to reorganize our thinking about individual classrooms in diverse communities throughout America. Although the issues may be complex and the emotions high, the process of collaboration will strengthen our educational foundation. In working with Dr. Tiegerman-Farber and Dr. Radziewicz over the years, I share their commitment to educational policy and the need for school reform. We must ask probing questions in order to reorganize the most fundamental experience for our children—education. Our schools must be reorganized to reflect our communities and our continued commitment to international standards of excellence in a world-wide economy. Education safeguards our American values and culture. An educated society protects the history and the heritage of which we are all proud.

The Honorable Dean G. Skelos
Deputy Majority Leader
New York State Senate

C O N T E N T S

CHAPTER 1
MAINSTREAMING AND INCLUSION: A HISTORICAL AND LEGAL OVERVIEW   1

The Impact of Legislation on Special Education   2
> *Education for All Handicapped Children Act*   2
> *Individuals with Disabilities Education Act*   3

Mainstreaming   4
> *Normalization Principle*   4
> *Least Restrictive Environment*   6
> *One State's Interpretation of Least Restrictive Environment*   8

Inclusion   10
> *Historical Review*   10
> *Inclusion Concept*   12
> *Legal Support*   15
> *Children's Characteristics*   17

Questions for Classroom Discussion   22

Bibliography   22

CHAPTER 2
PROGRAM AND PLACEMENT ISSUES   24

Program Descriptions and Options   26
> *Home Instruction*   26
> *Special Education Schools*   26
> *Special Education Within School Districts*   27
> *Self-Contained Classes*   27
> *Resource Room Program*   28
> *Special Education Within the School District with Partial Mainstreaming*   28
> *Consultant Teacher Services*   29

Practical Concerns Related to Inclusion   30
> *Child Diversity*   31
> *Levels of Ability and Types of Mainstreaming*   32

Classroom Environment 34
Type of Disability 36
Socialization 37
Communication 37
Teacher Staff Issues 38
Benefit 40
Curriculum Development 40

Teacher Issues 45
Teacher Attitudes 49
Special Education Teachers 51

District Issues 55
District Planning 55
Resources 55
Teacher Training 58

Conclusion 60

A Few Words from Cathy Ambrosio 61

Questions for Classroom Discussion 62

Bibliography 63

CHAPTER 3
THE COLLABORATIVE TEAM

65

The Inclusion Classroom 68

Teachers 70
Coequality and Coparticipation 70
Reciprocity 71
Common Goals 74
Team Teaching and Coteaching 77
Designing the Classroom 79
Curriculum 81
Administrators 84
Parents 87

Parents 88
Coequality and Coparticipation 89
Reciprocity 91
Common Goals 91
Parent–Teacher Teaming 95
Designing the Classroom 97
Curriculum 98

Teachers 99
Administrators 104

Administrators   104
  Coequality and Coparticipation 105
  Reciprocity 105
  Common Goals 106
  Designing the Classroom 106
  Teachers 108
  Parents 108

Conclusion   108

A Few Words from Lucy O'Sullivan   109

Questions for Classroom Discussion   110

Bibliography   111

CHAPTER 4
COLLABORATION FOR INCLUSION   **115**

Collaborative Teaming and Decision Making   116
  Identify the Problem 117
  Identify Ways to Solve the Problem 118
  Possible Results and Recommendations 118
  Responsible Decision Making 119
  Evaluating the Decision 120

Cultural and Linguistic Diversity   120

The Development of an Inclusive Curriculum   122
  Classroom Cultural Goals 122
  Academic Goals 123

Curriculum Modification   126
  Levels of Development 126
  Curriculum Development 126

Program Modifications   127
  Designing the Inclusion Classroom: A Prototype 127
  Equipment 128

Classroom Modifications: Building on Diversity   130
  Type of Disability 130
  Number of Children with Disabilities 131
  Level of Disability 131
  Age versus Stage of Children with Disabilities 133

Classroom Modifications   134

Teachers   134
Regular Education Teachers: Attitudes   135
Special Education Teachers: Attitudes   136
Professional Modifications   137

The Inclusion Experience: Determining Child Benefit   138
Catherine   138
Alex   142

Beginning the Inclusion Process   146
Early Intervention   146
Diversity of Needs   147
Twenty-First Century Vision   148

A Few Words from Millie Alpert   149

Questions for Classroom Discussion   152

Bibliography   154

CHAPTER 5
THE ROLE OF THE FAMILY IN THE COLLABORATIVE PROCESS   159

The Role of Parents   161

Parent and Family Issues   163
Cultural Determinism   164
Linguistic Differences   165
Economic Pressures   166
Alternative Family Dynamics   167
Gender and Ethnicity   168
Educational Expectations   169

Understanding the Needs of Parents   170
Parents of Children with Disabilities: Attitudes   172
Parents of Regular Education Children: Attitudes   172
Support Groups   173
Parent Network Groups   173
Parents in the Classroom   174
Parent Education Classes   174
Listening to the Concerns of Parents   174
Parent Advocacy and Empowerment   175
Parent Choice and Educational Coercion   176
Collaboration Modifications   176

Overcoming Differences   177
Developing a Family Profile   177
The Perceptual Report Card   178

Resolving Conflicts   182
Communication Feedback   182
Parent Meeting Room   183
Communication Problems: Confusing Messages   183

Conclusion   184

A Philosophical Point of View   185

Questions for Classroom Discussion   187

Bibliography   187

Chapter 6
Formalizing a Collaborative Model:
Questions and Answers   191

Question 1: Do You Have the Competency Skills Necessary for Collaboration?
How Are These Skills Developed within Your Discipline Area?   195
Response: Regular Education Teacher Surveys   195
Response: School Psychologist   195
Response: Regular Education Teacher   196
Response: Dance Movement Therapist   198
Response: Special Education Teacher   199
Response: Music Therapist   199
Response: Special Education Teacher   200
Response: Speech–Language Pathologist   200

Analysis and Discussion   201

Question 2:   How Do You Collaborate with Other Team Members and
Professionals in School? Does Collaboration Always Work?   202
Response: Regular Education Teacher Surveys   202
Response: School Psychologist   203
Response: Regular Education Teacher   204
Response: Dance Movement Therapist   206
Response: Special Education Teacher   206
Response: Regular Education Teacher   207

Analysis and Discussion   208

Question 3:   How Do You Collaborate with Parents?   210
Response: Regular Education Teacher Surveys   210
Response: School Psychologist   210
Response: Music Therapist   212
Response: Speech–Language Pathologist   212
Response: Special Education Teacher   212

Analysis and Discussion   213

Question 4:   Is Inclusion Appropriate for ALL Children with Disabilities?   214
    Response: Regular Education Teacher Surveys   214
    Response: School Psychologist   215
    Response: Music Therapist   215
    Response: Special Education Teacher   217
    Response: Occupational Therapist   218
    Response: Special Education Teacher   218
    Response: Speech–Language Pathologist   219
    Response: Speech–Language Pathologist   220

Analysis and Discussion   221

A Few Words from Toya Davis   224

Questions for Classroom Discussion   225

Bibliography   225

Appendix   227

Epilogue   233

Index   235

1

Mainstreaming and Inclusion: A Historical and Legal Overview

LEARNING OBJECTIVES

After you have read this chapter, you should be able to:

1. Identify the following acronyms:
   LRE
   FAPE
   IEP
   CPSE
   CSE
   IDEA
   REI
   P.L. 94-142
   P.L. 99-457

2. Trace the history of special education legislation from 1975 to the present and discuss the changes that have occurred.

3. Identify and explain the principle on which mainstreaming is based.

4. Discuss mainstreaming in terms of process and continuum of program options.

5. Discuss the concept of LRE and the controversy surrounding it.

6. Explain how REI has propelled school reform and inclusion programming.

7. Discuss the relationship between mainstreaming and inclusion.

8. Discuss what variables and considerations come into play when planning inclusion programming for the child with disabilities.

S ince 1975, special education has grown and expanded in terms of a proliferation of programs, educational philosophies, professional practice, and funding mechanisms. During the past two decades, special education programs (along with the special educator) have been monitored, regulated, evaluated, and critiqued by public officials, parents, and researchers interested in educational policy as it applies to program efficacy.

Over time, however, new issues have emerged. Limited resources and general dissatisfaction with American education have focused attention on the growing costs of special education. Clearly, education today serves more than just "school-age" children. There are now programs for infants, toddlers, and preschoolers with a variety of developmental disabilities. These populations and programs create a further demand and strain on an educational system that is already feeling the effects of decreased funding. Also, additional social problems compete with the public's demand for education reform: Equity issues, parental concerns, violence, teenage pregnancy, HIV-AIDS, alcoholism, drug abuse, school dropouts, welfare reform, and managed health proposals all require funding.

THE IMPACT OF LEGISLATION ON SPECIAL EDUCATION

Education for All Handicapped Children Act

Educators and legislators have been reviewing the Education for All Handicapped Children Act with a view toward reform. Two public laws, Public Law 94-142 (1975) and Public Law 99-457 (1986) make up the content of the Education for All Handicapped Children Act. The first of these laws, P.L. 94-142, enacted more than 20 years ago, continues to be a critical force in maintaining the educational rights of children with disabilities throughout the United States. This law details several important programmatic components:

- The development of an Individualized Education Program (IEP)
- The right to be educated in the least restrictive environment (LRE)
- The provision of appropriate services depending on educational and developmental needs
- Parental involvement.

The purpose of the Education for All Handicapped Children Act (EAHCA) was to assist states in providing children with disabilities with a series of educational opportunities and to establish minimum education requirements for obtaining eligibility for public funding. In addition to providing a free and appropriate public education, the EAHCA also requires that each state have a "plan which details the policies and procedures which ensure the provider of the right" [Section 1312(2)]. In other words, each state is required to establish procedural safeguards to ensure that local educational agencies within the state create the Individualized Education Programs required by this law—to formulate a plan for educating students with disabilities. Therefore, community and local school districts can no longer exclude children from participating in public school programs, services, and classrooms. Further, all of the rights and protections of P.L. 94-142 were extended to preschoolers with disabilities through the enactment of the amendments to the EAHCA in 1986. The expanded law provides for the development of comprehensive services and early intervention programs for infants, toddlers, and preschoolers with disabilities and their families.

Individuals with Disabilities Education Act

In 1990, Public Law 101-476 reauthorized Public Law 94-142. It also changed the name of P.L. 94-142 from Education of All Handicapped Children Act to Individuals with Disabilities Education Act (IDEA). The time line shown here outlines the development of these education laws and amendments.

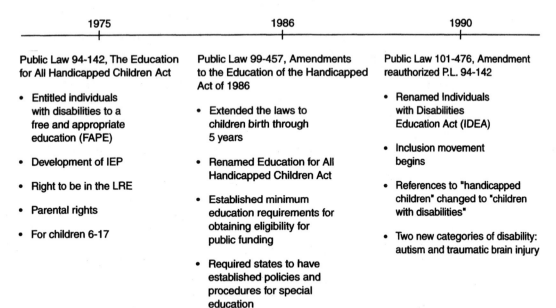

1975	1986	1990
Public Law 94-142, The Education for All Handicapped Children Act	Public Law 99-457, Amendments to the Education of the Handicapped Act of 1986	Public Law 101-476, Amendment reauthorized P.L. 94-142
• Entitled individuals with disabilities to a free and appropriate education (FAPE)	• Extended the laws to children birth through 5 years	• Renamed Individuals with Disabilities Education Act (IDEA)
• Development of IEP	• Renamed Education for All Handicapped Children Act	• Inclusion movement begins
• Right to be in the LRE	• Established minimum education requirements for obtaining eligibility for public funding	• References to "handicapped children" changed to "children with disabilities"
• Parental rights		
• For children 6-17	• Required states to have established policies and procedures for special education	• Two new categories of disability: autism and traumatic brain injury

In attempting to meet the needs of many children from diverse family and community backgrounds, educators are faced with three challenges:

1. Accountability
2. Quality
3. Individualized programming

Some legislators and other public officials seek to decrease educational costs by evaluating the efficacy of special education programs and focusing attention on "a return to general education." Educating children together is *not* a new idea. Prior to 1975, special education was not a nationalized, formalized, and recognized institutional process in American education. During the middle 1970s, students with disabilities were permitted to participate in general education when they were able to meet traditional academic expectations or when participating in recess or school assemblies. Perhaps we have completed a cycle by returning to an earlier time, but with a different perspective on educational programming. With these thoughts in mind, this chapter discusses the issues related to the mainstreaming and inclusion process.

MAINSTREAMING

Normalization Principle

Salend (1994) indicates that the philosophy of mainstreaming is based on the principle of *normalization*. Normalization for the child with disabilities involves the identification of activities, educational experiences, and social interactions that stimulate realistic and ongoing environmental events. This normalization process attempts to provide real-world challenges for children with handicapping conditions. Through these realistic experiences, children can more readily make the transition from institutional and self-contained settings to the natural, "uncontrolled" environment.

Mainstreaming is a process that incorporates a continuum of learning steps for the child with special needs; it involves a series of educational program changes that progressively approximate the general classroom experience and ultimately includes the general education classroom. Figure 1.1 describes placement options from the most specialized (residential care) to the least specialized (general education). As the child moves along the continuum of placements, the programmatic components change significantly. The program components listed in Figure 1.1 indicate some of the educational changes that may occur as the child moves along the placement continuum. Midway down the continuum, the majority of the child's academic instruction is given within the regular classroom. Other support services such as individual related services or resource room services are recommended according to the needs of the child. The last step on the continuum is inclusion in the regular classroom with regular monitoring from educational specialists to determine if the child is ready to be declassified or needs an increase in support services.

When you look at the continuum, you can clearly see the wide variety of options available to the child. It is the task of a school's Committee on Special Education (CSE) or Committee on Preschool Special Education (CPSE) to determine the needs of the individual child and which of these educational options meets those needs. It is also important to note that midway down this continuum, when the child with

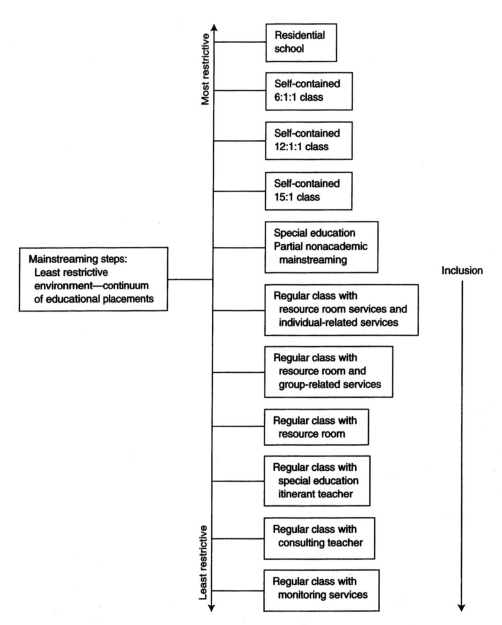

FIGURE 1.1
Continuum of placement and service options for children with disabilities.

special needs is placed in the regular education classroom, the inclusion process begins. Inclusion may take several forms. It is in reality one step along the mainstreaming continuum. It involves the social and instructional integration of children with handicapping conditions into the general education classroom. In every instance of inclusion there is an inherent responsibility to provide appropriate learning opportunities in the educational and social areas. This will often require that the academic program be adapted to meet the individual needs of the student being included.

Least Restrictive Environment

Though often used interchangeably, the *least restrictive environment* (LRE) is related to, but not the same as, the mainstreaming process. Briefly, LRE is the *mechanism* by which the child's individual needs are matched with an educational placement, whereas mainstreaming consists of a *series* of placement steps.

Because LRE has major implications for child placement and educational decision making, how each state defines the term *least restrictive environment* is often open for interpretation. School district CSEs and CPSEs use the meaning of LRE to determine the placement appropriate to meet the needs of the child with disabilities. As the child develops and progresses, his or her needs will ideally change from individualized instruction to group instruction and from special education to general education. Changes in development and educational needs of the child should be reflected in what constitutes the appropriate least restrictive environment.

Because mainstreaming and LRE are often used interchangeably by parents and teachers, it is important to separate the terms as well as the issues. Mainstreaming is a process that consists of a series of placement steps. LRE is the mechanism by which the child's individual needs are matched with an educational placement. It is the responsibility of each school's Committee on Special Education (CSE) to identify the child's individual needs based on a multidisciplinary evaluation and process of decision making. Once the committee does so, it must then decide if and how the child will be included in the general education classroom.

Figure 1.2 describes some of the factors that affect the CSE's decision-making process. A look at the factors listed will lead you to realize that some factors such as behavioral deficits, pervasive language deficits, and management needs present significant challenges to inclusion placement. Conversely, if the child has high-level communication skills, high-level socialization skills, and mild behavioral needs, the child will be readily included in a regular classroom. The CSE attempts to link the child's characteristics with his educational needs in order to identify the placement that can appropriately address those needs. In making its decision, the CSE must be able to construct an environment on paper that will benefit instructional learning and then identify a program that satisfies those educational criteria.

Figure 1.2 also describes the relationship between the child's level of functioning and the need for individualized instruction. The more severely impaired the child, the

Disorder Characteristics		Child's Needs
—Management Needs	LRE	—Small class
—Behavioral deficits	Most restrictive	—Self-contained
—Pervasive language deficits		—Individual programming
—Socialization deficits	Severe deficits	—Special education teacher
—Communication deficits	Highly individualized	
—Motor deficits		
—Self care deficits		
—Academic deficits		
—Mild behavioral needs		—Regular education classes
—Good socialization		—Inclusion programming
—Good communication skills	Least restrictive	—Regular education teacher
	Individualized	—Group learning
		—Peer facilitation

FIGURE 1.2
Factors affecting CSE decision making.

more he needs to be provided with a prescriptive individualized program. The child with severe disabilities requires a curriculum that includes intensive therapeutic programming and management instruction. This kind of curriculum often focuses on developing prereadiness and basic language–communication–social abilities and is best provided in a small self-contained classroom.

This child with pervasive learning needs may require assistive and adaptive devices if he is to be included within the general education classroom. This child's academic and social programming will require strong collaboration between regular and special educators as well as strong support personnel. Full inclusion may or may not be appropriate for this child. It is only through careful and intense assessment by the multidisciplinary team and strong communication between regular educators, special educators, and parents that an appropriate mainstreaming program can be created. Most important, however, this program must be one that enables the child with special needs to benefit socially as well as academically.

At the other end of the developmental continuum is a child with a mild disability. This is a child who can function more independently because the basic developmental building blocks of language–communication and socialization are emerging abilities within her repertoire. The child with a mild disability can socialize and interact within a larger group setting and can readily benefit from interaction with peers who do not have disabilities. She requires less individualized attention and adult-directed instruction. She can respond more readily to incidental cues and clues within the social context. She has also acquired an internal schemata that allows her to make judgments about the management of her own behavior within the social context; she can manage herself and her play interactions with peers. This is a child who presents with emerging self-regulatory behaviors, social judgment, and social awareness. Early on, prereadiness skills may not be as strong as her social skills, but it appears that she can benefit from a more challenging social context in a mainstream classroom. It is the *flexibility* in educational programming and accommodations to the child's learning style that provide for the transition into regular education for this child. As we discuss later, the inclusion process provides the transitional mechanism for the child to ultimately accomplish the regular education goal. The Opinion Box on p. 9 gives the opinions of teachers as to what kind of child should be placed in a regular classroom. Their responses clearly show that independence and high-level communication and socialization skills are critical for regular classroom placement.

One State's Interpretation of Least Restrictive Environment

New York State's definition of a least restrictive environment (LRE) indicates that the placement of students with disabilities in special classes and separate schools can occur only when the nature and severity of the disability are such that, even with the use of supplementary aides and services, education cannot be satisfactorily achieved in the regular classroom. The placement of an individual student with a disability in the least restrictive environment shall:

1. Provide the special education needed by the student
2. Provide for education of the student to the maximum extent appropriate with other students who do not have disabilities
3. Be as close as possible to the student's home

Historically, federal law described LRE as the placement that met the individual needs of the child with disabilities. As part of the placement decision-making process, school district committees were required to identify the child's individual educational needs and *then* the appropriate program that could address those needs. Some professionals and parents interpret the LRE to mean that only students with disabilities who can benefit should be placed in a regular classroom since the regular classroom is *not* the least restrictive environment for *all* children with disabilities—particularly those with severe disabilities (Carr, 1993). However we must ask ourselves, what does *severely disabled* mean? What does *benefit* mean? We must also ask, what changes can be made in the classroom environment to enable the student with disabilities to benefit?

> **❧ OPINION BOX ❧**
>
> **Question:** What kind of child should be placed in a regular classroom? Can you describe the primary characteristics that would determine placement?
>
> - Any child who has the ability to learn incidentally can be placed in a regular classroom. The child who can function independently and stay on task can probably be managed in a regular classroom.
>
> - I think that communication skills are essential for a child to get along in a regular class-room. A child with strong communication ability, no matter what kind of disability he or she has, might be able to succeed in a regular classroom.
>
> - I think socialization is the primary prerequisite for the inclusion success. Children with strong socialization skills will have the ability to network with peers and to establish friendships. Children who can socialize will be accepted by other children and by teachers. Socialization training should be a key element to inclusion preparation.
>
> - I think this is a very important question that must be answered *before* children with disabilities are placed in regular classrooms. We should not be experimenting with this process before we have answered this question.
>
> - I think the child with disabilities must be able to function independently by picking up on verbal and nonverbal social cues. Children with disabilities must also have the social judgment to respond appropriately to teachers and peers. Spitting, hitting, calling out, and cursing will not be tolerated very long by other children. We certainly do not want to create a situation in which a child with disabilities will be isolated, singled out, and picked at by peers.
>
> *Note:* Regular education teachers, special education teachers, and therapists in the local community and at School for Language Communication and Development (SLCD) were sent anonymous surveys. These responses are representative samples.

Other professionals and parents propose a slightly different interpretation. *All* children with disabilities should be placed in a regular classroom regardless of severity level as a means of ruling it out *before* special education is recommended. Still other professionals and parents argue a more basic procedural concern. The regular classroom is not appropriate for *all* children with disabilities. The intent of LRE was to link the individual needs of the child with an appropriate educational placement. The regular classroom is not the least restrictive environment if it is not going to be educationally beneficial. On what basis does the CSE decide whether the regular classroom is beneficial to the child? Many parents argue that the mainstreaming experiment has very limited research support and the real issue is cutting educational costs at the expense of children with disabilities.

Numerous questions arise when one considers these different perspectives. Should LRE mean that *all* students with disabilities be placed in a regular classroom first? What if the child fails? Should the regular classroom be a "fail first" step? Many parents and educators argue that the answer should be "no" (National Joint Committee on Learning Disabilities, 1991). Very often, children entering the school system at age 5 have already been classified at the preschool level as having a developmental disability. Should LRE be defined as the regular classroom? The intent of LRE was to place children in a setting that provides a learning benefit. LRE should change as the child grows and develops. The general education classroom should be available for consideration by the CSE for *all* children, but *all* children may not benefit. The CSE should pay close attention not only to the child's disabilities, but also to his or her ability to function within a regular classroom setting.

It is important to note that the original definition of LRE has changed over time. The original definition was *the placement that met the individual needs of the child*. The present definition is *the regular education classroom*. The problem for parents and school districts is how to safeguard the intent of least restrictive environment and address the individual needs of the child with disabilities. A clear example of upholding the least restrictive environment can be found in a recent proposal by the chancellor of the New York City Schools. He has submitted a plan that would affect approximately 40,000 students, or nearly a third of the number presently in special education. This plan would place students who were previously in segregated classrooms back into regular education classrooms. These students with minor learning disabilities and behavioral problems would be given extra help from teachers and/or therapists. The plan would evolve in phases over three years. To succeed, the plan requires the development of more stringent methods for evaluating children for special education, improving teacher training, making more efficient use of psychologists and counselors, increasing parental involvement, and improving ways of bringing trained special educators and therapists into regular classrooms. Interestingly, because this proposal would involve mainstreaming only the 70 percent of special education children who have minor disabilities, it will most likely diffuse opposition from those persons who fear that the children with the severest disabilities will be denied the intense special education programming that they require (Belluck, 1996). The following Opinion Boxes also support this idea of including children with mild disabilities. Many professionals and advocates are applauding the chancellor's efforts to include children with disabilities in the regular education classroom, and the next three years will be the litmus test for inclusion programming. What does "minor" disabilities mean? The proposal highlights the critical importance of developing a child profile that can identify the characteristics of a child with *mild* disabilities.

INCLUSION

Historical Review

During the past several decades, special education has become more specialized. Consequently, a proliferation of highly specialized programs, services, and curricula for specific populations of disabled children was created. Once mainstreaming and the

---

⋙ OPINION BOX ⋘

Question: Can a severely disabled child be placed in a regular classroom?

- The child with severe disabilities (physically and mentally challenged) would be very difficult to place in a regular classroom. The regular education teacher is not professionally equipped to address the needs of this child. The child with severe disabilities will interfere with the general instruction and learning within the classroom. There will be too great a difference between the needs of the child with severe disabilities and everyone else.

- I feel that children with severe disabilities can be placed in regular classrooms only if they are provided with individual teachers, equipment, and assistance. The regular teacher and the nondisabled child do not have the training background or skills to be responsible for the management of the child with severe disabilities.

- Without individual support, the child with severe disabilities could have a serious detrimental effect on all of the other children within the classroom.

- I think we need to define what we mean by *severe disability*. Do we mean physically, mentally, socially, or linguistically challenged? Most regular teachers would probably not object to any child, as long as he or she did not disrupt the instruction within the classroom.

- I think severely disabled means a disruptive, behaviorally impaired child. This child's needs cannot be met in a regular classroom.

- Are we talking about education in the public schools? We cannot even educate children who are not handicapped!

Note: Regular education teachers, special education teachers, and therapists in the local community and at SLCD were sent anonymous surveys. These responses are representative samples.

---

regular education initiative were introduced, the educational trends started to shift in the opposite direction (Peck et al., 1989). The *regular education initiative* (REI) proposes that the regular classroom be the starting point for the provision of services to the child with special needs. The REI was developed to enhance general education and to maintain students who are experiencing learning difficulties in general education. It facilitates the mainstreaming process and it attempts to decrease the need for referral to special education by addressing a student's learning difficulty first in the regular education classroom. If the regular education classroom does not satisfactorily meet the child's needs, then and only then can the child be considered for a segregated classroom. The least restrictive environment, which previously meant the placement that met the individual needs of the child, changed to mean the normalized environment. Because the Individual with Disabilities Educational Act did not use the term *inclusion,* the Department of Education did not directly define the term. However,

```
╔══════════════════════════════════════════════════════════════╗
║  🔹      OPINION BOX       🔹                                   ║
╟──────────────────────────────────────────────────────────────╢
```

Question: Can a child with mild disabilities be placed in a regular classroom?

- I feel that if the child is high functioning socially, there is a possibility that inclusion will be successful. The child with mild disabilities who has social skills will have the best chance of networking and being accepted by nondisabled peers. The academic differences will have to be addressed with the appropriate teacher, consultant support.

- I think that *only* children with mild disabilities should be placed in regular classrooms. Inclusion is *not* for all children with disabilities. We need to learn first about the inclusion process from the children who will probably benefit—children with mild disabilities. This population has the greatest opportunity for success and will provide parents and teachers with the chance to work out the instructional problems within the inclusion classroom. All children with disabilities cannot benefit from regular programming. The least restrictive environment is not the regular classroom. Parents and teachers need to make individualized decisions concerning the placement of children with disabilities.

- It is my belief that children with mild disabilities will be more readily accepted socially by peers and teachers. This child will probably require fewer special education services and will have the greatest chance for success. Inclusion should begin with defining what we mean by a *mild* handicap. Is it a disability? Does it refer to level of functioning?

- Parents and teachers need to develop a child profile for placement. Which skills must the child possess in order to succeed in a regular classroom? Which child is most likely to succeed? Certainly, parents and teachers do not want to create a situation where children are likely to fail; child failure would be devastating for all children.

- Let us begin the inclusion process by placing children with mild handicaps. We need to determine how the regular classroom is going to change once the child with disabilities is introduced. Educators need to understand how learning changes as a function of the special education student.

Note: Regular education teachers, special education teachers, and therapists in the local community and at SLCD were sent anonymous surveys. These responses are representative samples.

IDEA does require that school districts place students in the least restrictive environment, to the maximum extent appropriate. As a result, another concept was introduced—inclusion (Behrmann, 1993).

Inclusion Concept

Inclusion conceptually means the integration of children with and without disabilities. In its "purest" form it is the belief that students with disabilities should be integrated into general education classrooms regardless of whether they can meet traditional academic standards. The Opinion Box that follows reflects the personal feelings of teachers and therapists about inclusion. Many professionals and parents however, disagree about:

- When inclusion should be provided to a disabled child
- How inclusion should be accomplished within the regular classroom
- Whether inclusion is appropriate for *all* disabled children

One thing parents and professionals do agree about is that inclusion can be accomplished much more easily and readily during the early childhood years with children with mild disabilities. Early intervention programming within special

---

❧   OPINION BOX   ❧

Question: What do we do if inclusion fails? What happens to the child with disabilities? How will the family react?

- If inclusion fails, the child with disabilities will be the person who is penalized. This will be a terrible disaster for the child and the family. The child will probably be placed back into special education. The family will want to know why inclusion has failed. Is it the child's fault or the teacher's fault? Who is to blame? Unfortunately, failure sets up a process of blame.

- Parents and teachers need to look at the inclusion classroom as an experiment. It should be a learning experience for all involved. We do not want parents and teachers to feel like failures if the child cannot be maintained within the regular classroom. Clearly, we do not understand enough about learners with disabilities to place all children within the regular classroom.

- I think the results will be disastrous when the child with disabilities fails. A great deal of time will be wasted. How will parents put the pieces back together? Will teachers have the courage to indicate that inclusion is not appropriate? Who has failed here, the parents, the child, or the teachers? Will educators be able to analyze why the child with disabilities has failed in the inclusion classroom?

- When the inclusion experience fails and the child with disabilities is removed, what explanation can be provided? Do we say that the child did not have the appropriate skills to make it in the inclusion classroom? Do we say that the teachers were not adequately trained to maintain the child in the classroom? Do we say that there were not adequate resources to develop instructional techniques to maintain the child in the classroom? We must be very careful about placing children and very clear about how we made our decisions.

Note: Regular education teachers, special education teachers, and therapists in the local community and at SLCD were sent anonymous surveys. These responses are representative samples.

education settings or early childhood programs provides an ideal framework for exploring inclusion as a program option—for children who are disabled and those who are not. Odom and McEvoy (1988) believe that during the preschool years parents and professionals can more easily work together toward an educational goal because there is *choice* about the placement of the preschool child. Because preschool education is not mandated in the United States, parents choose to remain involved in specific programs in which they have placed their children, and are committed to the outcome of those programs. They have placed their children into these programs because they believe they are educationally sound and meet their children's needs. Leister, Koonce, and Nisbet (1993) believe that the young age of the preschool child facilitates a successful inclusion process during the preschool years. Preschool programming emphasizes socialization and prereadiness and is ideal for beginning the inclusion process and there is a great deal of legal support for the practice of inclusion. If a child in a regular education preschool is identified as having special needs, parents welcome the opportunity for their child to receive special education intervention in the regular education preschool in which the child had originally been placed. Furthermore, even if the child has never been in a regular education preschool but has been identified as having special needs, parents are eager for their child to be placed in the least restrictive environment. They want their child to have regular education peers and friends.

Legal Support

The Individuals with Disabilities Education Act and the Americans with Disabilities Act both facilitated the inclusion of children with disabilities into educational environments such as nursery schools, preschools, and day care programs. Several legal cases have been resolved in federal courts, establishing the framework for school districts to educate children in general education classrooms, using supplementary aides and services whenever parents requested such a placement. These cases are particularly interesting, given the diversity and differences among the children, as well as the degree of severity of the disabling conditions. Before enactment of IDEA, the children in these cases would have received services within special education classrooms. In *Oberti v. Board of Education of the Borough of Clementon School District (New Jersey)* (1992), a dispute arose when school officials recommended special education programming for Rafael Oberti. Rafael is a child with Down syndrome and has a tested mental age below the first percentile. The school district argued that Rafael required special education programming, given the fact that his behavior was too disruptive to be managed in a general education classroom. The parents did not agree with the decision of the school district's CSE. The parents argued that the LRE requires "that to the maximum extent appropriate," children with disabilities should be educated with nondisabled children. The court ruled for the parents, indicating that the district had failed to prove that Rafael could not be educated in a general education classroom and that his presence in the mainstream would interfere with the learning of other children in school.

In *Sacramento Unified School District v. Holland,* (U.S. Court of Appeals, 1994), a child with severe cognitive disabilities had been denied placement in a general classroom. Rachael Holland, who was 11 years old, has an I.Q. of 44. The school district's officials recommended that Rachael's day be split between a general education classroom for music, art, and other nonacademic subjects and a special education classroom for individualized and instructional learning. The parents insisted on a program of full inclusion within the general classroom and appropriate supportive services provided therein. The court ruled in favor of full inclusion and the school district has appealed the ruling.

The Association of Supervisors and Curriculum Development and the National Association of State Boards of Education have advocated in favor of full inclusion. Many educational groups have advocated for dramatic reforms in education that would result in dismantling the special education system that presently exists. The result would be a single inclusive system of education, providing services to all children within the regular education classroom (Behrmann, 1993).

When considering inclusion, it is important that we consider not only the general philosophy of inclusion but also the specifics of inclusion. In so doing, we must focus on the profiles of the children who will be included.

Children's Characteristics

One basic and critical assumption underlying inclusion involves the issue of benefit to children with disabilities. The REI suggests that students with disabilities are not different from students without disabilities in any meaningful way. Children with disabilities can be better served in regular classrooms rather than in resource rooms or separate settings. Further, all regular education teachers can teach students with disabilities in regular classrooms and are willing to do so. The REI assumptions go on to say that special education is in general too costly, fragmented, and inefficient (Behrmann, 1993). Even the child with the most severe disabilities can be served within the general education classroom when it is done properly. REI challenges educators to develop a process and system that facilitates including children with disabilities. The following Opinion Box reflects teachers' ideas about these REI assumptions and the concerns of teachers regarding the ability of the regular education teacher to handle the student with special needs in the classroom. Clearly, there is an overwhelming concern regarding the regular education teacher's ability to manage and or meet the needs of the child with special needs. They fear that they will be faced with a "sink or swim" situation, one in which they must frantically try to teach the child with special needs without any background knowledge or experience in that area. Their concerns highlight the need for intense teacher training and support within the classroom. These are necessary components of successful inclusion.

Carr (1993) discussed her feelings as a parent of a child with learning disabilities. She questions whether education has changed in some significant way. Is education more effective today in servicing the needs of regular students? If so, perhaps the needs of the child with disabilities can be met within the regular classroom. She argues, however "nothing has radically changed in most classrooms when the door is closed." There are more violent and behaviorally impaired children than ever before. There is more diversity and problems within regular education than ever before. She further comments that students with learning disabilities may not be able to function in classrooms with large numbers of diverse learners. As the increased degree of diversity creates further demands within the classroom, the individual needs of the child with learning disabilities will be ignored. "Special education services for children with learning disabilities will no longer be available anywhere in America's public schools." If inclusion programming is based on the findings of long-term empirical investigation with ample support and training available to all teachers involved, it is hoped that these concerns will be addressed.

LEVEL OF DISABILITY

Polansky (1994) indicates that *not all* students may be ready for the inclusion classroom. Inclusion programming provides an alternative for some children; the question is, which children? Is the inclusion classroom the appropriate learning environment for the child with mild disabilities, the child with moderate disabilities, and/or the child with severe disabilities? Polansky inquires, "Who decides if a child is ready for

❧ OPINION BOX ❧

Question: Do regular education teachers have sufficient training to understand and meet the needs of children with developmental disabilities?

- Regular education teachers have some training to understand the needs of children with disabilities; experience adds knowledge. Most regular education teachers are resistant to having children with disabilities in their class because they feel special educators are more appropriately trained.

- All teachers have learned basic techniques that allow them to teach the general education student. The special techniques necessary to teach children with specific handicapping conditions require specialized academic training and clinical practice. No teacher can ever learn enough to enable her to teach all children in her classroom. The greater the diversity of children, the more problems for the regular education teacher.

- Regular education teachers do not have sufficient training to meet the needs of children with disabilities. I am a certified elementary education teacher and I know personally that professionals in my area possess only minimal skills and knowledge concerning children with disabilities.

- I am a regular education teacher in a school district. My professional experience is that colleagues indicate that most regular education teachers do not have the background, training, or the inclination to teach children with disabilities, particularly children with behavior orders. There is a great deal of concern about how these types of children will interfere with generalized instruction within the classroom.

- As a special education teacher who has worked with children with severe disabilities for many years, I find it hard to believe that autistic children and children with mental disabilities will be able to benefit from a regular education classroom. Certainly, most regular education teachers do not have the training or skills to provide these children with the attention and intervention that they need on an individual basis. If the child with a disability does not stand to personally benefit, why is a regular education classroom being considered? If the child is not going to learn or advance his abilities in a regular education classroom, why is it being considered? The teacher is very important to the child's learning and development.

- Although inclusion programming is being pushed by many school districts, teachers are not prepared. There has not been enough teacher preparation or teacher training. Teachers need to retool their skills to create a profession between the regular education teacher and the special education teacher—the inclusion teacher.

Note: Regular education teachers, special education teachers, and therapists in the local community and at SLCD were sent anonymous surveys. These responses are representative samples.

inclusion?" Part of the controversy relates to the definition of least restrictive environment. A placement cannot be restrictive if it is appropriate to the individual needs of the child. When LRE is defined as the regular classroom, tension results between the needs of the child and the artificial definition of LRE; there are clear cases of the regular classroom being inappropriate for certain types of disabilities. Is it the type of child—his learning characteristics and behavioral needs—that represents the critical variable to decision making? Is it the level of the child that may be the critical variable? There are no clear-cut answers to these questions. However, the fact remains that the special education system as it currently exists has not adequately met the needs of many students with disabilities. The segregated education of the past has not always led to the inclusion and acceptance of students with special needs into our society. Instead, in many instances it has resulted in social isolation. Reform is necessary and LRE and REI are pillars of this reform movement.

Clearly, many teachers and parents feel that LRE cannot be the regular classroom for *all* children; however, efforts must be made to explore the idea seriously and determine its feasibility. Polansky suggests that the definition of LRE should remain to be the placement that meets the individual needs of the child—wherever that is. LRE needs to be defined in terms of the child, not the other way around. If LRE is only *one* place—the regular classroom—there is no longer a continuum of programs and services. If on the other hand, the process of mainstreaming children carefully along the continuum of services is performed in an educationally sound manner with consideration given to appropriate learning goals, achievement, and social normalization, inclusion will be achieved in an exemplary manner.

When considering severity of disability as a factor of inclusion, the following variables may be important to consider:

1. A finite number of children with disabilities can be placed in the regular classroom when careful consideration is given to the individual needs of the students and the supports necessary to maintain them in the classroom.
2. Individualized teacher instruction must increase according to the level of severity of the child's disability.
3. Management and behavioral support must increase according to the level of severity of the child's disability.
4. The greater the degree of disability, the faster the *tipover effect* within the regular classroom. This means that two distinctive subgroups are created: a subgroup of children with disabilities and a subgroup of children without disabilities. If these two groups are to socialize together, teacher instruction and facilitation must increase.
5. As the level of the child's disability increases, development of her social and communication skills will require more direct modeling.
6. As the level of the child's disability increases, more support will be needed to enable him to learn incidentally within a classroom context.
7. Long-term clinical research needs to be conducted that describes the impact of inclusion programming on nondisabled children.

🙙 OPINION BOX 🙙

Question: Speculate or predict how parents of children with disabilities are going to react to having their children within the regular classroom.

- Some parents might be delighted with the thought of mainstreaming their child without thinking about some of the consequences. Initially parents of children with disabilities will focus on the benefits of a neighborhood program and the opportunities for socialization. Over time, these parents will be faced with the realities. Schools are not prepared to facilitate socialization. Most teachers do not know how to teach children with disabilities and those without to interact with each other. Parents will become disillusioned and angry about the fact that there are no inclusion curricula.

- Some parents of children with disabilities will be happy about the fact that their child will have an opportunity to be in a regular classroom. It will give parents the feeling of hope that something magical will occur within the general education classroom. It is my belief that inclusion offers parents of children with disabilities the hope that their child will be accepted. In our society, acceptance must be taught. There is no curriculum at this point to facilitate this child's learning process.

- I would speculate that most parents would love to place their child in a regular classroom. In their hearts, I think parents want what is best, and in most cases special education provides individual services and represents the least restrictive environment.

- I see this as an issue of choice. This whole issue makes me very angry because I feel that parents are being forced into a regular education classroom. Parents should be allowed to make decisions about their children. Inclusion is not for every child. The parent needs to be a key player in deciding what is the least restrictive environment for their child.

Note: Regular education teachers, special education teachers, and therapists in the local community and at SLCD were sent anonymous surveys. These responses are representative samples.

All of these variables focus on the degree of disability or the severity of the handicapping condition. There is clearly a need to research the relationship between the level of disability—social and communicative behaviors—and the degree of support needed for the child to benefit from general education instruction.

Many educators and parents fear that REI and LRE will disregard the individual needs of the child, and deny his or her disability. In recognizing cultural and linguistic diversity within schools, educational reform must maintain its sensitivity to students with disabilities. To say that *all* children must be included is as restrictive and segregating as the alternative extreme—that all children with disabilities must be in self-contained classrooms. The critical parameter that must be safeguarded in decision making relates to placement opportunities along a transitional continuum of programs and services (Webb, 1994).

≈.   OPINION BOX   ≈.

Question: Speculate or predict how parents of nondisabled children are going to react to children with disabilities being placed within the regular education classroom.

- Parents only want the best for their children, and many parents of nondisabled children feel that the child with disabilities will take too much of the teacher's time and, therefore, nondisabled children will suffer instructionally.

- Initially, parents will resist inclusion. If the child with disabilities does not disrupt the regular education classroom, the parent community will probably be much more accepting of the entire process.

- I would predict that parents of nondisabled children will feel that the attention given to the child with special needs will interfere with their own child's learning. I think most parents are concerned about the quality of education as classes get larger. As it is, the regular education teacher has problems dealing with multicultural diversity, and normal children present their own learning differences. The child with disabilities will not receive the instructional time that he or she needs, and will probably interfere with the quality instruction for the regular children.

- I think most parents of nondisabled children are not free to express their true feelings. Most parents are concerned about the modeling process that will occur when children with disabilities are introduced to the regular classroom. Will the young, normal child know enough not to pick up and imitate socially inappropriate behaviors? How will the quality of education be changed? What about grading and classroom management? If education cannot adequately address the needs of normal children, how can a mix of children with and without disabilities be appropriately educated together? There just is not enough research in this area. This is a social experience that will create disastrous educational results.

- Because the issue of inclusion has been described in terms of segregation, most parents are afraid to express their fears and concerns.

Note: Regular education teachers, special education teachers, and therapists in the local community and at SLCD were sent anonymous surveys. These responses are representative samples.

The Opinion Boxes on pp. 19 and 20 reflect some ideas about how parents of regular education students and special education students feel about inclusion placement. Interestingly, the opinions stated refer to either an initial feeling of hope and delight on the part of the parents of children with special needs that would soon be tempered by the reality that schools are not prepared for inclusion, or feelings of resistance to inclusion by the parents of regular education children. It is not surprising that there is a prediction of nonacceptance by the parents of regular education children. Today, many parents are feeling distressed over the state of public education, overcrowding,

A Reaction to Full Inclusion
A Reaffirmation of the Right of
Students with Learning Disabilities
to a Continuum of Services

The National Joint Committee on
Learning Disabilities

The National Joint Committee on Learning Disabilities (NJCLD) supports many aspects of school reform. However, one aspect of school reform that the NJCLD cannot support is the idea that **all** students with learning disabilities must be served only in regular education classrooms, frequently referred to as **full inclusion.** The Committee believes that full inclusion, when defined this way, violates the rights of parents and students with disabilities as mandated by the Individuals with Disabilities Education Act (IDEA).

Because each student with learning disabilities has unique needs, an individualized program must be tailored to meet those needs. For one student, the program may be provided in the regular classroom; yet for another student, the regular classroom may be an inappropriate placement. Therefore, the NJCLD supports the use of a continuum of services and rejects the arbitrary placement of all students in any one setting.

In *Issues in the Delivery of Educational Services to Individuals with Learning Disabilities (1982)* . . . the NJCLD stated its support and commitment to "a continuum of education placements, including the regular education classroom that must be available to all students with learning disabilities and must be flexible enough to meet their changing needs." This was reaffirmed in 1991 . . . in *Providing Appropriate Education for Students with Learning Disabilities in Regular Education Classrooms,* which recommended that public and private education agencies should "establish system-wide and state-based plans for educating students with learning disabilities in the regular education classroom when such placement is appropriate. The responsibility for developing plans must be shared by regular and special educators, parents, and student consumers of the services. Once developed, a plan must be supported at all levels of the educational system."

In summary, the NJCLD supports educational reform and efforts to restructure schools. As stated in "School Reform: Opportunities for Excellence and Equity for Individuals with Learning Disabilities" (1992) (see *Newsbriefs,* Jan./Feb. 1993, p. 3), "NJCLD demonstrates a deep concern and desire that parents, professionals, and policy makers work cooperatively in planning and implementing reforms. We strongly urge that strategies be developed within the reform movement for students with learning disabilities." As these strategies are developed, it is necessary to ensure that each student with a learning disability is provided a continuum of service options that will guarantee a free, appropriate public education based on the student's individual needs.

Author's Note:

This position paper was developed by the National Joint Committee on Learning Disabilities and approved by the member organizations, January, 1993. Reprinted by permission.

FIGURE 1.3
The National Joint Committee on Learning Disabilities' position on full inclusion.
Reprinted with permission from NJCLD (1982), Issues in the Delivery of Educational Services to Individuals with Learning Disabilities, *ASHA 33,* 15–17, and from NJCLD (1991), Providing Appropriate Education for Students with Learning Disabilities in Regular Education Classrooms, *ASHA 33,* 15–17.

and lack of funding. They believe their children are not being educated properly or being prepared to enter the work demands of the twenty-first century. It does not make sense to them to place students with disabilities into regular classrooms. They fear the quality of education will be compromised. These responses highlight the need for schools to connect with parents and alleviate such fears by developing "action plans" that would take into account the needs of all children. Full inclusion would not necessarily be the final goal for all students with disabilities.

The National Joint Committee on Learning Disabilities has also expressed concern about "the idea that *all* students with learning disabilities must be served only in regular education classrooms, frequently referred to as full inclusion." Figure 1.3 presents the Committee's position on full inclusion. With this position statement in mind, let us consider the individual child characteristics and placement decisions that need to be made when planning for inclusionary experiences for special needs children. Chapter 2 will examine these issues.

QUESTIONS FOR CLASSROOM DISCUSSION

1. Why must a continuum of placements be an option for children with disabilities?
2. What fears do parents of children with disabilities have about inclusion programming?
3. What fears do parents of regular education students have about inclusion programming?
4. How has special education legislation changed during the last 20 years? What impact do these changes have?
5. What exactly is the inclusion concept and what effect will it have on society?
6. Discuss the pros and cons of inclusion and what solutions are available to address the concerns of persons who do not support it.

BIBLIOGRAPHY

Americans with Disabilities Act (1990). P.L. 101-336, 42 U.S.C. at 1201.
Behrmann, J. (1993). Including everyone. *Executive Educator, 15* (12), 16–20.

Belluck, P. (1996, November 26). A plan to revamp special education. *The New York Times,* pp. 1, B4.

Board of Education, Sacramento City USD v. Holland, 786 F.Supp. 874 (ED Cal. 1992).

Carr, M. N. (1993). A mother's thoughts on inclusion. *Journal of Learning Disabilities, 26* (9), 590–592.

Education for All Handicapped Children Act (1976). P.L. 94-142, 20 U.S.C. at 1401 *et seq.*

Education for All Handicapped Children Act Amendments of 1986 (1986). P.L. 99-457, 20 U.S.C. at 1400 *et seq.*

Individuals with Disabilities Education Act (1993). A reaction to full inclusion: A reaffirmation of the right of students with learning disabilities to a continuum of services. *Journal of Learning Disabilities, 26* (9), 596.

Individuals with Disabilities Education Act, Part B. (1990). P.L. 101-476, 20 U.S.C. at 1411–1420.

Leister, C., Koonce, D., & Nisbet, S. (1993). Best practices for preschool programs: An update on inclusive settings. *Day Care and Early Education, 21* (2), 9–12.

Lewis, R. B., & Doorlag, D. H. (1987). *Teaching special students in the mainstream* (2nd ed.). New York: Merrill/Macmillan.

National Joint Committee on Learning Disabilities (1991). Providing appropriate education for students with learning disabilities in regular education classrooms. *ASHA, 33,* 15–17.

Oberti v. Board of Education of the Borough of Clementon School District, 789 F.Supp. 1322 (D.N.J. 1992).

Oberti v. Clementon School Board, 801 F.Supp. 1392 (D.N.J. 1992).

Oberti v. Clementon School Board, 995 F.2d 1204 (3rd Cir. 1993).

Odom, S., & McEvoy, M. (1988). Integration of young children with handicaps and normally developing children. In S. Odom & M. Karnes (Eds.) *Early intervention for infants and children with handicaps: An empirical base.* Baltimore, MD: Paul Brooks.

Peck, D., Richarz, S., Peterson, K., Hayden, L., Mineur, L., and Wandschneider, M. (1989). An ecological process model for implementing the LRE mandate. In R. Gaylord-Ross (Ed.) *Integration strategies for persons with handicaps* (pp. 281–297). Baltimore: Paul H. Brooks.

Polansky, H. B. (1994). The meaning of inclusion: Is it an option or a mandate? *School Business Affairs, 60* (7), 27–29.

Salend, S. (1994). Effective mainstreaming: Creating inclusive classrooms. New York: Macmillan.

Schultz, J. B., & Turnbull, A. P. (1983). *Mainstreaming handicapped students* (2nd ed.). Boston: Allyn & Bacon.

United States Court of Appeals for the Ninth Circuit (1994). *Sacramento Unified School District v. Holland.* San Francisco: Barclays Law Publishers.

Webb, N. (1994). With new court decisions backing them, advocates see inclusion as a question of values. *The Harvard Education Letter, 10* (4), 1–3.

2

Program and Placement Issues

LEARNING OBJECTIVES

After you have read this chapter, you should be able to:

1. Define the various program descriptions and options available to children with special needs.

2. Identify the pertinent issues that impact the development of inclusion programs.

3. List the developmental domains of the child with special needs that must be considered when making program and placement decisions.

4. Define the different types of mainstreaming.

5. Discuss the concerns of special education teachers regarding the inclusion movement in education.

6. Discuss the concerns of regular education teachers regarding the inclusion movement in education.

*A*t the Committee on Special Education (CSE) or Committee on Preschool Special Education (CPSE) a decision is made whether or not the child is in need of special education services. In addition, the CSE and CPSE have the responsibility of determining what inclusion opportunities can be made available to the child. In Chapter 1 the continuum of services was outlined. As one looks back at this continuum, it becomes evident that decision making at this level is complex and multifaceted. A balance must be struck between a child's individual special education needs and placement in an environment that provides opportunities to be with regular education peers. This chapter carefully addresses placement options and programming that is available to children with disabilities.

PROGRAM DESCRIPTION AND OPTIONS

What specific placements and educational options are available to children with developmental disabilities? What programs best fit each child's skills, abilities, and readiness? How are the child's needs linked to program services? Let's discuss these topics in terms of environments, beginning with the description of the environment for the child with the most needs through the description of the environment for the child with the fewest needs.

Home Instruction

Home instruction is provided to pupils who are temporarily unable to attend school. Pursuant to the recommendations of the student's physician, longer term home instruction may be provided pursuant to the recommendation of the district's CSE. As in all other instances of CSE placement, a recommendation from the CSE and parental consent are required. Pupils receive at least an hour a day of instruction at the elementary school level. At the secondary school level, pupils receive two hours of instruction per day.

Special Education Schools

Self-contained programs are often conducted in schools that provide day treatment services to children with disabilities. Some of these schools may be highly specialized in terms of meeting the needs of children with very specific disabilities. For example, Henry Viscardi School located in Albertson, New York, has an outstanding reputation for providing services to children with physical challenges. The physical facility has been constructed to provide individualized educational instruction and services. However, not every school district has the financial resources or expertise to develop this type of specialized program for a single population of children with severe physical disabilities.

In a special education school, the primary instruction is provided by a special education teacher. The specialty or related services such as occupational therapy, physical therapy, dance movement therapy, music therapy, auditory training, and language therapy are tailored to the individual needs of the particular population. For example, the Association for Children with Down Syndrome services children from birth through 21 years of age. At this school the collaborative team is very knowledgeable about Down syndrome and addresses issues that are particular to the Down syndrome child, such as different subtypes of Down syndrome, specific problems with successive processing, and fine motor and oral motor problems.

Special Education within School Districts

As a function of the passage of P.L. 94-142, most school districts in the United States provide special education services. These programs range from classes for autistic children, children with mental deficiencies or hearing disabilities, to classes for mixed populations of children. Communities have established different special education classrooms either as a function of the number of children with a specific disability and/or as a function of a general philosophy concerning special education programming.

Many parents complain that school district programs are just as restrictive and separate as the specialty schools. In fact, parents feel strongly about the fact that the specialty schools provide more individualized services with teachers and specialists who are better trained to meet the needs of children with very specific disabilities. This is usually true. Because school districts must meet the needs of *all* children with disabilities, their programs tend to be more generic in nature. Although the primary instruction is provided by a special education teacher, specialty and related services are often more difficult for school districts to acquire, particularly medically based services, such as occupational therapy and physical therapy. Because individual services are costly, school districts tend to emphasize group-related services.

Self-Contained Classes

At the elementary and secondary school levels, self-contained classes are maintained for pupils whose educational needs are best met within a self-contained class unit with a teacher-to-pupil ratio of one teacher for 12 pupils. All self-contained classes are taught by teachers certified in special education. Teaching assistants are available for at least one-half of the instructional day. The school day is equivalent to that offered to other pupils in the building. At the elementary level, instructional groupings may consist of pupils within a three-year chronological age range who evidence similar educational needs.

At the high school level, pupils often participate in vocational programming. This programming is considered part of the students' half-day instructional program because it would be impossible for them to participate in a half-day instructional program and also participate in the vocational program.

Mainstreaming for both elementary and high school students is scheduled whenever the students evidence the capacity to participate.

Resource Room Program

This program is designed to meet the needs of pupils with educational disabilities who can best profit from being mainstreamed into regular classes with the assistance of supportive individualized instruction in basic skills and tutorial assistance in their mainstream subjects. Resource room teachers have a teaching load of not more than 20 pupils. Instructional groups are kept to 5 or fewer pupils. All resource room teachers are certified in special education. Teaching assistants are assigned to the resource room throughout the instructional day. Generally, there is at least one full-time resource room teacher located in each elementary school building, with additional special education teachers' time assigned as needed. High school students can also be programmed into resource rooms. Resource room pupils receive at least three hours of resource room instruction per week depending on their individual needs.

Special Education within the School District with Partial Mainstreaming

During the past 10 years, some school districts throughout the United States have attempted to facilitate formalized programming between learners with disabilities and those without. Very often a CSE will identify opportunities for student interaction in the nonacademic areas of educational instruction: lunch time, library, music, and gym. These nonacademic activities can represent the beginning of an interactive process that teaches:

- The child with disabilities about nondisabled peers in a larger more challenging context
- Nondisabled children about the individual differences in students with disabilities
- Parents of students with disabilities and those without about an educational process that includes all children
- Teachers about the need for an instructional curriculum that focuses on teaching both groups of children to learn together

Evaluators indicate that the primary developmental skills that signal a readiness for educational transition are:

- Increased social skill
- Increased communication skills
- Decreased behavior management problems

Mainstreaming is a process that attempts to link the child's individual learning needs with an appropriate educational placement. At one end of the mainstreaming continuum is a small self-contained special education classroom with minimal mainstreaming activities; at the other end is the general education classroom.

When the CSE makes its decision about mainstreaming a child with disabilities into nonacademic instructional areas, it must evaluate whether the child can *benefit* from such learning activities. Part of the controversy relates to the definition of the term *benefit* and how the multidisciplinary team decides whether the child with disabilities is ready to interact and to learn within a less restrictive setting. The final step in the mainstreaming process is inclusion—instruction within the regular classroom. The first step in the decision-making process for the CSE is to "rule out" the regular classroom; this process often creates an adversarial relationship between parents and the committee.

All of these placements are already in place. If we are to make a transition to more inclusive programming for students with special needs, we must consider some very real issues related to this kind of programming.

Consultant Teacher Services

Consultant teacher services are recommended for pupils who can benefit from a full-time regular education program with assistance from a special education teacher. Pupils receiving this level of service typically require only a minimal level of supportive assistance, and generally are either in transition to declassification or require weekly follow-up. Pupils in this category receive a minimum of two hours of instruction per week. The assistance may be indirect, to help the child's regular education teacher modify instruction to meet the unique needs of the child with special needs and to help the child adjust to the learning environment. The assistance may also be direct, in which case the pupil receives specialized instruction from his or her special education teacher. In this case, the instruction is provided in the child's regular classroom.

This consultant teacher model lends itself well to the philosophy of inclusion and is currently being utilized by some schools. The special education teacher consults with several regular education teachers who have children with developmental disabilities in their classes. Her or his role in this instance is to help the regular education teacher structure the classroom environment with a range of materials and activities so that the children with developmental disabilities can learn and interact with their regular education peers. When a youngster with developmental disabilities moves from a special education setting to a regular education classroom, he or she must adjust to different instructional formats, curriculum demands, teaching styles, classroom behavioral expectations, and new peer socialization patterns. It is the responsibility of the special education teacher to work with the regular education teacher in order to highlight the needs of the special learner and what teaching strategies and environmental supports help the student meet the challenges of the regular education classroom. Preteaching, utilizing visual aids, and teaching text comprehension strategies such as surveying textbooks are just a few of the necessary bridging techniques that learners with special needs require to function in the regular education classroom.

PRACTICAL CONCERNS RELATED TO INCLUSION

Most parents and professionals support the idea and the ideal of providing inclusion programming to children with disabilities. The problems concerning the intent, the interpretation, and the implementation of P.L. 94-142 present pragmatic-practical difficulties for schools, educators, teachers, parents, and children. The following issues represent some of the concerns expressed by parents and professionals:

1. What are the benefits of inclusion programming for the child with developmental disabilities?
2. Are there any criteria or developmental profiles that need to be met before a child with disabilities is placed in a general education classroom?
3. What kind of training must be provided to regular education peers so that the environment appropriately supports the social inclusion of the child with disabilities?
4. What kind of training must be provided to the regular education teacher so that she or he can meet the demands of the inclusion process, the needs of the regular education children within the classroom, and the individual needs of the children with disabilities within the classroom?
5. How is inclusion accomplished within the classroom? Does inclusion mean physical integration, social integration, educational integration, or communicative integration?
6. How do we assess on an outcome basis the placement of the child with disabilities within a general education classroom? On what basis do we decide if inclusion has been successful for the included child?
7. Is it reasonable for education to establish a mission goal that *requires* inclusion for *all* individuals with disabilities?
8. Does inclusion really mean participation rather than education for the child with disabilities in the regular classroom?
9. What kind of parent education and training must be provided to parents of children with disabilities and regular education children to facilitate inclusion within the general education classroom?
10. How many children with disabilities can be placed within one general education classroom?

These are some of the issues that have arisen over the years that need to be addressed *before* school districts launch a massive inclusion program and run the risk of inclusion failure. School districts need to begin the process of dialogue with parents, teachers, and administrators within their community before the "policy runs away with the reality" of the issue (Webb, 1994). Professionals and parents need to answer some of the questions and address some of the issues. Clearly, the general education classroom will change in content and organizational design. Expectations of educational performances and outcomes will be different. Interactions between children, teachers, and parents will be dynamically altered by inclusion reforms. The participants in the inclusion classroom must all have an investment in its change and its ultimate success or failure. As contributors, the children, teachers, and parents must be part of the decision-making process.

The redefined least restrictive environment (LRE) for the child with disabilities emphasizes the placement of all children with disabilities in general education classrooms. Rather than viewing inclusion as a *final* step along the mainstreaming process, the new definition suggests that the general education classroom is the first step. The National Joint Committee on Learning Disabilities believes that the regular education classroom may not be possible for *all* children with disabilities (1991). Before we place a child in an inclusion setting we must ask ourselves to identify and/or develop a child profile that will ensure child success within the general education classroom. Three points can be highlighted that may serve to resolve this critical issue:

1. Identification of the characteristics that determine child readiness for the inclusion experience.
2. Identification of the environmental characteristics that must be addressed to ready the classroom for the child with a disability.
3. Identification of outcome measures that can be used to determine whether it is appropriate to place a child within an inclusion classroom. Specifically, we must assess inclusion success for a particular child with a disability.

Child Diversity

Part of our problem regarding inclusion placement relates to the fact that we are not dealing with a single population of children with developmental disabilities. There are many different *categories* and groups of children with developmental disabilities with many different educational needs. There are also different *levels* of disability within each category. The traditional organization of the general education classroom must be changed to reflect a diversity of children. Rather than developing general education classrooms with a homogenous population of children, general education classrooms must now be developed with a developmental diversity in mind (Polansky, 1994). This might include consideration of various developmental domains: social skills, language development abilities, cognitive functioning, gross and fine motor abilities, emotional skills, and motivational factors. The diversity in children's abilities will provide the framework for developing inclusion classrooms.

An ideal inclusion classroom will require a focus on (1) each child's instructional needs and (2) how each child can contribute to group learning. Educational diversity will require and facilitate a process of peer instruction, multiple levels, and multiple grades within each classroom. This will require that the *roles* of the teacher, the parent, the student, and the classroom be redefined; educational alternatives will also have to be developed to redesign the relationship between school and home environments.

Levels of Ability and Types of Mainstreaming

Reynolds and Birch (1988) describe three types of mainstreaming: physical, social, and instructional. Figure 2.1 describes the relationship between the types of mainstreaming that can be provided to a child with disabilities, given a particular level of functioning. In Chapter 1, we noted that in order for children to transition along the educational continuum, significant changes within the child must occur in three developmental areas: social, communicative, and behavioral. Figure 2.2 presents a social interaction scale, which can be used by members of the educational team to determine the child's readiness to function within a more challenging social context. The social interactional scale can be utilized by the classroom teacher, the school psychologist, the parent, and the individual therapist. The scores generated by each member of the team would provide a mechanism for decision making about the mainstreaming experience appropriate for the child.

Figure 2.1 indicates that for the child with *severe* behavioral and communication needs, physical mainstreaming may be appropriate as an initial interaction experience. Physical mainstreaming involves the placement of children with and without disabilities within the same environment. Physical mainstreaming does not however ensure

---

Child's Level of Functioning

Severe

Type 1: Physical Mainstreaming
Children with disabilities share the same physical environment. This does not ensure that there will be any social interaction between typical children and children with disabilities.

Moderate

Type 2: Physical Social Mainstreaming
The contextual setting is structured to facilitate the interactions between children with disabilities and those without. The educational staff provides opportunities for children to interact as peer partners.

Mild

Type 3: Physical Instructional Mainstreaming
Typical students and students with disabilities are educated in the same contextual setting. The regular classroom provides an inclusive opportunity for typical children and children with disabilities.

FIGURE 2.1
Types of mainstreaming.

SCHOOL FOR LANGUAGE AND
COMMUNICATION DEVELOPMENT
2351 Jerusalem Avenue
North Bellmore, New York 11710
516-783-7523

Social-Interactional Scale

Team Members

_____
_____
_____
_____

Date: _____
*1–28   6:1:1 or 12:2:2 class
*29–40 12:1:1 class
*41–56 Inclusion class

Child's Name _____
D.O.B. _____ CA _____ Group _____

Directions: Read each item below carefully and decide how much you think the child fits the descriptions based on developmentally appropriate peers.

Behaviors	Not at all 0	Occasionally 1	Sometimes 2	Most of the time 3	Always 4
1. Can share toys and objects spontaneously.					
2. Can play with peers.					
3. Cooperates with adults.					
4. Attends to structured lessons with minimal prompting.					
5. Can tolerate frustrating events and situations.					
6. Can transition easily from activity to activity both in and out of class.					
7. Can respond spontaneously and verbally to a variety of "wh" questions.					
8. Can respond to verbal directions appropriately.					
9. Can handle conflicts in an appropriate manner without resorting to tantrums, explosive outbursts, or unpredictable behavior (hitting, biting, spitting).					
10. Can wait his or her turn.					
11. Can function appropriately in a low structured activity.					
12. Can complete tasks or activities with minimal verbal prompting.					
13. Can initiate verbal interactions with peers.					
14. Can handle conflicts without isolating self from peers and/or adults.					
Total					

Special Comments:

FIGURE 2.2
Social interaction scale.

that there will be formalized or programmatic social interaction between typical children and children with disabilities. Parallel activities are ongoing, and there is always an opportunity for limited and preliminary integration of activities.

For children with *moderate* educational needs, there may be an opportunity to expand the mainstreaming process to include physical as well as formalized social interaction. The child with a moderate disability may have communicative and social abilities such that he or she can benefit from peer interactions with nondisabled children. In this case, the educational staff consisting of a regular education teacher and a special education teacher may develop organized activities based on daily living events, activities, and routines that would provide opportunities for formalized interactions between children with disabilities and their regular education peers. The prerequisite skills, however, for children with disabilities would require a level of social and communication functioning. An important question that comes to mind is "What is the level of functioning?" This question is not so easily answered.

The final type of mainstreaming involves ongoing instructional activities within a general education classroom. This means that students with and without disabilities can receive instruction in the same contextual setting at the same time. Although academic abilities and educational levels of functioning may differ, the prerequisite social and communication skills of *all* the children are present and ensure the success of inclusion instruction in the classroom. Here, children with mild disabilities may present the readiness skills to benefit from such an instructional context. Again, we must ask ourselves "What are the prerequisite social and communication skills that the child with disabilities needs?"

The three levels of mainstreaming can also be combined with other variables: classroom, children, and teacher. Figure 2.3 attempts to show that the levels of mainstreaming can be overlapped with three educational issues: (1) classroom environment, (2) children's characteristics, and (3) teacher–staff issues. Each of these can be a means of identifying barriers to inclusion. A successful inclusion experience is more likely when the physical, social, and instructional supports are solidly in place. Without these supports in place, the inclusion experience will crumble into failure, just as a building with poor support structure would crumble over time. In attempting to understand the barriers that affect the inclusion process, we can assume that this overlap provides a continuum of experiences for children, teachers, and parents. Physical interaction is the first step along the continuum followed by social and instructional interaction.

Classroom Environment

To work toward instructional inclusion within the classroom, obvious dramatic changes must occur in space in order to achieve this initial physical step (Pierce, Rasdall, & Ferguson, 1993). As children with disabilities enter the regular education classroom, space must be allocated to accommodate the needs of these children. The traditional classroom of 500, 600, or 700 square feet may not provide enough space for wheel-

Successful Inclusion
Higher level of abilities
More peer interaction
Greater academic integration

Physical	Social	Instructional
Classroom environment	Children's characteristics	Teacher-staff issues

FIGURE 2.3
Mainstreaming overlap.

chairs, special equipment, or subgroups of children attempting to learn within the same environment. Teachers, parents, and administrators must look critically at the size of the room and the width of doorways, given the need for communication technologies, wheelchairs, toilets, computers, special tables, and chairs that are appropriate for children with disabilities.

To accommodate the needs of children with disabilities within the general education classroom, space accommodations are going to translate into additional personnel time, facility costs, construction, remodeling expansions, consultants, and specialized technical equipment and supplies. McCormick and First (1994) indicate that custodial and maintenance services within a building will be affected dramatically. Children with disabilities who have health and or physical needs will require alterations in space as well as maintenance procedures. One must consider special cleaning and refuse disposal for items such as battery-powered wheelchairs, which could leak acid on floors and surfaces.

Many educators, administrators, and school districts have suggested that inclusion may be a way to reduce educational costs in general. The reality may be quite different. McCormick and First (1994) suggest that inclusive education represents a social policy "with a blank check" (p. 30). The concern expressed by many educators is that general education has not adequately met the needs of regular students, and now children with disabilities are being introduced into the general education classroom. If the ideal for inclusive programming is to be met, school boards, administrators, teachers, and parents must take into consideration the adaptations in the physical space that will be required within each classroom.

Preplanning, staff training, and supervision are critical to the achievement of inclusion within the general education classroom (Evans, Harris, Adeigbola, Houston, & Argott, 1993). Each school district should complete a building survey that analyzes each school building in terms of the accommodations required to meet the needs of children with disabilities within the specific building. McCormick and First (1994) stress the fact that inclusion decision making will have financial implications for program costs. Initially, classrooms may be too small, and districts may not have the financial resources to reorganize building space into larger rooms. To begin the inclusion process within existing classrooms, class size may have to remain relatively small. This would mean two teachers and two classes coexisting within the same room (York, Doyle, & Kronberg, 1992). A special education teacher would provide services in one part of the classroom for 6 to 10 disabled children. A general education teacher would provide instruction for 12 to 15 regular education students in another part of the classroom. Instruction would be separate, but there would be opportunities for interaction during the course of the day, particularly during nonacademic activities: individualized reading, creative arts, computer instruction, music time, etc.

During the course of the academic year, the two teachers could develop a classroom Individualized Education Program (IEP) that would specify opportunities for nonacademic areas for social interaction and instructional areas for learning interaction along a time line. Team teaching opportunities would also allow both instructors to learn about their children separately and look for common areas of overlap and instruction, so that during the course of the academic year children would be provided with a greater number of opportunities for interaction (Chalmers, 1993).

Type of Disability

An additional variable that should be considered in developing a child profile for classroom placement may relate to the type of disability. Different developmental disabilities present specific learning problems and stylistic concerns. This would suggest that in order to identify an appropriate educational placement, the disability characteristics must be translated into the learning needs of the child. In understanding the child's learning style needs, appropriate classroom accommodations may be attempted in order to maintain the child within a regular classroom setting. For a child with learning disabilities who is easily distracted, a smaller classroom placement with peer groups may facilitate learning. For a child with cerebral palsy, physical accommodations in space and equipment must be developed to meet his or her needs. For a child with hearing impairment, an auditory trainer, FM system, or classroom seating arrangement may be utilized to manage the child's learning needs within a regular classroom. The point here is to emphasize the need to identify specific child variables that are going to have an impact on the child's ability to learn within the classroom. Several researchers stress the significance of socialization and communication behaviors to the maintenance of children with disabilities within the general education classroom.

Socialization

Leister, Koonce, and Nisbet (1993) describe the significance of socialization learning in preschool environments. Social skills involve exchanges of behaviors that initiate and/or maintain verbal and nonverbal interaction between children. Although creating an environment that provides an opportunity for interaction is critical to the process, children must have a repertoire of learned social behaviors. Creating the environment creates the necessary conditions for interaction to occur for children with developmental disabilities. Specific prescriptive training must take place to develop social behaviors that can be utilized across various classroom routines. Teaching social skills to children is of paramount importance in ensuring that the teacher will be able to maintain and reinforce interactions with their nondisabled peers.

Although it may be desirable for social skills to be age appropriate, the reality is that the more severe the child's disability, the more primary and primitive the social behavior. One mechanism to facilitate exchanges of social behaviors involves peer facilitation and instruction. Nondisabled children may be encouraged to interact with classmates who have disabilities through direct modeling and instruction by the teacher. These children must also learn to utilize their words as an alternative to nonverbal negative behavior. The time spent in socialization learning for the *entire* class is a well-spent long-term investment. Socialization involves a "learning to learn" process for children with disabilities. The more a child with disabilities socializes, the better she becomes at the socialization process. The better a child is at socialization, the more she seeks to socialize with others. Part of the IEP for the entire classroom should involve a development plan for peer instruction and social learning.

Communication

The communication process involves a complex exchange between a speaker and a listener. Information is exchanged verbally and nonverbally in a turn-taking sequence. Children with disabilities often present with severe communications deficits (Leister, Koonce, & Nisbet, 1993). They cannot initiate, maintain, or terminate communicative interactions with peers and adults. If a child is to communicate effectively, he must acquire a set of behaviors that can be used to exchange information, a reason to communicate, and an event to communicate about. Many children do not present with the ability to communicate verbally by means of words and sentences; as a result some alternative form or system may have to be utilized. Sign language and communication boards represent two alternatives for children with productive language deficits. Children with disabilities who cannot express what they want or need in a standardized or recognized format (1) become easily frustrated when they are not understood and (2) cannot respond appropriately to the verbal exchanges initiated by nondisabled peers. The nondisabled child must be taught to understand the language and learning differences in his classmate with disabilities. The nondisabled child must also learn to regulate his communication and form of communication to the level of his peer with special needs. This simple regulatory accommodation facilitates a degree of communicative exchange between peers. Often, nondisabled facilitators may assume that the child with disabilities is *uninterested,* rather than *unable* to understand. It is important for the classroom teacher and the nondisabled children to understand how each child with disabilities communicates. The communication process is as individualized in children with developmental disabilities as it is in regular education children. Peer dyads consist of a child with disabilities and a nondisabled child learning about each other's communicative style and behaviors in order to develop a personalized system of interaction that may be nontraditional, but effective.

Teacher Staffing Issues

The primary assumption in the inclusion classroom is that the needs of all children can be met within the classroom and not outside it. To achieve instructional inclusion within a classroom, the special education teacher and the general education teacher must work together to develop a socially responsive environment for children. Each teacher contributing her skills, her training, and her knowledge in a collaborative effort to meet the needs of a diverse population of children would share a common space. The classroom functions as a learning laboratory for children, parents, and teachers. There is no longer a need for pull-out related services and there is also an assumption that children with disabilities will benefit from their interaction with higher functioning and higher achieving nondisabled peers. As a result, the classroom laboratory includes children with a greater diversity of skills, cultural backgrounds, linguistic competencies, educational needs, instructional requirements, and behavioral supports. These needs are identified by the collaborative team and are addressed by them within the classroom. This process is prerequisite to the child transitioning from physical to social to instructional interaction.

In attempting to restructure and reform general education, there has been a parallel attempt to develop inclusion within the classroom. There are many models of inclusion programming that describe various attempts at the building level to achieve inclusion programming. The diversity of the models suggests that different communities recognize the unique needs of students with disabilities. The predominant model for most inclusion programs involves the student with mild disabilities. Evans, et al. (1993) describe the Florida Uniting Students With Exceptionalities (FUSE) Public School/University Collaboration. The FUSE program unites school districts and universities in an attempt to restructure collaboratively classroom programming.

Coteaching and collaborative teaching are utilized as a means of reducing pull-out services and resource room services to children with disabilities. Students with mild disabilities are assessed in terms of self-esteem, motivation, interactions with nondisabled peers, satisfaction, achievement, discipline referrals, and suspensions.

The course discipline, communication and collaboration, shared decision making, and problem solving that occur between general and special education teachers provide a mechanism for an increased understanding of student needs within the general education classroom. Significant planning and educational change in programming require teacher, administrator, and parent support. Children with mild disabilities present diverse needs. According to Evans et al. (1993), the FUSE program also requires significant changes in philosophy, policy, and logistical planning as children are "included" within the general education classroom. Teacher and parent stress has to be addressed as problems occur within the classroom. Some of the other issues include "resistance to change, lack of trust or credibility, time, financial and personnel resources, and discomfort with new roles and responsibilities" (p. 145). With all of this in mind, we must still ask: "Can the inclusion classroom meet the needs of all children?" "What will occur when the number of children with disabilities increases?" "How will the classroom dynamics be affected as children with severe disabilities are included within the classroom?"

Benefit

The underlying assumption in the mainstreaming process involves whether the child with disabilities will benefit from a specific program and service. The issue of benefit may be viewed in terms of outcome-based criteria that can be observed and measured in the child with disabilities; benefit should be linked to child characteristics (York, Doyle, & Kronberg, 1992). Two behaviors that may assist in determining benefit are social and communication competencies, which can be directly facilitated by teachers and children within a dynamic context that serves to generalize these skills across other partners. The degree to which social and communication behaviors can be facilitated in children with disabilities increases the likelihood that the child can be maintained with nondisabled partners. Social and communication abilities provide the child with disabilities with autonomy and independence within the classroom. These behaviors also ensure a degree of acceptance from and interaction with nondisabled peers.

Often children with disabilities present with social and communication behaviors that are divergently different from nondisabled learners and can interfere with educational instruction. Many teachers express a high degree of concern about disruptive behavior in the classroom (Volk & Stahlman, 1994). Instructional inclusion can be achieved more readily if the child with disabilities has the social and communicative competencies to manage herself within the dynamics of the classroom. The complexities related to a teacher's lecture on an academic subject (i.e., "The Pilgrims and Thanksgiving") and sitting in one's seat for a half hour listening and paying attention may be very difficult for a child with disabilities. Given the characteristics of the child with severe disabilities, is it reasonable to assume that this child can benefit from such instruction? Given the characteristics presented by a child with moderate disability, can she benefit from such academic instruction? Is it reasonable to assume that a child with mild disabilities given the characteristics that she presents, can benefit from the academic instruction within the classroom? To answer these questions, it becomes critical for members of the multidisciplinary team to identify the child's learning profile along with her educational needs. Child benefit must be measured over time to determine if the educational programming facilitates changes in the child. Benefit must be defined in terms of child outcomes.

Curriculum Development

Another significant issue affecting placement of children with disabilities in regular classrooms involves the development of curricula. Curricula and instructional procedures must be modified in order to address the increased heterogeneity and diversity within inclusive classrooms. Can we teach children individually within the inclusive classroom? Can we teach children in the same way as we used to? How do we grade children? Can we teach children with the same materials?

In designing a curriculum for the inclusive classroom, learning must be individualized with a view toward specific classroom outcomes. Whereas traditional instruction focused specifically on the content of learning, the inclusive classroom may shift the focus to the process of learning. Along with specific academic objectives, direct instruction may have to expand to target interactional competencies.

York, Doyle, and Kronberg (1992) describe the use of a core curriculum and how children at different developmental levels may learn skills, given their own individual abilities. While some children are learning mathematical concepts, others may be instructed in math computation skills. Some children may be reading grade-level materials while others are learning to listen to stories. The classroom becomes a laboratory for individual student learning. Students with different abilities work at different levels within the core curriculum. Each child's level of learning is individualized; the IEP is extended from the child with disabilities to the nondisabled child and represents a classroom goal. A core curriculum provides a mechanism for the *type* and the *level* of disability to be factored into the learning equation of the classroom. The individual needs of children are viewed in terms of group goals and outcomes in a core curriculum. Academic, multicultural, and interpersonal goals are generated for each child's IEP from the classroom core curriculum. There is a "wide array of opportunities for students to learn important and individually relevant skills, attitudes and values for life," (p. 4). To achieve these outcomes for children and the classroom, there needs to be an ongoing collaboration between general and special educators.

With all of this in mind, let us consider a child for whom the CSE is determining placement. Figure 2.4 describes Bryan, a child with special needs. Bryan's evaluation results can be summarized as follows:

BRYAN'S CHARACTERISTICS	RECOMMENDED PROGRAMMATIC COMPONENTS
Emerging language skills	Regular education classroom with support
Emerging social skills	Services from the special education and
Independent behaviors	speech language pathologist
Emerging prereadiness skills	

Figure 2.5 illustrates the CSE decision process and outcome for Bryan.

In the past, a child like Bryan might have been recommended for a special education self-contained classroom for academics and mainstreaming in nonacademic areas for the rest of the school day. However, the CSE recommended full inclusion with a consultant teacher. The consultant teacher will spend two hours each day in the regular education classroom. She will work with the regular education teacher to adapt reading instruction to meet Bryan's individual learning characteristics. Together they will decide which approach is best: a phonetic approach or a whole-word approach. The special educator will also familiarize the regular education teacher with the instructional modifications that Bryan needs. Subgrouping utilizing multisensory materials that combine visual, auditory, kinesthetic, and tactile modalities, and some individual instruction time each day would be useful for a child like Bryan. Because Bryan has difficulty in the area of peer relationships and play skills, he will need to be taught

BRYAN

Likert Scale

- Use the following Likert Scale to assess severity of functioning.
- Use values from 1–7 to rate *each* characteristic
- 0 = Age Appropriate
- less severe — more severe — most severe

  $\boxed{1}$ 2   3 $\boxed{4}$ 5   6 $\boxed{7}$

Language and Communication Profile

Language Use

Deficit Characteristics (1–7)

1	range of pragmatic functions
2	awareness of social rules
3	eye gaze behaviors
4	relatedness
5	speaker–initiator/ speaker–listener roles
1	initiates new topic
4	elaborates on topic
2	maintains topic
4	terminates topic
5	metapragmatic skills

1	perseveration
5	tangential language
0	ritualized
0	routinized
0	echolalia
0	gestures/facial expressions
1	physical proximity/ contacts
0	vocal intensity/ quality/prosody
0	jargon

Social/Interaction Skills

4	play skills
0	behavioral issues
4	peer relationships
1	management needs
0	transitional abilities
0	temper tantrums
5	distractibility
2	generalization of use

Language Content

Deficit Characteristics (1–7)

2	range of semantic functions
2	relational meaning
2	categorization skills
2	association skills
3	spatial concepts
5	following directions
3	comprehension of wh- questions
4	lexical development
3	concept development

2	production of wh- questions
1	nonverbal sequencing
3	verbal sequencing skills
4	narrative development
5	word finding/retrieval
3	descriptions
6	meaning expansion (multiple meanings)
2	absurdities
1	nonverbal problem solving
3	verbal problem solving
2	integration of communicative use and meaning
5	metasemantic skills
4	readiness skills (preschool)

School Age

___	reading
___	math
___	written language

Information Processing

5	attending skills
1	Gestalt processing
3	retention skills
6	auditory/visual discrimination
6	auditory/visual figure-ground
4	short-term memory
5	retrieval skills
5	organization of information
6	metacognitive skills

FIGURE 2.4
CSE decision process and outcome for Bryan.

Language Structure

Deficit Characteristics (1–7)

1	mean length of utterance	1	production of morphological structures	1	phonetic repertoire
2	structure of utterances (declarative, imperative negative, questions)	3	organization of utterances (word order)	2	phonological processes
3	comprehension of complex utterances (simple, compound, complex)	3	integration of content and structure	1	phono-syntactic skills
		2	morpho-syntactic skills	1	metaphonological skills
2	production of complex utterances (simple, compound, complex)	0	oromotor competence	0	intelligibility in known contexts
3	comprehension of grammatical morphemes			0	intelligibility in unknown contexts
				1	stimulability
				1	generalization of form
				0	intonation
				2	dysfluencies

Severity Scale
>300 → Severe
200-300 → Moderate
<200 → Mild to Moderate

Kindergarten Placement

Fall

√ Related services
√ Regular education classroom
√ Special education services
√ Consultant teacher
___ 15:1 classroom
___ 12:1 classroom
___ 12:1:1 classroom
___ 12:2:2 classroom
___ 6:1:1 classroom

Total Score 187
Level of functioning:
Mild range

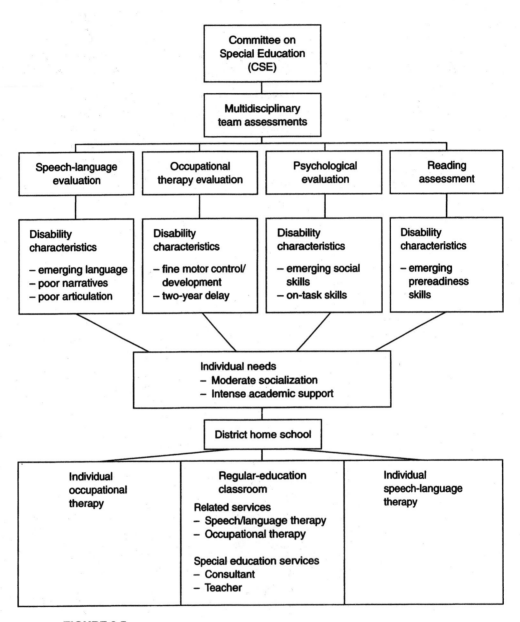

FIGURE 2.5
Mainstreaming decisions: The road to inclusion.

appropriate behaviors for establishing and maintaining positive peer relationships. The special educator will assist the regular education teacher to use techniques such as direct instruction modeling and frequent practice to facilitate Bryan's acquisition of appropriate social skills. In addition, the special education teacher will highlight for the regular education teacher those areas that may present the greatest challenge to Bryan. Because Bryan was in a special education preschool, entering the mainstreamed kindergarten requires that he adjust to different instructional formats, teaching styles, and behavioral expectations. All of these accommodations must be explored in order to provide an environment for Bryan that allows him to be educated with his regular education peers. All of these accommodations require a strong collaborative approach between the teachers.

Now let us consider another child, Michael. Figures 2.6 through 2.11 present his Assessment Profile from his multidisciplinary team, which consists of an administrator, a psychologist, a parent, a special education teacher, and a speech–language pathologist. The Assessment Profile would be based on the team's review of both formal and informal tests that assess Michael's psychological, language, communication, motor, social, and behavioral needs.

Michael's evaluation results can be summarized as follows:

MICHAEL'S CHARACTERISTICS	RECOMMENDED PROGRAMMATIC COMPONENTS
Management needs	Small, self-contained classroom
Limited language abilities	Multiple individual therapeutic services
Socialization deficits	
Impulsivity	
Motor delays	

Figure 2.12 presents the least restrictive environment statement that might be generated by Michael's CSE team. The result of this statement is Michael's placement within a special education classroom. However, partial mainstreaming in nonacademic areas is recommended for three periods during the school day: lunch, physical education, and art. A paraprofessional will be provided as a means of support to transition the child from the special education classroom to the mainstream sessions. In the past, because of Michael's aggressive and impulsive behaviors he might have had no opportunities for mainstreaming. However, with the support of a paraprofessional, Michael will have opportunities to experience inclusion programming in nonacademic areas.

TEACHER ISSUES

The development of inclusion classrooms requires a shift in the way in which children and teachers function within the classroom. The challenge of integrating children with

MICHAEL

Likert Scale

- Use the following Likert Scale to assess severity of functioning.
- Use values from 1–7 to rate *each* characteristic
- 0 = Age Appropriate
- mild   —   moderate   —   severe

  1   2   3   4   5   6   7

Language and Communication Profile

Language Use

Deficit Characteristics (1–7)

6	range of pragmatic functions
6	awareness of social rules
4	eye gaze behaviors
5	relatedness
6	speaker-initiator/ speaker-listener roles
6	initiates new topic
6	elaborates on topic
7	maintains topic
7	terminates topic
7	metapragmatic skills

7	perseveration
7	tangential language
1	ritualized
1	routinized
1	echolalia
1	gestures/facial expressions
6	physical proximity/ contacts
4	vocal intensity/ quality/prosody
1	jargon

Social/Interaction Skills

6	play skills
7	behavioral issues
6	peer relationships
7	management needs
6	transitional abilities
6	temper tantrums
6	distractibility
6	generalization of use

Language Content

Deficit Characteristics (1–7)

3	range of semantic functions
3	relational meaning
4	categorization skills
3	association skills
3	spatial concepts
5	following directions
3	comprehension of wh- questions
4	lexical development
3	concept development

4	production of wh- questions
5	non-verbal sequencing
5	verbal sequencing skills
5	narrative development
3	word finding/retrieval
5	descriptions
5	meaning expansion (multiple meanings)
2	absurdities
1	non-verbal problem solving
5	verbal problem solving
4	integration of communicative use and meaning
2	metasemantic skills
1	readiness skills (preschool)

School Age

___	reading
___	math
___	written language

Information Processing

7	attending skills
4	Gestalt processing
5	retention skills
4	auditory/visual discrimination
6	auditory/visual figure-ground
4	short term memory
3	retrieval skills
6	organization of information
3	metacognitive skills

FIGURE 2.6

Language and communication profile.

Language Structure

Deficit Characteristics (1–7)

__2__	mean length of utterance
__3__	structure of utterances (declarative, imperative negative, questions)
__6__	comprehension of complex utterances (simple, compound, complex)
__6__	production of complex utterances (simple, compound, complex)
__3__	comprehension of grammatical morphemes

__5__	production of morphological structures
__4__	organization of utterances (word order)
__4__	integration of content and structure
__4__	morpho-syntactic skills
__1__	oromotor competence

__1__	phonetic repertoire
__1__	phonological processes
__1__	phono-syntactic skills
__2__	metaphonological skills
__1__	intelligibility in known contexts
__1__	intelligibility in unknown contexts
__2__	stimulability
__2__	generalization of form
__1__	intonation
__1__	dysfluencies

Severity Scale

>300 → Severe
200-300 → Moderate
<200 → Mild to Moderate

Kindergarten Placement

Fall
___ Related services
___ SE district
___ 12:2:2 classroom
_√_ 6:1:1 classroom

Fall: Individual Aide: No

Total Score <u>307</u>
Level of functioning:
Severe range

```
┌─────────────────────────────────────────────────────────────────┐
│  Michael                                                          │
│  D.O.B.: 7/27/90                                                  │
│                EXPRESSIVE ONE-WORD PICTURE                        │
│              VOCABULARY TEST—REVISED (EOWPVT-R)                   │
│  Name: Michael                                                    │
│  Date of Birth: 7/27/90                    Date of Test: 1/31/95  │
│  Chronological Age: 4.6                                           │
│  Test Results:                                                    │
│              Raw Score: 18                                        │
│              Language Age: 3–2                                    │
│              Language Standard Score: 77                          │
│              Percentile: 6                                        │
│              Stanine: 2                                           │
│  Comments:                                                        │
└─────────────────────────────────────────────────────────────────┘
```

FIGURE 2.7
Vocabulary test results.

disabilities into the regular classroom involves a change in the roles of the general education and special education teachers. In the process of developing inclusion classrooms, intensive in-service training must be provided to members of the staff who will be involved with inclusion classroom issues such as (1) integrating children with disabilities, (2) teaching nondisabled children about their disabled peers, (3) parent education, and (4) training for related staff.

The immediate staff issue involves providing teachers with knowledge and skills so that school districts can begin the process of mainstreaming. Long-term staff development issues can be addressed at the university level so that ultimately the inclusion teacher will be educationally formulated and created before he is ever hired by a school district. Today, immediate demand involves a bootstrapping process to retool and reeducate the existing staff. A great deal of time and energy must be spent by school districts if this is going to be accomplished during the next year. School districts must make a commitment to the inclusion process philosophically and pragmatically. Administrators must set aside the time, the personnel, and the resources to address teachers' schedules, attitudes, and building resources in order to meet classroom needs.

Michael
D.O.B.: 7/27/90

TEST OF LANGUAGE DEVELOPMENT—PRIMARY
SECOND EDITION

Child's Name: Michael

Date of Birth: 7/27/90   Date of Test: 1/20/95

Chronological Age: 4.5   Examiner: M.R.

SUBTESTS

		Raw Scores	Percentiles	Standard Score
I.	Picture Vocabulary	5	16	7
II.	Oral Vocabulary	0	16	7
III.	Grammatical Understanding	3	9	6
IV.	Sentence Imitation	2	16	7
V.	Grammatical Completion	0	9	6
VI.	Word Discrimination	0	9	6
VII.	Word Articulation	9	25	8

FIGURE 2.8
Language development test results.

Teacher Attitudes

Many general education teachers who have functioned as professionals for several years, feel that they are poorly prepared for working with children with disabilities (Volk & Stahlman, 1994). General education teachers also indicate that their academic training, coursework, and experience do not provide them with the knowledge base to deal with instructional problems and differences, behavioral difficulties, and management concerns. The underlying problem for teachers is an overwhelming sense of inability, which underscores a frustration and anger. Many teachers are frustrated about the fact that they have not been historically part of the decision-making process. As administrators, legislators, attorneys, and parents make decisions about the classroom, teachers are often left out of the process. If the classroom is going to be redesigned with a direction toward multicultural diversity and inclusion programming

Michael
D.O.B.: 7/27/90

Bracken Basic Concept Scale

Child's Name: Michael

Date of Birth: 7/27/90   Date of Test: 1/19/95

Chronological Age: 4.5   Examiner:

Subtests		Raw Score	Standard Score	Percentile Rank
I-V.	SRC	18	5	5
VI.	Direction/Position	17	6	9
VII.	Social/Emotional	12	7	29
VIII.	Size	6	6	22
IX.	Texture/Material	5	6	22
X.	Quantity	8	9	37
XI.	Time/Sequence	16	7	29
Total Test Score		82	78	7

FIGURE 2.9
Bracken basic concept scale results.

for all children, then a key player in the process must be the educator. It is not surprising that teachers are frightened of the mainstreaming process and are angry about being forced into a situation that they feel poorly equipped to manage and handle (Volk & Stahlman, 1994). In addition, parents have fears too. The Opinion Box on p. 56 discusses some of the fears they have about placing children with developmental disabilities in regular classrooms.

It is important to take teachers' feelings and attitudes into consideration as the district works toward the development of a plan or program to meet the mandate of inclusion programming. Administrators need to take the time to provide teachers with a safety network of intensive in-service programming. The self-esteem feelings of the teacher will be reflected in her willingness to face the changes and the challenges necessary within the inclusion classroom. School districts have had a history of problems with educational reform. The process of developing inclusion programming that will meet the individual needs of diverse groups of children will be difficult enough. Administrators and school districts do not want to waste time and energy fighting with their staff. Part of the success related to inclusion involves the philosophical agreement and commitment of the staff to the long-term process.

Michael
D.O.B.: 7/27/90

**PATTERNED ELICITATION SYNTAX TEST
(PEST)**

Child's Name: Michael
Date of Birth: 7/27/90   Date of Test: 1/21/95
Chronological Age: 4.5

Score: 23
Percentile Rank: <10%
Mean For Age: 35

LANGUAGE AND EDUCATIONAL PROFILE:

Goals of Therapy:

GOALS: **LEVEL OF FUNCTIONING:**

I. To develop pragmatic/social interactional skills.

   A. To demonstrate relatedness.   Emerging with maximal prompting

   B. To demonstrate topicalization skills.   Emerging with maximal prompting

   C. To demonstrate the use and knowledge of
       pragmatic functions.   Emerging with maximal prompting

   D. To demonstrate speaker/listener roles.   Emerging with maximal prompting

II. To develop speaker/listener skills.

   A. To respond with the appropriate information
       to simple "wh" question forms (who, what, where). Emerging with maximal prompting

   B. To encode simple "wh" question forms
       (who, what, where) to gain further information.   Emerging with maximal prompting

   C. To follow 3–4 step related directives.   Emerging with maximal prompting

   D. To improve lexicon through categorization skills. Emerging with maximal prompting

FIGURE 2.10
PEST results.

Special Education Teachers

Special education teachers are concerned about how the inclusion changes will affect
them personally and professionally (Volk & Stahlman, 1994). The process of inclusion
alters how and where children with disabilities will be educated. As children with developmental disabilities are shifted from special education classrooms, what will

Michael
D.O.B.: 7/27/90

GOALS:	LEVEL OF FUNCTIONING:
E. To improve accuracy of word retrieval for members of a semantic class (categorization).	Emerging with maximal prompting
F. To construct a narrative schemata.	Emerging with maximal prompting
III. To develop morpho-syntactic structure.	
A. To develop/improve morpho-syntactic structures commensurate with age level expectancies.	Emerging with maximal prompting
IV. To develop cognitive skills.	
A. To demonstrate developmentally appropriate attending behaviors.	Emerging with maximal prompting
V. To develop play/social interactional skills.	
A. To engage in cooperative play skills.	Emerging with maximal prompting
B. To participate in social/play games of low structure and organization.	Emerging with maximal prompting
VI. To demonstrate developmentally appropriate behaviors.	
A. To socialize appropriately within the classroom context.	Emerging with maximal prompting

GROUP SPECIALTY:

The aforementioned goals are integrated throughout a variety of group specialty services utilizing a transdisciplinary approach. In addition to these goals, dance movement therapy addresses gross motor development and social interactions. Music therapy provides an opportunity to communicate through songs, rhythmic patterns, and the use of various melodic instruments. Auditory training employs instructional techniques for basic listening skills. Creative arts concentrates on fine motor skills and exploration of a variety of materials. All specialty services are provided one time per week for 30-minute sessions, with the exception of dance movement therapy, which is provided two times per week.

INDIVIDUAL SPECIALTY SERVICES:

Individual Dance Movement Therapy

Michael has been receiving individual dance/movement therapy two times per week for 30-minute sessions. Goals have focused on developing appropriate social interactions and body im-

FIGURE 2.11
Language and educational profile.

age awareness while engaging in gross motor/creative movement activities. Michael demonstrates poor impulse control and has difficulty with turn-taking. He requires frequent verbal and physical prompting to gain his attention and to focus him onto task. Michael's interactions with the adult during individual dance/movement therapy sessions are often limited and restricted by his need to remain within a set routine. Michael requires 1:1 attention to focus on developing impulse control, social skills, body boundaries, spatial awareness, and awareness of self and others. Individual dance/movement therapy is recommended to continue two times per week for 30-minute sessions.

PSYCHOLOGICAL ASSESSMENT:

Michael's most recent psychological evaluation was conducted on January 13, 1995. Michael was administered a *Stanford-Binet Intelligence Scale: Fourth Edition* and attained a test composite of 105, placing his cognitive abilities in the average range overall. Michael's individual skills showed significant variability, ranging from low average to superior. Relative strengths were expressed in spatial–analytical tasks; relative weaknesses were seen in short-term memory abilities, apparently due to attentional difficulties. Although verbal reasoning abilities were average overall, Michael displayed expressive language difficulties that included phonological and syntax errors, language-organization deficits, and pragmatic difficulties. Additional formal testing yielded performances generally consistent with Michael's *Stanford-Binet* results.

The *Connors Rating Scales* were administered independently to Michael's teachers and to his mother. These are questionnaires designed to compare Michael's reported problem behaviors in the classroom and home environments to a standardized sample. Both rating scales indicated significantly elevated scores on the hyperactivity index; thus, follow-up was suggested.

Throughout the evaluation, Michael displayed a limited attention span and impulsive behavior, often grabbing materials and ignoring directives. Due to these behaviors as well as his young age, the evaluation should be viewed as a minimal estimate of Michael's potential and not predictive of future intellectual functioning.

Informal observations within the classroom reveal Michael to be a lively, animated youngster. Michael still requires adult supervision to follow classroom routines and prevent conflicts with peers. Michael is an alert, curious child yet his high activity level and short attention span appear to prevent sustained involvement in structured tasks. At times he may ignore teacher directives and remove himself from an activity to engage in attention-seeking behaviors that are distracting to his peers. On a one-to-one basis, however, Michael's participation is more consistent.

Although Michael is a friendly, affectionate youngster, he has some difficulty sustaining cooperative play interactions with peers on a consistent basis. Michael may engage in aggressive behavior (hitting or pushing) when confronted with a conflict, such as sharing toys. Attempts at verbal and physical redirection provoke tantrums, at times. A formal behavioral plan is in effect to address the above-mentioned behaviors. Significant improvement has been seen, as Michael responds well to reinforcement techniques. Individual counseling is also recommended to address remaining difficulties. The goals are to limit aggressive behavior and increase positive social interactions.

Child's Name: Michael   Date of Birth: 7/27/90

1. Michael is at risk for being socially isolated, and frustrated in a regular classroom.

2. Michael is at risk for not receiving the attention and individualized instruction that he needs in a regular classroom.

3. Michael is at risk for experiencing social and academic failure within the regular classroom.

4. Michael may become disruptive to instruction and to peer learning in a regular classroom. The severity of disruption is such that education in a regular classroom even with the use of supplementary aids or services cannot be achieved satisfactorily.

5. Michael is at risk for regressing in a regular classroom.

6. The regular classroom is not appropriate to meet the individual and academic needs of the child. Michael requires instructional modifications that cannot be made in the general education classroom by the regular education teacher.

7. Given the nature of Michael's learning needs, education in a regular classroom even with the use of supplementary aides or services cannot be achieved satisfactorily.

   a. The regular classroom is not appropriate to meet the needs of Michael because he requires a highly individualized structured classroom setting.

   b. The regular classroom is not appropriate given Michael's disability because he cannot function independently in terms of social or academic skills.

   c. The regular classroom is not appropriate because Michael cannot manage or regulate his own behavior.

8. Removal from special education may have a potentially harmful effect on Michael's learning and educational development.

9. Because Michael needs opportunities to experience social integration with regular education peers, partial mainstreaming in nonacademic areas is recommended for 3 periods during the school day: lunch, physical education and art. A paraprofessional will be provided as a means of support to transition the child from the special education classroom to the mainstream sessions.

FIGURE 2.12
Least restrictive environment statement.

become of the special education teacher? As universities begin to shift and alter teacher preparation programs, will the special education teacher be phased out of the instructional system? For the special education teacher, there is also a concern that her services will no longer be required within the new system. The reality, however, will probably include the special education teacher, but her professional role will be quite different. Consequently, special educators have the extraordinary opportunity to redefine their professional responsibilities (Hines, 1994). They also have the opportunity to redesign their relationships with other professionals. Of primary importance is that the special education teacher needs to understand that inclusion must incorporate the abilities, skills, and competencies of special educators within the general education context, and that if inclusion is to succeed, the special education teacher must be part of the general education classroom. This relationship, however, may vary from school district to school district as various models are created to meet the mandate of inclusive programming. Creative planning and collaboration will be key factors to program development.

DISTRICT ISSUES

District Planning

School districts should create an inclusion committee that is charged with the responsibility of developing a district-wide plan to develop an inclusion program within a specific time period. The committee should consist of administrators, general education teachers, special education teachers, psychologists, and parents. All of these individuals have an investment in the success of the inclusion process and, as a result, they should all be involved with the development of a workable plan. Inclusion cannot be accomplished all at once, nor can districts utilize existing models. Inclusion programs should be community based and should take into consideration the multicultural diversity of the unique setting in which it will be used. Clearly, this is not an issue of "reinventing the wheel," but rather an understanding that inclusion must be culturally based and community sensitive in its origin if it is going to be successful. There cannot be too much time spent on planning (York, Doyle, & Kronberg, 1992). The commitment of parents, teachers, administrators, and resources to the development of a long-term district vision will clarify the community's thinking about the roles and responsibilities of all of the decision makers. The plan should be disseminated and circulated for review and commentary. PTA meetings and hearings should be scheduled for open discussion. All voices should be heard and modifications should be made in plans and programs. The first step should be the plan, not the program.

Resources

To implement an inclusion program, the district plan should detail the commitment of teachers, resources, space, and children first in a pilot program. It is important to detail the financial impact that must be committed to educational reform. How much will it cost to put in the ramps? How much will it cost to reallocate space? Will there be a need for additional teachers? Does the district have to hire a consultant? Do teachers need additional time to plan, study, and schedule? Do teachers need special meeting

---

Question: Do you have any fears about placing your child with disabilities in a regular classroom? What are the problems and issues?

- My child was in a regular classroom for two years. David's behavior was not understood. He was lost in a class of 28 children. The regular education teacher felt he was misbehaving on purpose. My child was lost and I am extremely afraid of inappropriate inclusion of kids with special needs for the wrong reasons.

- A child with disabilities has special needs that cannot be adequately met in a regular classroom. They tend to "fall through the cracks." Special needs require special skills, time, and understanding that a classroom teacher is unable to provide due to the number of children in the classroom and/or the time involved to support the special child. Not *all* disabilities should be included. Each child is an individual and needs an individual evaluation.

- I feel that overcrowding in the classroom might be an issue with my son who does need extra attention.

- I want more than anything for Anthony to be able to function in a regular classroom, but he has to be ready. I think we're getting our priorities confused. Yes, schools help to socialize children, but their main function is education. All children should be in an environment that is conducive to learning. Most classroom teachers at the moment are ill prepared to deal with the problem posed by children with disabilities, especially if we put a whole group of them in without adequate support. Inclusion affects everyone. Children are our most vital asset, and a good education is the greatest gift we can give them and society in general. We have to stop kowtowing to the almighty dollar and think of what's best for the children.

- I feel that a lot of regular classrooms are very crowded. Large groups of children and one teacher cannot always fulfill these children's needs of giving them enough individual attention as it is. Never mind dealing with a child with disabilities who may need more time and more special help. The teacher will bend over more for the child with disabilities and devote less time to the regular class. In the long run, the children will pay the price in either direction that it can go.

- I feel that inclusion does work in many cases. As for my child, inclusion is not a solution. A one-on-one classroom setting works best for my child. Inclusion may work for some, but I feel that in my child's situation, it just is not the answer.

- I do not feel that the average teacher in my school district can handle a child with a disability in a *normal* classroom environment. Most children with disabilities have problems interacting with others who do not have disabilities. This causes the child with disabilities to be singled out and ridiculed. This does not help the child with disabilities who in most cases already has low self-esteem. In a normal classroom there are too many children for a teacher to provide the extra individual attention that is needed for a child with disabilities. It is our goal to have our child mainstreamed; however, my child must be ready physically and mentally before it can happen.

- I trust that if my child is put in inclusion then he or she is ready and fully prepared for district schooling. However, if after inclusion there are still some language skills that need to be worked on, the district should notify the proper district speech and/or language teachers for continued support and work with the appropriate kindergarten or first grade teacher, so as to not hold up the child's academic learning skills.

- The problems are twofold: (1) Children in a regular classroom who do not have a disability may not treat a child with disabilities kindly. Children by nature can be cruel to anyone who is different from themselves. (2) Parents of so-called "normal" children will not appreciate having a child with disabilities in a regular class. The parents may or may not say anything in public, but whatever they say at home might be overheard by the "normal" kids and be repeated to the children with disabilities. An inclusion program is a setup for failure for kids with disabilities and unfair to "normal" kids. No one's needs are being met completely in an inclusion program.

- The only real problem is the lack of training on the part of the classroom teachers. Also, many of them are angry because if they wanted to deal with students with disabilities, they would have chosen special education. These are the complaints I hear in the faculty room.

- I am a teacher. Until I had a child with a disability, I really did not know how to modify my lessons. Even in regular classrooms, there are children who are not placed in special education settings because parents do not want it. For many years (and even now), I have taught children with problems. I have not really got the skills that a special education teacher may have or a speech pathologist. I just do my best. I have to learn on my own. In my school (N.Y. City), I give preps to the teachers. Now, I am teaching social studies. No one ever alerts me to special needs. I see 750 children each week. It is hard to learn each child's needs in dealing with this academic subject. I also supervise in the lunchroom. We serve 600 children each lunch period. Not much is done for the children who cannot handle the lunchroom environment.

- I worry that my child won't get the extra attention he might need and also other children will make fun of him. He likes school and I don't want to force him into something he is not ready for, which will make him hate school. He gets mad very fast if he is forced into doing something and he cannot do it. His attention is not always there either. He still needs help with things.

- A regular education teacher paces the class too quickly for a child to move along. The child loses his or her place, gets more easily frustrated and begins to behave inappropriately. He or she then disrupts class and gets in trouble a lot *and* doesn't learn what is being taught. The child is tormented, teased, etc., by "normal" classmates with references to being "stupid," "a dunce," "slow," etc.

Note: Parents of children with special needs in the local community and at SLCD were sent anonymous surveys. These responses are representative samples.

times? Will new teachers have to be hired? Will teachers have to be fired? Which district children will be placed in regular classrooms? What will administrators and teachers tell parents? These are just some of the questions and issues that must be discussed prior to the initiation of an inclusive classroom. The more resources a school district is willing to commit to the development of the inclusion classroom, the greater the likelihood of success for all concerned. It will be the responsibility of administrators to work with school boards to gain the financial support needed.

Teacher Training

Once the school district has developed a plan, a teacher-in-service training and support program must be established to encourage teachers to express their feelings and address their instructional concerns. A consultant may be helpful in organizing discussions and activities that will address classroom issues. Teachers need training in academic areas concerning the exceptional child, technical assistance in terms of child management issues, and consultation about classroom arrangements.

It may be important to network regular and special education teachers. Creating the link and a collaborative working relationship would allow teachers not only to work together but to contribute their diverse skills to a common goal—development of the inclusion classroom. Coteaching and team teaching may provide a short-term resolution to teacher training issues. Rather than teaching the regular teacher about special education, the district may assign both teachers to the inclusion classroom. The competency to meet the needs of typical children and children with developmental disabilities is then available in the classroom.

Instructional differences may become a concern as teachers begin to collaborate. The general education teacher and the special education teacher must learn to meet each other's needs interpersonally and instructionally within the same classroom. The classroom does not belong to the general education or the special education teacher; neither one is in charge. The two teachers have different skills and each must contribute equally to the success of the classroom. In learning to collaborate with each other, they will learn to rely on their differences (see Chapter 3). Teachers must help each other understand how they can both contribute to the physical, social, and instructional interaction that must occur in an inclusion classroom. They must be able to give each other advice, support, and information on (1) children with disabilities and those without, (2) facilitating parent support, (3) special equipment, (4) instructional supplies and materials, (5) classroom organization, (6) appropriate teaching techniques, (7) managing and positioning children within the classroom, (8) the development of a core curriculum, and (9) the development of an IEP for each child. It may be helpful early in the process to provide teacher teams with in-service training that would include visiting other inclusion programs. This field observation may provide teachers with an opportunity to observe how inclusion programming is achieved in other districts.

To achieve inclusion programming, teachers need to redefine their roles and responsibilities within the classroom. Teachers need to rethink who they are and what they do. Hines (1994) describes the fact that regular educators may redefine themselves as "content experts" while special educators may redefine themselves as "learning strategists" for both types of students in the inclusion classroom. The collaborative relationship between teachers filters down to a collaborative relationship between children; the teachers' relationship provides a working model for the children to learn about.

Coteaching and teaming may provide the instructional design for implementing the inclusion mandate. The inclusion classroom may initially be a nontraditional classroom, and as a result teachers need to be creative in resolving anticipated barriers. The inclusion team must seek to find creative solutions to parent–teacher, teacher–child, and child–child problems. Just as regular and special education teachers must accommodate each other's strengths and skills, administrators must make accommodations for teachers. Teachers must be provided with a greater degree of flexibility in terms of scheduling meetings and professional networking. Teachers need to spend time sharing ideas and materials with colleagues. The interdisciplinary networking among professionals will encourage instructional creativity within the classroom.

As school districts develop in-service programs that support the development of the collaborative relationship between regular and special education teachers, classroom coverage must be addressed. Teachers should be provided with the opportunity to spend time making curriculum modifications, instructional adjustments, and discussing creative solutions to child problems. One mechanism to release teachers from classrooms involves the use of floating teachers (Chalmers, 1993). Floating teachers provide the mechanism for the regular staff to engage in in-service instruction for large blocks of time. Floating teachers can also provide the mechanism for large groups or small groups of teacher teams to meet on a regular weekly or monthly basis. School district administrators must make a commitment of resources to the concept of teacher flexibility. Administrators must also see that the success of inclusion involves a redefinition of the role of the teacher. The inclusion classroom is a new classroom; it requires a new type of teacher who can function in a creatively different manner within the classroom. The inclusion teacher, in attempting to redefine herself or himself, requires support from colleagues, administrators, and parents. To function as a new teacher, she or he must develop the insight to reorganize thinking about the teaching process and the classroom. This will enable the inclusion teacher to meet the challenge of the integrated classroom with new ideas that will generate instructionally creative teaching techniques.

CONCLUSION

In this chapter, we discussed some of the historical issues that underlie the controversies concerning inclusion programming. What was the intent of P.L. 94-142, and its resulting mandate? Was the intent to include *all* children with disabilities? If the least restrictive environment is defined as the regular classroom, school districts will have to proceed through an exhaustive process to place the child with disabilities in a self-contained class. Many associations, educators, and parents argue that the least restrictive environment must continue to be individually based on the educational needs of the child with disabilities. Perhaps what is most challenging about inclusion is that it very much reflects a social process. American society has invested a great deal of legal time and energy to ensure the rights of minority groups. How can the inclusion mission safeguard the rights of those with disabilities while providing individualized instructional services?

Aside from the definition of least restrictive environment, we must consider the changing roles of special education and general education teachers within the inclusion classroom. Professionals are anxious about their competencies to meet the challenges of the diverse multicultural mix of children. Inclusion must be seen as a site-based and community-based program. Each community must decide for itself on how the inclusion mandate will be met; it is important for school district personnel to talk among themselves as well as with parents. Just as the role of teachers will change, so too must the role of parents (see Chapter 5). Very often, administrators and teachers talk about the fact that educational reform must be accomplished, but parents are not included in the decision-making process. If inclusion is going to reflect the community, its population, its issues, and its concerns, then parents must be major contributors to educational reform.

Inclusion cannot be accomplished in a month or even in a year. Each school district must engage in a dialogue process with the intent of developing a mission statement, a program proposal, and an implementation plan. Time is an investment that underlies the success of all inclusion programs. The more clearly defined the issues, the greater the likelihood that inclusion will ultimately be implemented. Parents, teachers, and administrators need to discuss their feelings and fears about educational changes and reforms. If all of the players are not committed to the process, a great deal of time and energy will be wasted on interpersonal infighting and control issues.

In the last analysis, as educators, we must address the questions raised by Billingsley (1993). Inclusion assumes that children with disabilities will benefit from the regular classroom. This is a great leap of faith. Will they? Can *all* of them benefit? How do we decide if they are "ready" to face the challenge of a regular classroom? Is the real agenda here financial savings? If inclusion fails, then what? Built into the inclusion process should be a fail-safe network for children with disabilities. Administrators, teachers, and parents need to develop a child profile for children who will enter the regular classroom first and then decide the alternatives if specific children are not able to manage and/or benefit. Inclusion is a challenge for *all* children. What will educational reform teach us about child learning? What will educational reform teach us about ourselves as professionals?

❧   *A Few Words from Cathy Ambrosio*   ❧

My son Joseph had an opportunity to receive services as a preschool child in a highly specialized program for language disordered children. I believe that Joseph would not have achieved mainstreaming without the opportunity for early intervention programming. I am mortified and terrified for other parents of children with special needs when I think that the federal and state governments are considering cuts to early intervention and preschool program services. My son is an example of the fact that early intervention works. The earlier a problem is addressed, the more likely a child is to achieve mainstreaming education. Developmental disabilities do not disappear. Our basic experiences with simple medical problems and illnesses should have taught us that when a simple problem is not addressed or treated, it develops and progresses into a severe unmanageable illness or disorder. As a parent of a child with special needs, to know that a child has a problem and not address it is a terrible social injustice. I have always believed "small children, small problems"—get in early and intervene. Because I have had the opportunity to proceed through special education during the past several years, I can share my tears and fears with all of you.

I do not believe that *all* handicapped children will benefit from being in a regular classroom. It depends on the child's social, behavioral, and academic level of functioning. Also, the classroom teacher's training and her ability to modify the instruction to meet the individual needs of the child become important to the child's integration within the classroom. Having been through this with Joseph this past year, I also realize that the makeup of the classroom provides an important backdrop for the child with special needs. The regular classroom must be "readied" to receive such a child. All of these issues must be taken into consideration before a child with special needs is placed in a regular classroom. Such a child should only be placed in a regular classroom if he is "ready." I define this word in terms of his maturity, his confidence, and his ability to function independently. A child who can socially integrate himself with other children can benefit from interaction with normal peers. The child who is disruptive or unable to work with others cannot benefit from the regular experience. In fact, the regular classroom may negatively affect not only the child with the disability but all of the other children.

I think most parents know their child well and also know if the child is ready to be in a regular classroom. Parents should play an important role in the decision-making process. Currently, parents do not serve as voting members of the CSE. If inclusion programming is going to be part of the educational process, the role of parents must change.

My son Joseph had problems once he was placed in a regular classroom. The children in my son's class teased him a lot and even resented that he got "baby" work to do. Fortunately, the teacher did not stand for any teasing or name calling, and by the second half of the school year, many children came to accept Joseph. I think the size of the class affected the way that children interacted with each other. More than 20 students does make a difference; it is very difficult for the teacher to handle so many children. With the introduction of children with special needs into a regular classroom, the teacher needs to modify her lessons to meet each child's individual needs. Joseph needed a great deal of individual instruction and support.

Joseph entered a regular classroom as a fourth grader. There was one other child with a disability in the room. My biggest fear was that the normal children would not accept him and that his self-esteem would suffer. Joseph does feel bad at times that he cannot do the same work as the other children; the teacher does try to give him the same material, but at his level. My concern is that the learning gap will get bigger each year and that his disability will become more apparent. Each year I worry that the majority of what takes place in the classroom is going over his head. It is clear that without a caring and well-trained teacher, Joseph will become depressed and frustrated and find school to be a waste of time.

Luckily, Joseph's teacher has a master's in special education. My district did provide a training session, but did not require that all teachers attend. I feel that any teacher who has a student with a disability in her class should be required to receive educational training on inclusion issues. Teachers need to be given a tremendous amount of support and instruction on inclusion programming. They have a responsibility and an obligation to learn about the process. Regular education teachers who are going to be involved in inclusion programming need to have an outside consultant who is an expert in inclusion.

I have thought a great deal about the parents of the nondisabled children in Joseph's class. I have not found them to be as understanding and supportive as I would have liked. They are fearful that their "normal" child will be affected or slighted by my child. I think there needs to be a training program for children, as well as their parents, on feelings and differences—on the subject of how we need to respect each other.

I think my district is trying to make inclusion work, but there just has not been enough training for administrators and teachers. They seem to have the concept, but not the changes and goals that are necessary to implement programming. The idea may be wonderful, but the reality may involve something quite different—particularly for the child with disabilities.

I have learned that child advocacy is my responsibility. Over the years, I have realized that this is true; Joseph can only succeed if I continue to be an effective advocate for him. I have had the necessary training as a parent advocate, and I will continue to use these skills throughout Joseph's education. If I did not advocate for my son, he could easily slip through the cracks. Every teacher I have ever spoken to has confirmed the fact that parents need to advocate for their children. Teachers do not have the interest or the time to do that. Parents have a vested interest in their children and their children's success in school.

Cathy Ambrosio

QUESTIONS FOR CLASSROOM DISCUSSION

1. Why must the special educator and the regular educator collaborate when providing inclusion programming for the child with special needs?

2. What type of child would most easily be included in the regular education classroom?

3. What type of child would have the most difficulty being included in the regular education classroom?

4. What do you consider to be the most critical issue when implementing inclusion programming in a school district?

5. What kind of district planning would be necessary when developing a district-wide inclusion philosophy and program?

BIBLIOGRAPHY

Billingsley, F. (1993). In my dreams: A response to some current trends in education. *Journal of the Association for Persons with Severe Handicaps, 18,* 61–63.

Chalmers, L. (1993). Successful inclusion in rural school settings: How one rural Minnesota school district made it work. *Rural Educator, 14*(3), 31–32.

Evans, D., Harris, D., Adeigbola, M., Houston, D., and Argott, L. W. (1993). Restructuring special education services. *Teacher Education and Special Education, 16*(2), 137–145.

Hines, R. A. (1994). The best of both worlds? Collaborative teaching for effective inclusion. *Schools in the Middle, 3*(4), 3–6.

Individuals with Disabilities Education Act (1993). A reaction to full inclusion: A reaffirmation of the right of students with learning disabilities to a continuum of services. *Journal of Learning Disabilities, 26*(9), 596.

Leister, C., Koonce, D., and Nisbet, S. (1993). Best practices for preschool programs: An update on inclusive settings. *Day Care and Early Education, 21*(2), 9–12.

McCormick, C., and First, P. (1994). The cost of inclusion: Educating students with special needs. *School Business Affairs, 60*(7), 30–31, 34–36.

National Joint Committee on Learning Disabilities (1991). Providing appropriate education for students with learning disabilities in regular education classrooms, *ASHA, 33,* 15–17.

Pierce, J., Rasdall, J., and Ferguson, J. (1993). A bridge over troubled water: Facility needs for inclusive classrooms. *Educational Facility Planner, 31*(5), 10–15.

Polansky, H. B. (1994). The meaning of inclusion: Is it an option or a mandate? *School Business Affairs, 60*(7), 27–29.

Reynolds, M. C., & Birch, J. W. (1988). *Adaptive mainstreaming: A primer for teachers and principals* (3rd ed.). New York: Longman.

Volk, D., and Stahlman, J. (1994). "I think everybody is afraid of the unknown": Early childhood teachers prepare for mainstreaming. *Day Care & Early Education, 21*(3), 13–17.

Webb, N. (1994). With new court decisions backing them, advocates see inclusion as a question of values. *The Harvard Education Letter, 10*(4), 1–3.

York, J., Doyle, M., and Kronberg, R. (1992). A curriculum development process for inclusive classrooms. *Focus on Exceptional Children, 25*(4), 1–16.

3

The Collaborative Team

LEARNING OBJECTIVES

After you have read this chapter, you should be able to:

1. Discuss the relationship between collaboration and the development of inclusive classrooms.

2. Discuss the various stakeholders in collaborative decision making.

3. Describe the interactive process between the stakeholders. The process can be diagrammed by means of a match–mismatch model.

4. Describe the concerns presented by parents, teachers, and administrators that act as barriers to decision making.

5. Describe various kinds of modifications that can be made by parents, teachers, and administrators to facilitate inclusive education.

6. Discuss why the inclusion concept requires a great deal of preplanning before programs are implemented.

*I*n the last chapter, we discussed some of the programmatic results that have been occurring as a function of legislative changes in the definition of least restrictive environment. Once least restrictive environment (LRE) changed from "the placement that met the individual needs of the child" to "the general education classroom," decisions about educational programs and services began to change. With the emphasis changing toward general education for *all* children, schools need to develop classroom models that provide opportunities for children with developmental disabilities. In discussing issues related to the collaborative team, we attempted to make a distinction between the Committee on Special Education (CSE) and the collaborative team(s) that must be created to deal with the decision generated by the CSE to provide inclusion for a specific child.

The Committee on Special Education, which was discussed in the last chapter, is a federally defined and legally constituted multidisciplinary team. Members of the CSE collaborate and make an individual educational decision about a specific child. Inclusion represents an opportunity for *all* children. As authors and educators, we recognize that inclusion may not be a practical reality for all children although it is an opportunity that must be considered. The primary responsibility of the CSE is to decide whether a child can benefit from an inclusive educational experience. As we discuss in this chapter, the definition of *benefit* is not only controversial, but also requires collaborative consensus within each and every school. Part of the decision-making process of the Committee on Special Education is to explore inclusion as an educational opportunity and option because there is, and must remain to be, an educational continuum for all children. Once the CSE has decided and recommended for or against inclusion, the assumption of benefit becomes the primary responsibility of the collaborative team, which is the topic of this chapter. At this point, given the "newness" of inclusion, the assumption of benefit becomes a weighty responsibility for members of the collaborative team. The primary responsibility of the collaborative team is to ensure inclusion success and, therefore, the stakeholders must develop a model that will remove all of the barriers to the inclusive classroom. Collaboration involves a process of ongoing discussion that begins with the question, How do we achieve inclusion?

In this chapter, collaboration is discussed as a creative partnership that can be used by teachers, parents, and administrators to achieve inclusion within the regular classroom. Effective collaboration provides the framework for developing the inclusion classroom. Collaboration is a learning process. Collaboration requires that the participants within the process—parents, teachers, administrators, and children—engage in shared decision making. Collaboration cannot be achieved all at once, just as inclusion cannot be achieved all at once. The success of collaboration involves the commitment of people to a long-term self-discovery process. Just as inclusion establishes a challenge to education, collaboration requires a redefinition of the roles of parents, teachers, and administrators so that they can reorganize educational learning within the regular classroom. "Collaboration consultation is an interactive process that enables people with diverse expertise to generate creative solutions to mutually defined problems.

The outcome is enhanced, altered and produces solutions that are different from those that the individual team members would produce independently" (Idol, Paolucci-Whitcomb, & Nevin, 1986).

Collaboration consultation cannot be achieved if we continue to use the traditional time constraints, organizational structure, clinical roles, and professional responsibilities that have been utilized by educational institutions in the past. Each school must embark on a process of self-exploration and development in order to create a working model that uniquely reflects the issues of teachers, parents, children, and administrators within a specific multicultural community. In this chapter, we discuss some of the strategies, procedures, and variables that should be considered by a school for modifying traditional ideas to achieve educational reform. In viewing itself as a model school, each educational program has the opportunity to create a highly specialized environment that is collaboratively designed to meet the needs of all children within the inclusion classroom (Marston & Heistad, 1994).

Coufal (1993) said that collaboration defines how participants interact with each other as equal contributors in a decision-making process in order to generate common or shared goals. Collaboration requires the reciprocal acknowledgment of all participants in a decision-making process that assigns an equal status to each contributor. The collaborative process requires that professionals and parents be coequal and coparticipate in the dialogue exchange (Coufal, 1993). This suggests that all of the "players"—administrators, teachers, and parents—should share goal decision making, status, accountability, and resources in an ongoing working relationship (Friend & Cook, 1992).

The process of "coming together" in education requires a reevaluation and recreation of roles, responsibilities, and relationships. If inclusion is to be achieved, administrators, teachers, and parents must learn to work together as equal partners. To do this, collaboration teams must pay close attention to interactional variables, communication skills, problem-solving skills, and conflict resolution strategies. The formation and development of a collaborative team involves a learning process that includes a set of competencies. Members of the team must consider the following communicative competency skills (Crais, 1993):

- Willingness to listen to others
- Being supportive of someone else's ideas
- Being receptive to input
- Managing differences of opinion and conflict
- Accepting and integrating the suggestions of others
- Expressing opinions and ideas without criticism
- Acknowledging and using the ideas of others
- Being flexible

These interactive behaviors contribute to the effectiveness and efficiency of collaboration. By developing these behaviors and adopting a collaborative style, the participants ultimately create and generate:

1. A working relationship
2. Communication goals
3. An inclusion classroom
4. A model school, which is "uniquely different" from anything that the individual collaborators could produce independently (Idol et al., 1986)

The significance of collaboration to the success of inclusion is critical. Collaboration is the determining process by which inclusion will either succeed or fail. As schools become more interested in inclusive education, the need to identify a process for decision making will become more intense. Inclusive classrooms require shared decision making and problem solving. Parents, teachers, and administrators as stakeholders must believe that a shared effort will result in a better outcome than an individual effort (Dettmer, Thurston, & Dyck, 1993). The social and psychological dynamics of contributing to a group's decision-making process create a premium on maintaining positive communicative relationships (Friend & Bursuck, 1996).

THE INCLUSION CLASSROOM

The classroom is an ecological environment that must be created and organized by the collaborative team. The classroom can be viewed as a complex clinical model. The purpose of a clinical system is to provide the team with a representational structure that can be used to highlight why specific interactions do or do not operate effectively. Chess (1986) described a set of relationships that could contribute to an operational model within the classroom. The use of such a model underscores the fact that there is a synergy of factors that interface within a classroom. The collaborative team needs to understand these variables and how they affect one another in making decisions about children, learning procedures, classroom organization, and curricula. The use of an interactional model allows the team to analyze on an ongoing basis the effectiveness of classroom decision making.

Chess (1986) described "a goodness of fit" concept, which can be utilized as a starting point for decision making. Tiegerman-Farber and Radziewicz (1995) described decision making in terms of an interactional process between individuals; this model is helpful in understanding how parents, teachers, and administrators can develop the characteristics and behaviors of a collaborative style in order to create the inclusion classroom. Figure 3.1 describes the collaboration that must occur in order for the inclusion classroom to be developed. The cooperative working relationship and commonality of mission will facilitate decision making that provides the impetus for change in traditional programming.

If we look more closely at this model within the collaborative framework, we realize that all members of the collaborative team need to be aware of each other's educational perceptions. Once these baseline perceptions are discussed and agreed on, joint expectations arise. These joint expectations manifest themselves in mutual goals, parity, shared participation, and accountability, all of which are inherent in collaboration.

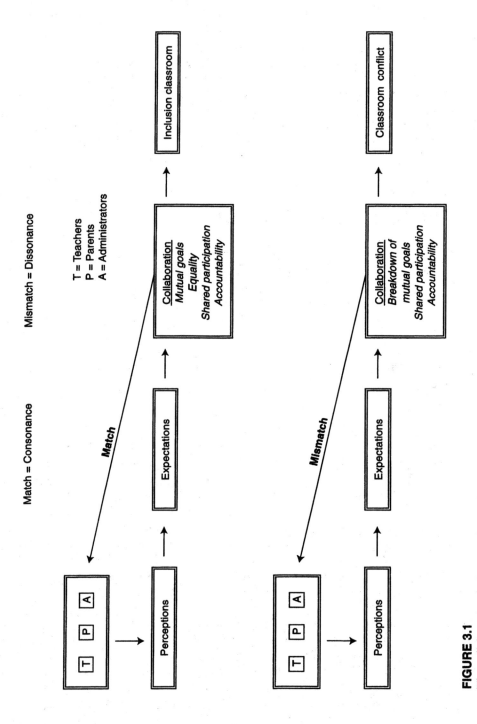

FIGURE 3.1

The collaborative decision-making process—developing a shared perspective.

The consequence of this matching process is an inclusion classroom that promotes success for both children with special needs and regular education peers.

The inclusion classroom as an ecological environment is different from the traditional classroom. The goals are different, the teacher is different, the environment is different, learning is different, child outcomes are different, and the curriculum is different. The inclusion classroom stimulates a synergy of change focused within one small space—the classroom. The agents of change, the collaborators, must all share a common focus and commitment to create the necessary change. The characteristics and behaviors contributing to a collaborative style are described with parents, teachers, administrators, and children in mind. The characteristics of

- Coequality and coparticipation
- Reciprocity
- Commonality in goals and
- Accountability

are discussed given the framework of a goodness of fit model. The collaborators and contributors to the final product, which is the inclusion classroom, are described in terms of the interactional variables just listed (Coufal, 1993).

TEACHERS

Coequality and Coparticipation

Within the collaborative process, the role of the teacher will be different. Who the teacher is and how the teacher functions within the inclusion classroom suggest many challenging changes for the new classroom professional. Teachers need to be provided with intensive in-service instruction over a long period of time (Chalmers, 1993). As children with disabilities are introduced into the general education classroom, regular education teachers need to receive formal instructional training on the organizational changes that will occur within their classrooms. Teachers need to know about developmental disabilities and what they mean educationally and behaviorally. They need to know what to expect from chiid with a disability. They also need to know about management strategies, about the kinds of procedures and techniques that can be used to integrate the child with a disability into ongoing classroom activities.

Coteaching or team teaching may provide one educational mechanism for beginning the inclusion process. This would mean that the role of the special education teacher would change from that of providing direct services to children with disabilities in a separate classroom to providing services to *all* children in the same classroom (Chalmers, 1993). Team teaching allows the regular education teacher and the special education teacher to work within the classroom as equal partners who coparticipate in teaching. Classroom goals are developed by both teachers working together to achieve a common educational concept—individual achievement for each child. Team teaching provides a mechanism for each specialist to support and to respect the unique contributions of the other teaching professional. The special education teacher can assist the regular education teacher and the regular education children to develop an understanding of the individual needs of children with disabilities within the classroom. The special education teacher has a set of specialty skills that includes management techniques, task analysis skills, and instructional procedures that can facilitate individualized programming for *all* of the children in the inclusion classroom, because children who have been classified as special education are not the only ones with individual needs. The special education teacher can also assist in facilitating interactions between the regular education teacher and the children with disabilities, as well as between child peer groups.

The regular education teacher can contribute to the inclusion classroom by providing instructional and modeling skills for the special education teacher and the regular education students. The regular education teacher is uniquely skilled in identifying academic curriculum goals that provide a level of motivation and skill opportunity for the children with disabilities. Each teacher has something to share with colleagues. Each teacher has something to contribute to the transdisciplinary curriculum and to the integration of students within the classroom. The professional difference creates a strength in the inclusion classroom. Each teacher contributes her or his expertise to an educational curriculum that could not have been developed by either separately. Figure 3.2 describes how equality in roles and participation can enhance collaborative decision making between teachers. Coteachers need to acknowledge their academic–professional differences as a starting point to inclusion development. Dynamic collaborative decision making through dialogue exchange creates a new classroom product and an exciting interpersonal process (Coufal, 1993). When there is a mismatch between teachers, collaborative decisions cannot be generated. Teachers need to analyze the interactional dialogue by evaluating their perceptions and expectations concerning classroom factors.

On closer examination of Figure 3.2 we see that the special education teacher and the regular education teacher need to share their perceptions of various classroom factors such as children, procedures, organization, goals, and curriculum. From these shared perceptions comes a set of shared expectations. If the collaborative process is operating correctly, these expectations are based on clear communication, active listening and responding, effective brainstorming, and creative integration of ideas. Consequently, good decision making regarding all classroom factors is generally achieved and an overall condition of consonance between teachers exists. If on the other hand, the two teachers do not clearly communicate actively, listen to each other and respond to each other, or maintain a good rapport, there will be no attainment of shared perceptions or expectations. A state of dissonance will arise and result in independent decision making rather than shared problem solving.

Reciprocity

Many special education teachers are concerned that with the development of inclusive classrooms, they will lose their jobs. Special education teachers express the frustration that their skills and training are being phased out of the educational system. The

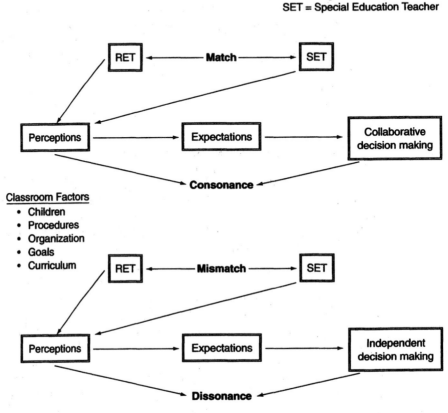

Match = Consonance   Mismatch = Dissonance

RET = Regular Education Teacher
SET = Special Education Teacher

FIGURE 3.2

Teacher collaboration—working toward a shared vision of the inclusive classroom.

regular education teacher, on the other hand, describes an inability to meet the challenge of inclusive instruction. Many teachers claim that they are poorly prepared to work with the child with disabilities in a regular classroom. Many teachers express negative attitudes about children with disabilities because of the necessary changes that must occur as these students are integrated. Many regular education teachers pinpoint behavioral disruptions and the inordinate amount of time that children with special needs will take away from general education instruction. Most teachers express feelings of incompetence, fear, anger, and frustration about being coerced into inclusion classrooms (Volk & Stahlman, 1994).

Professional change must include a process of personal growth. Teachers need to talk about their feelings, their fears, and their concerns. If teachers do not have control over their classrooms, what do they have control of? Teachers need to speak to each other and see themselves within a supportive environment. The inclusion classroom must be supportive of teacher change. If the classroom is seen as a battleground in which teachers are fighting with each other and fighting with students, nothing will be accomplished.

The reciprocity of interpersonal exchange allows the regular teacher and the special education teacher to work toward recognizing how they can support each other in their personal and professional growth. They must each see that they have an investment in the inclusion classroom. Inclusion cannot occur without each of them; in fact, it cannot occur unless both of them are working together (White & White, 1993). They must learn how to talk to each other about children, curriculum, and management issues. They must learn that inclusive education cannot succeed with "territorial" thinking.

The inclusion classroom can only be developed when each teacher recognizes her or his uniqueness, contribution to the inclusion classroom, and interdependence with the other teacher. Looking at Figure 3.3, you can see that when the regular education teacher and the special education teacher do not "match" in terms of providing sup-

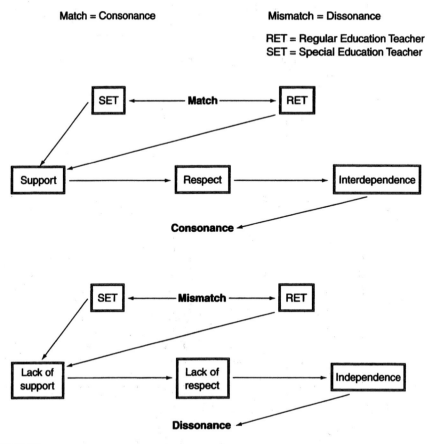

FIGURE 3.3
Teachers' attitudes are important in creating collaborative interdependence.

port and respect, they will work independently and an atmosphere of dissonance will result in an unsuccessful inclusion classroom. Reciprocal exchange between coteachers suggests that the inclusion classroom is really a bridge that spans across a professional divide; each teacher from her or his side builds toward and reaches toward a common meeting place in the middle (see Figure 3.4). Ultimately, inclusion within the classroom can only be achieved when the bridge between teachers provides a firm foundation for all children—regular education and children with disabilities—to walk across.

Common Goals

Because special education and regular education teachers will be working together within the inclusion classroom, it may be of critical benefit to both if they conceptualize the classroom as a working model (Denton & Foley, 1994). This conceptual approach allows both teachers to design the new classroom as an integrated setting. Teachers can approach the process pragmatically. Given specific child and resource limitations, they can also approach the process creatively, given common goals and innovative curricula.

Goal setting is a task that requires a considerable amount of time. When the teachers are recommending goals, they should consider the following items (Pogorzelski & Kelly, 1993).

FIGURE 3.4
The inclusive classroom can only be developed through the shared professional and personal countributions of different teachers.

- What are the desired outcomes of the program?
- How will these outcomes be measured?
- Are the parents in agreement with these outcomes?

The purpose of inclusion is to diminish the isolation of children with disabilities from their regular education peers and to provide socialization experiences for both groups of children. The following Opinion Box describes some of the theoretical, procedural, and programmatic complexities that must be discussed when developing an inclusion classroom. The inclusion classroom requires that teachers, parents, and administrators think about educational learning in a different way. Teachers, parents, and administrators must be willing to change their roles and responsibilities in order to create a diverse instructional environment to meet the needs of all children. With this in mind, two common goals that should be on the Individualized Education Plan (IEP) are

1. To provide the least restrictive environment
2. To provide maximum socialization experiences

In addition to these goals, the special education teacher and the regular education teacher must determine the academic and social levels of functioning for all children in the inclusion classroom. Once the teachers match perceptions regarding these questions, they can then set common classroom goals (Jayanthi & Friend, 1992). Figure 3.5 illustrates both a match and mismatch of teachers. One results in consonance and the development of common classroom goals, the other results in dissonance and the development of unclear or inappropriate classroom goals. The perceptual variable in Figure 3.5 relates to the perceptions and related beliefs of the teacher approaching the problem that needs to be resolved. These beliefs, which are often based on old information and past experiences, result in a cumulative effect that provides the foundation for viewpoints and proposed recommendations. Each teacher's belief system generates specific expectations in terms of (1) behavior, (2) the outcome of events, and (3) the interpretation of experiential data. When the perceptions and expectations match the realities of the environment, there is a synchrony or confluence that flows from perceptions to expectations to environmental occurrences. Alternatively, when there is a mismatch between perceptions, expectations, and the reality of an environmental occurrence, dissonance results that requires conflict resolution. Each teacher utilizes an individualized representational system which serves to frame her or his decisions based on learned knowledge and past experience. This operational schema functions as an information processing loop in decision making. It also explains the divergence of thinking and the difference in decision-making patterns that result from independent professionals. Teachers must translate their differences in educational training, procedures, and content into common inclusion themes. Establishing a common classroom focus can facilitate the generation of interdependent goals. Teachers must agree about the educational needs of each child as an interdependent learner in the classroom. The child with disabilities must be programmed given his or her particular learning strengths. Instructional and academic modifications can only be generated and implemented if the teachers agree on each child's learning needs and contributions to the classroom.

❧   OPINION BOX   ❧

"It becomes clear that there are common traits and indicators of successful inclusion" (Beninghof 1993). In order to ensure this endeavor, everyone involved must clearly understand the individual's needs, and understand that the end results may be distinctive; however, the core components of the program must be common.

The common and necessary components are:

- A closely monitored support team which includes related service providers. This team must have time to work together in establishing scheduling, modifications and goals. The classroom teacher is always the "responsible" party and needs to develop an "ownership" of the child. The classroom teacher needs to be selected or volunteer for this position based on her teaching style which would (complement) the team and child.

- A system must be in place. System by definition is the "plan" which includes team meetings, parent intervention and dialogue and an established list of "what if" related problems.

- And finally the education of parents, teachers and aides which will assist in determining if the individual child would be a successful candidate.

The school district must face all contributing internal and external factors which will affect the program. The district must be willing to accommodate program needs and establish processes that are fair and measurable to determine acceptance into the program. As well, the parents must understand that not every classroom teacher will transform their level of involvement into the main provider. Some teachers will not take full "ownership" of this special child. Inclusion is an option that needs to be available to all special education children; however, it is not a mandate for everyone. Inclusion is best when there are clear specific pre-established goals and when the parent, team and when possible, child agree that this option is in the best interest of the individual child.

ZoeAnn Walker
Acting Coordinator of Special Education Services
Lindenhurst Public Schools

Source: Beninghof, A. M. (1993). Ideas for inclusion: The classroom teacher's guide to integrating students with severe disabilities (Chap. 1, p. 7). Longmont, CO: Sopris West.

Teachers who are beginning the process of working together in a novel creative environment such as the inclusion classroom, need to spend time designing the classroom and recreating their roles, responsibilities, and relationship (Adams & Cessna, 1991). This requires a process of self-analysis, self-investigation, and self-inquiry. Teachers must challenge themselves personally and professionally. The discord created between teachers will require that they evaluate their perceptions and beliefs about

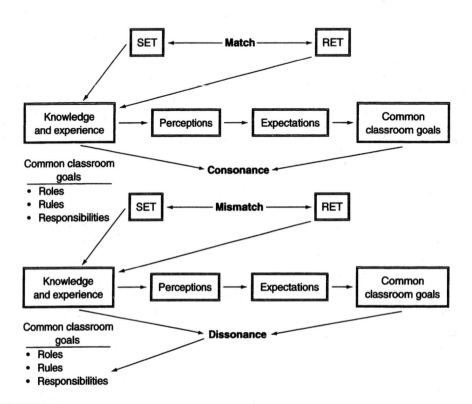

FIGURE 3.5
Teachers must work toward a common perspective of classroom learning.

children, learning procedures, goals, educational expectations, and their own personal–professional performance (Hines, 1994).

Team Teaching and Coteaching

The fact that there will be two teachers within the inclusion classroom presents many challenges for the teachers who have been trained in different discipline areas (Chalmers, 1993). Regular education and special education teachers have highly specialized and divergently different foundations for knowledge. They approach the teaching experience from different vantage points; their academic coursework has been different, their teaching experiences have been different (see Figure 3.6), and the classrooms in which they have worked have been different. Perhaps the first and most immediate problem involves an understanding of the working relationship that must be created between the two of

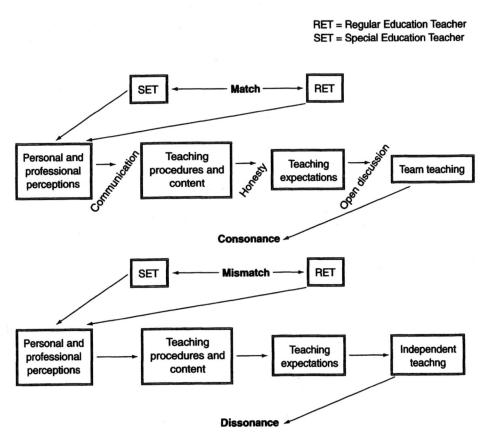

Match = Consonance   Mismatch = Dissonance

RET = Regular Education Teacher
SET = Special Education Teacher

FIGURE 3.6
The significance of the communication process to successful collaborative decision making.

them. Team teaching is an interactional exchange and process. The dynamic interface between teachers must be learned "on the job" since there are no teacher training internships available to facilitate this stylistic form of interaction. Can two different teachers with very different backgrounds work together with the same mission of goals? Here, communication interchange, honesty, and open discussion become primary factors in contributing to the success of the working relationship. Without this, only dissonance and an unhealthy, unsuccessful classroom will result.

Teachers must learn to express their concerns and fears to each other with the view of providing support in the development of a new working relationship. Again, teachers must learn that they each contribute different skills to the inclusion classroom. The success of the inclusion classroom can only be achieved if each teacher contributes what she or he knows best to child learning. Coteaching provides a mechanism to develop common goals by pooling perceptions, training and expertise to the development of an IEP for each child. It should be clear, however, that designing a classroom requires a creative and nurturing personal–professional relationship between teachers.

Designing the Classroom

Having addressed some of the interpersonal and interprofessional issues related to roles and responsibilities within the classroom, the teachers next need to design a supportive integrated environment (Johnson, Pugach, & Hammittee, 1988). The inclusion classroom is an ecological environment. Teachers, children, and organizational dynamics contribute to the success of ongoing learning. Schools should provide staff training and flexible schedules so that teachers have enough preparation time to design and implement the goals related to the inclusion classroom. In the process, the teachers should consider (1) classroom space, (2) the number of regular education students and children with disabilities, (3) the specialty needs of the children with disabilities, and (4) the individual learning needs of all of the children. The teaching team needs to develop an IEP for the classroom as a whole, and then for each individual child.

In reviewing the educational model for the classroom, teachers first need to agree about a common set of goals for the 25 or 30 children within the inclusion classroom. What goals can everyone achieve together as a group? How can the class function as a group? One common goal might be to provide maximum socialization experiences between children with special needs and regular education children. Figure 3.7 describes the fact that an educational match must occur between teachers in terms of their philosophy of inclusion and their expectations for the children as a group to accomplish a common set of goals during the course of the year. The group goals of establishing friendships, self-esteem, mutual respect, and understanding and recognition of personal differences can only be achieved when there is consonance between the regular education teacher and the special education teacher. Indeed, the aforementioned group goals of the classroom are already achieved at a personal level between the regular education teacher and the special education teacher.

Teachers must discuss their perceptions and expectations of regular education students and children with disabilities (Sardo-Brown & Hinson, 1995; Wilczenski, 1992). They must make decisions about how children will behave and interact with each other. They must make some decisions about each child's performance before he or she enters the classroom and about how each child's behavior can ultimately affect classroom learning. Figure 3.7 also suggests some common classroom goals that highlight achievement for all of the children within the inclusion classroom. A mismatch occurs when the two teachers cannot agree about the integration of children, the organization of space, the curricula, and/or the learning outcomes for the group. Differences in training and professional expertise will require that the teaching team discuss their differences and resolve their conflicts (Hines, 1994).

In designing the classroom, teachers may benefit from viewing each child in two ways: as a contributor to the group and as an individual learner. Teachers should develop group goals that will facilitate friendship relationships and child–child interactional learning. Understanding individual differences can be part of classroom

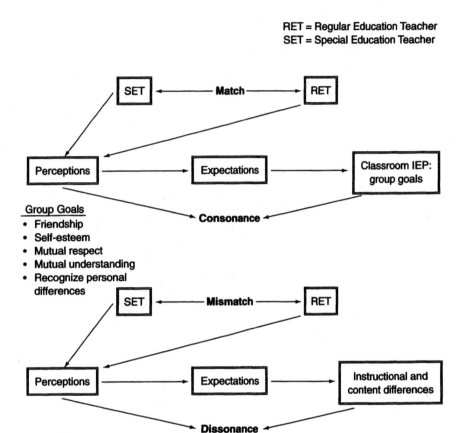

Match = Consonance   Mismatch = Dissonance

RET = Regular Education Teacher
SET = Special Education Teacher

FIGURE 3.7
The common goals for *all* children in the inclusive classroom.

development and discussion to facilitate collective contributions to a social consciousness. Learning to understand and to help others must be taught to children within the framework of the classroom curriculum. These goals provide children with a common focus and vision of their classroom as a social network and community. Children must be taught the process of building personal bonds and social links to each other.

The child with disabilities will be affected by the perceptions and expectations of teachers and peers. His learning and ultimate behavioral performance will be a function of classroom variables. The teaching team must understand the child with disabilities in terms of these contextual variables; ongoing analysis may be helpful in modifying decision making for the child with disabilities who is presenting disruptive behaviors. Integrating this type of child within the inclusion classroom represents a challenging new experience for all (VanGunday, 1988). Figure 3.8 describes how a mismatch between the child and the classroom can provide a mechanism for further brainstorming. Each problem can be diagrammed as an opportunity for learning further about the inclusion process. Each problem for the classroom and child with disabilities within the classroom can provide teachers and peers with an opportunity to remove a learning barrier (Volk & Stahlman, 1994).

Curriculum

Inclusion learning may not involve traditional expectations of child outcomes. The educational experiences that stimulate learning in developmental areas and academic domains may not require that all children achieve the same level of outcome in the inclusion classroom. Let us consider a special needs child with disabilities, Alyssa, in Figure 3.9. To set appropriate reading goals for Alyssa, the teachers must recognize that she is not at grade level for reading and may very well be below her peers in terms of decoding skills and comprehension skills. Nevertheless, Alyssa is able to participate

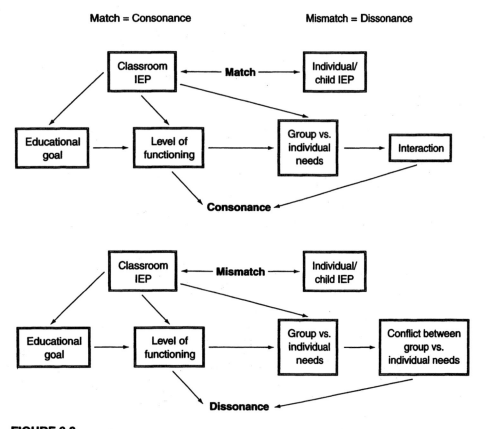

FIGURE 3.8
The need to engage in an ongoing collaborative analysis to understand the individual needs of *all* children in relation to group learning needs.

in some reading activities of her regular education peers. For example, the class reading assignment is the book *Sarah, Plain and Tall* (MacLachlan, 1985). Alyssa's peers are able to read this book independently; however, Alyssa is unable to do so and requires an audiotaped version of the book since she is a strong auditory learner. On completion of the book, Alyssa can participate with her peers in discussions regarding main characters, story events, and outcomes. Her individual goals for this reading activity included story listening and narration, which she can achieve. Her peers' goals include achievement of grade-level decoding and comprehension of the book. Although Alyssa's individual goals were different, she was just as successful as her peers. A consonance between level of functioning and individual outcome was achieved because her teachers collaborated and integrated her learning differences into the group assignment.

If the teachers had not recognized that, in order for Alyssa to comprehend and analyze the assigned book, she would need to hear it on tape, dissonance would have occurred. Alyssa would not achieve grade-level reading and would not have been ready

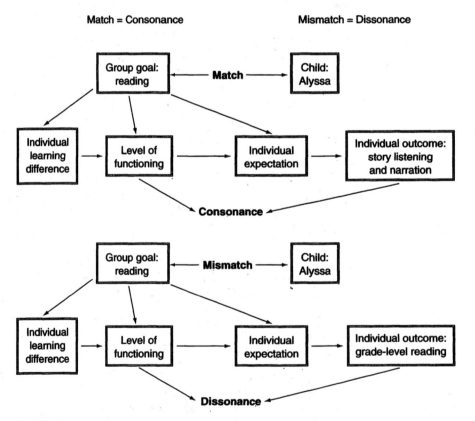

FIGURE 3.9
The individualized decision making that must occur for curriculum programming.

to participate with her peers in their classroom reading activities. The concept of inclusion programming involves the development of individualized education programs for each child. This IEP is a plan for teaching the child, based on her or his specific skills and abilities. Her strengths may be quite different from those of her peers. The teaching team needs to develop long-term and short-term educational goals, based on each child's level of functioning. The goal of providing individualized programming within a group classroom setting is a monumental task that requires intensive discussion, resource support, and administrative and parental input.

Teachers need to strike a balance between teacher-directed and child-initiated activities (Leister, Koonce, & Nisbet, 1993). Peer learning and facilitation also require careful consideration. Teaching children to interact and learn together is an important part of the inclusion experience. Regular students must learn about their peers who have disabilities. They must also learn about the learning differences which are a normal part of the social process. Every child is different, and every child has a learning difference. Learning differences are an acceptable part of a classroom, and should not interfere with the development of child friendships, peer instruction, and individual learning. Children must learn to help each other and accept each other. Built into the inclusion classroom and part of the educational curricula should be peer instruction; individual achievement can be facilitated by children teaching children. The more opportunities for social interaction, the greater the probability for social skill acquisition. The inclusion classroom provides opportunities for all. In individualizing programming for each child, the teacher team must identify optimal learning experiences through materials, classroom organization, learning centers, and individual activities for learning. The inclusion classroom provides one of the most important tools for facilitating interactional behavior and academic learning. Each child needs to be understood in terms of his or her specific learning skills, style, goals, and rate of acquisition.

In maintaining a balance between the individual child and the group, realistic outcome measures must be established for each child. As you can see in Figure 3.10, teachers need to modify and individualize their expectations for their students. Figures 3.10 and 3.11 describe the match that should occur between the child and the curriculum goal. The child's individual strengths and abilities should determine the outcome performance (Silliman, Wilkinson, & Hoffman, 1993). In the case of Alyssa, the curriculum reading goal may involve listening to a story. For Bryan (see Figure 3.11), the same reading goal may involve an outcome behavior of reading grade-level material. A mismatch occurs when the individual needs of children are lost within the diversity of differences. All children cannot learn in the same way, at the same rate, or with the same procedures. In respecting the individual needs of each student within the inclusion classroom, classroom goals must be generated, given each child's individual needs. This underscores the significant balance of understanding the learning needs of the individual child in relation to the needs of the group. Each child must be individually assessed in order to determine how he or she can contribute to the group learning process. The inclusion classroom should provide the context for each child to achieve maximal learning potential in addition to contributing to a dynamic group social process. The teachers' understanding of the child safeguards the child's individual

To include all children with disabilities and provide opportunities for social interaction and learning, consider the fact that inclusion requires changes in thinking about child learning.

The following suggestions are provided to facilitate some thought-provoking adaptations in the way parents and teachers need to change their thinking about child learning.

- Changing expectations about child learning.
- Adapting the curriculum to meet the needs of *all* children.
- Inclusion requires that teachers change their expectations about child performance.
- Inclusion requires instructional variations:
  - Individual and group learning
  - Children teaching children; peer facilitation
  - Subgrouping children
- Inclusion requires changing the measurement outcomes for child learning.
- Inclusion requires that parents and teachers acknowledge that children learn different skills in the classroom.
- Not all children in the inclusion classroom are at the same academic or social level; instruction is based on child diversity.
- The inclusion classroom highlights diversity in learning and child competencies.
- Not all children in the inclusion classroom achieve the same competencies or the same level of academic accomplishment.
- Not all children in the inclusion classroom learn in the same way; inclusion focuses on individualized learning abilities.
- Parents and teachers must acknowledge that in the inclusion classroom children learn different skills in different ways.

FIGURE 3.10
Strategies for inclusion: Modifications in child expectations.

learning needs and defines his or her contribution to the development of classroom cultural society.

Administrators

How do teachers feel about their administrators and supervisors? Most often, teachers describe a sense of ambivalence. Teachers need to feel that administrators are there to support them as well as the inclusion process. This means the administrators should be interpersonally flexible, supportive, and willing to commit time and financial resources to the inclusion classroom. It is one thing for administrators to set a goal of achieving integration within a classroom; it is another for administrators to set a goal without providing the prerequisite in-service training, substitute teachers, flexible schedules, consultants, curriculum resources, special equipment, and ongoing class-room support. The inclusion classroom requires cooperative learning, reorganization, and redesigning of roles and responsibilities—between teachers *and* between teachers

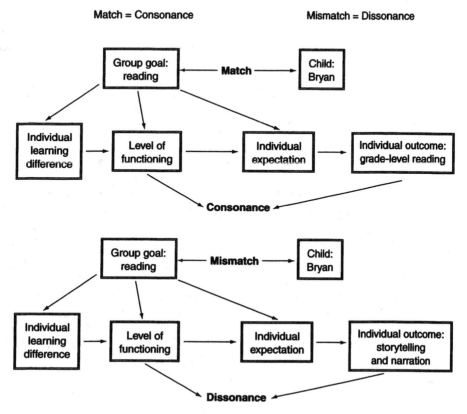

FIGURE 3.11
The effective use of the same process for another child with a different learning profile.

and administrators. The same interactional variables—personal and professional—that we discussed earlier apply here when considering the changes that must occur between teachers and administrators.

Teachers express the same negativity about administrators as administrators express about teachers. They need to address their concerns, fears, and attitudes before the school district embarks on implementing inclusion classrooms. The territorial battle in decision making between teachers and administrators will serve only to delay the inclusion process and ultimately undermine the mission of inclusion programming. Teachers and administrators must sit down together to discuss and decide collaboratively what each will contribute to the inclusion classroom. Teachers and administrators need to be clear with each other about the goals of inclusion, the school district's inclusion philosophy, and a time line for inclusion implementation (Salisbury, Palombaro, & Hollowood, 1993). Since this should be a collaborative process, teachers and administrators must agree that there will be a coequality, coparticipation, reciprocity, commonality of goals, accountability, and commitment of resources to the inclusion process. Teachers and administrators must discuss each of these variables and agree to an operating framework, an interactional schema that describes roles, rules, and responsibilities. Figure 3.12 describes the match–mismatch possibilities that may occur between teachers and administrators as they interact to develop an inclusion classroom.

If there is a dissonance because teachers and administrators have mismatched perceptions and expectations and the goal of successful inclusion is not met, teachers and administrators must sit down together and analyze why inclusion goals were not achieved. They must look at their goals, how they were implemented, and evaluate the outcomes (Peck, Carlson, & Helmstetter, 1992). Because the targeted outcomes were not achieved, modifications will need to be made. For instance, perhaps proper consideration was not given to the academic functioning of all the students, or perhaps the feelings of the staff were not considered. Both of these areas of mismatch need to be examined and modified to rectify the situation. Figure 3.13 lists a set of perceptions that need to be shared by teachers and administrators in order to facilitate successful inclusion.

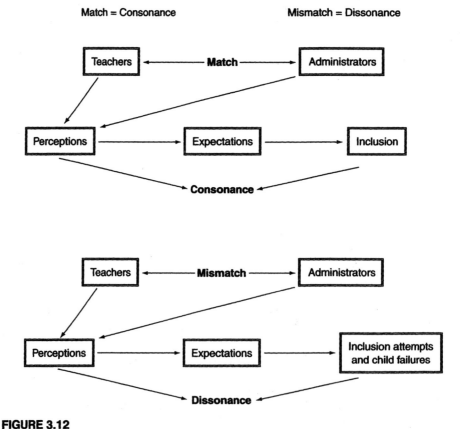

FIGURE 3.12
The need for administrators and teachers to collaborate on developing inclusive classrooms.

Parents

How do teachers feel about parents and the changing role of parents in education? Many teachers take the position that the classroom is a sacred domain that only educators can enter. Teachers are also confronted with the problems related to parents who are uninvolved in their children's daily routines and educational instruction. There is nothing more frustrating to a teacher than having to deal with a disruptive child and an uninvolved parent.

The inclusion classroom provides an extraordinary opportunity for parents to be involved with teachers in collaborative decision making. Historically, parents have not been directly involved in decision making concerning educational goals for their children. The balance between involvement, participation, and parental input often relates to the teacher's self-esteem and assurance about his or her decision-making control over classroom issues. Teachers often ask if parents can appropriately make decisions about a process about which they have little knowledge, training, and expertise. Parents clearly have a different perspective of the classroom problem and history of educational failure with general education children. Parents and teachers must work together to create this

- Inclusion redefines how teachers interact and function in the classroom:
  - Teachers become primary decision makers about classroom learning.
  - Teachers collaborate on content issues related to classroom instruction.
  - Teachers and parents collaborate on classroom decisions.
- Successful inclusion involves allowing teachers to decide about educational instruction and child performance outcomes.
- Successful inclusion redefines the role of the administrator as a facilitator rather than supervisor.
- Successful inclusion requires that teachers become more independent as decision makers about daily classroom issues.
- Successful inclusion requires flexibility in traditional educational notions:
  - Flexibility and schedules for meetings
  - Significant time commitment to staff development and training
  - Extending education beyond normal hours of 9:00 A.M. to 3:00 P.M.
  - Utilizing *more* instructional staff within the classroom, such as additional teachers and aides
- Successful inclusion includes parents within classroom decision making.
- Successful inclusion requires changes in how teachers function
  - Team teaching
  - Coteaching
  - Consultation
  - Individual instruction: teacher–child dyads
  - Teaching small versus large groups

FIGURE 3.13
Strategies for inclusion: modifications in classroom decision making.

new classroom model; a committed focus and philosophy are critical to inclusion success (Oberti, 1993). Parents and teachers need to share in the decision-making process *and* in the operation of the classroom. Parents have a responsibility to "show up" as collaborative members of the educational team. Figure 3.14 lists the perceptions that parents and teachers need to share to develop successful collaborative relationships.

PARENTS

The inclusion classroom leads to a recognition of the unique characteristics of families and the role of parents as members of the collaborative team (Leister et al., 1993). The inclusion classroom encourages a culturally sensitive, family-centered process of educational decision making. The collaborative team includes the parent as a decision maker. Developmental information, knowledge, and input concerning the child are shared across team members. Information networking across discipline boundaries provides a common focus to the understanding of the child's needs.

The parent as caregiver has highly specialized concerns, insights, and priorities regarding the child. Historically, the role of parents has changed within the educational system. As children receiving services have become younger, it has become more important to incorporate parents into the decision-making process.

Coequality and Coparticipation

Parents provide critical information about family issues and cultural concerns (Laadt-Bruno, Lilley, & Westby, 1993). The parent serves as the primary caregiver and mediator of change in the child's home environment. The parent can contribute to child learning and educational generalization. Parents play a role in the identification of the child's communication needs and of events that critically affect developmental changes within the child. Although the parent may not have clinical knowledge, a parent's insights, input, and intuition often provide valuable information that can be used by professionals to determine educational objectives.

As a member of the collaborative team, the parent participates as a respected equal contributor in the decision-making process. A parent's insights can provide information that is helpful in prioritizing and organizing the IEP. The collaborative team needs to incorporate the feelings, concerns, and directives of the parent when establishing short-term and long-term classroom goals. By being a member of the team, parents become supportive of the inclusion process. They have invested in the outcome and success of the inclusion experience. Having contributed to the goals and decisions related to the child and the classroom, the parent continues to plan and collaborate on the inclusion experience. As a recognized team member, parents can contribute a great deal of knowledge and support to the inclusion classroom.

- Successful inclusion requires that parents become part of the collaborative team.
- Education must redefine the role of parents within classroom decision making.
- Successful inclusion develops a process for parent collaboration:
  - Changes how parents contribute to the education of their children.
  - Changes how parents and teachers interact.
  - Changes how parents contribute to the decision making of the classroom.
  - Changes child outcomes by incorporating parent input into problem-solving solutions.
- Successful inclusion involves making parents responsible and teaching parents about educational issues.
- Successful inclusion involves parent empowerment, parent advocacy, and parent collaboration.
- Meet with parents on a regular basis during the day and at night.
- Establish parent–teacher teams for each classroom.
- Include parents in ongoing classroom programming.
- Formalize parent education programs with working parents in mind.
- Acknowledge the primary role of parents in inclusive classrooms.

FIGURE 3.14
Strategies for inclusion: modifications to create parent partnerships.

In the process of contributing to decisions and educational outcomes, the parent becomes invested in the success of the inclusion program (see Figure 3.15). As you read the Opinion Box responses on pp. 92–93, you will realize that parents are sometimes fearful that they will make the "wrong" decisions about their children. Another group of parents is quite confident that they "know" their children best and know what their children need. From their responses we see that just as teachers and administrators need to learn how to be good partners in the collaborative process, so too do parents. Clearly, there are some things that parents do better for children and some things teachers do better for children; as a collaborative team they need to identify their similarities and differences. The inclusion classroom involves an inclusion of people; parents have never been acknowledged as decision makers. The inclusion philosophy expands the roles of teachers, administrators, and parents. Parents have historically complained bitterly about their exclusion from the classroom and the minimalized role as organizers of "cake sales" and fund-raising events. The inclusion of parents in team decision making is an investment; it ensures that parents will main-

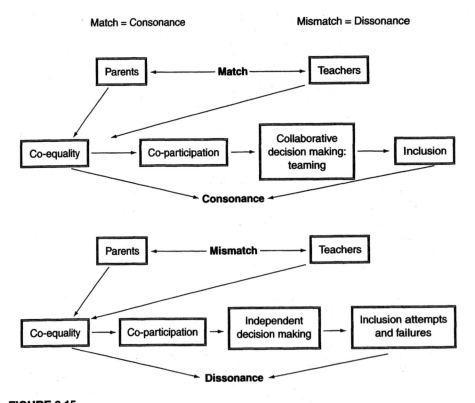

FIGURE 3.15
The inclusion of parents in the collaborative process is important. Parents must be part of the decision-making team.

tain a working relationship at home in order to generalize educational behaviors across different contexts. Parental empowerment requires that parents be recognized as decision makers and, therefore, serve as acknowledged members of the collaborative team. It is not enough for parents to participate if they cannot contribute substantively as decision makers to the process. It has been suggested by Pogorzelski and Kelly (1993) that parents should become active with the regular PTA and join regular education committees that deal with district-wide issues.

Reciprocity

The term *reciprocal exchange* suggests that a relationship is ongoing which involves modification over time. Part of the process that occurs between equal partners—parent and teacher—involves such an exchange of information. Parents and teachers need to work together when making decisions about child change and educational needs. A mutual respect for each other and differences in perspectives create a healthy tension between parent and teacher as collaborators. Reciprocal exchange does not mean that the teacher "hears what the parent has to say." Reciprocal exchange does mean that the teacher hears and incorporates what the parent has to say into the ongoing educational programming provided for the child (Coufal, 1993).

It is interesting to note that historically the issue of parent participation has related specifically to parents of children with disabilities. The legal cases concerning advocacy, least restrictive environment, and educational placement all involved families of children with disabilities (Yell, 1995). The opportunity to challenge traditional relationships and ideas within the inclusion classroom may also provide an interesting by-product and benefit for parents of regular education students. Because the inclusion classroom will include an integration of regular education students and children with disabilities, parents of regular education students may also seek to expand their relationship with teachers and professionals. Just as the inclusion classroom provides a comingling of experiences for all children, it should also provide a collaborative experience for all parents. The Opinion Box on pp. 94–95 shows that parents are ready and willing to embrace their role as team members. They certainly are the "experts" when it comes to knowing about their children. During the inclusion process parents will learn what it means to be a collaborative team member and how decisions are made.

Common Goals

Parents and teachers need to work closely together in order to develop inclusion goals that reflect each child's development within the classroom, as well as goals that will meet his or her individual educational needs. The classroom goals will reflect goals that are common to all children—regular education students and students with disabilities; goals that transcend cultural and gender biases, goals that create a universal social

---

OPINION BOX

Question: Explain what kinds of problems parents face in trying to be part of the educational team. What are your fears and your worries? What kind of time problems do you have?

- I think parents are naturally intimidated in the presence of school personnel. If a parent makes the wrong decision, the parent then loses the confidence to concern herself in decision making. I fear that there will come a time when I am unable to advocate fully for my child, that the school personnel will not inform me of all the problems that arise during the day. I do not want to feel powerless. Advocating for your child takes your time, energy, and mental strength.

- My fears are not about being part of my child's educational team, but about my child getting the best education, with the best professionals delivering the kind of help my child needs in order to function in this world. The educational team cannot understand my child if I am not part of the discussion.

- I am concerned that parents are not given enough information in a clear and concise manner to make reasonable decisions for their children. The scores on many specialty tests have no significance to a parent.

- Parents do not always have the patience it takes to teach a child. This could affect the child's learning. The problem I have is that my son gets frustrated if you don't understand him. My biggest fear is that he will get hurt by other children.

- Parents may have different ideas than the educational team because they do not have the training and experience. My fears are that the educational team does not see the "whole" child—just the child in a classroom setting.

- I think "time" would be a big issue in being part of a team. Some parents cannot choose to give up working time for educational reasons. My husband and I have

---

context for children. To generate these common classroom goals, parents of regular education students and children with disabilities need to work closely with teachers to identify areas of social and communication development that would benefit interactional exchange within the classroom. Inclusion classroom goals reflect the development of a cohesive working group of children. Teaching children to interact with, facilitate for, and understand each other underscores the philosophy of the inclusion experience and the Regular Education Initiative (REI) (Peltier, 1993). Common classroom goals such as self-esteem, friendship, socialization, peer facilitation, and leadership, should be reflected on each child's IEP. Parents and teachers can work together to identify common goal areas that will impact the success of the classroom; short-term goals could reflect developmental differences in children within each of these goal areas.

decided that I will make the extra time and be with my daughter. Sometimes I worry that I am not doing enough to help her overcome her disability.

- The biggest problem I have had was not being recognized as part of the team. I needed to assert myself more and at times I had to demand to be heard and considered. Luckily my time problems are minimal. I meet with the teachers during school hours.

- Some parents do not have the educational background. I fear that decisions will be made solely on an emotional basis by parents. Time problem: I teach during the same hours my son goes to school. However, if needed I can leave at a moment's notice.

- One of the problems I have been confronted with is the teacher claiming that she is knowledgeable and I am not. My worry is that someone who has no concern about my child will make a decision that will affect my son negatively for the rest of his life.

- I am afraid that I might not be as informed as I should be to make the proper decisions for my child. As far as time problems, I have another child who will need to be looked after if I'm in meetings during the day. My husband works late at night so evening meetings would be difficult. But one way or another if the issue is very important and my presence is needed, I will make myself available.

- I feel teachers are not the "experts" as far as educating my child is concerned. Why don't schools provide parent education courses?

Note: Parents at SLCD in school districts all over Long Island were sent anonymous surveys. These responses are representative samples.

Inclusion cannot be achieved within the classroom all at once. As a result, the process of inclusion should be reflected in a set of common goals that describes interpersonal changes and achievements that children, teachers, and parents will work toward (Farlow, 1996). The goals that are identified for children and the inclusion classroom by parents and teachers will obviously reflect their philosophy, beliefs, and attitudes about the inclusion classroom. For inclusion to succeed and ultimately be achieved, interactional goals must be collaboratively identified and mutually established by teachers and parents. For children to achieve, teachers must establish behavioral guidelines for the classroom. Behavioral expectations need to be identified and collaboratively supported in the classroom by parents and teachers. The inclusion classroom, given its child diversity, must establish behavioral and social goals for *all* children. How should children behave in the classroom? How should children behave

```
┌─────────────────────────────────────────────────────────────────┐
│                    ❧   OPINION BOX   ❧                            │
├─────────────────────────────────────────────────────────────────┤
```

Question: As a parent, do you feel that you have the *skills* to collaborate and make decisions for your child with teachers?

- I understand my child's needs very well. I read a lot and I feel that I'm very well informed on many issues that come up.

- I will answer yes, although I don't have any degrees in education or psychology or speech therapy. I think of myself as a level-headed, educated adult and parent interested in what's best for my child; I read a lot, ask questions, and I'm not afraid to speak up if I don't agree with the system. I try to assist my child at home with learning experiences, social, verbal, and communicative skills and reading a lot.

- I have the skills to collaborate and make decisions for my child with teachers and specialists. As a parent, I have the most hands-on knowledge of my child's personality, capabilities, and idiosyncrasies. I also understand my child's needs and his developmental history. I have my child's best interests at heart.

- I know that as a parent I have the skills to collaborate and make decisions for my child. I have developed the ability to determine whether the programs developed or initiated have helped or not. I have my son's best interest in mind at all times.

- As a parent and educator I feel that I have the educational background to collaborate and make decisions. I also have experience in teaching special education. Also I have researched my son's condition and spoken to many specialists about it.

- I believe that all parents have the basic skills to make decisions. The issue is simple, they are the parent and know that child better than any other person.

```
└─────────────────────────────────────────────────────────────────┘
```

toward one another? Common goals for all children provide an opportunity for the ecology of the classroom environment to be "seeded and nurtured." This provides an opportunity for the classroom to be viewed as a learning laboratory (Behrmann, 1993). Figure 3.16 highlights the perceptions that teachers, parents, and children need to share in order to facilitate successful inclusion.

Inclusion cannot be achieved for children with disabilities without the presence and support of regular education peers. Children with disabilities must be readied, taught, and facilitated to meet the challenges of interactional and communicative exchanges. Parents of regular education students and children with disabilities must spend a great deal of time talking about their feelings, fears, and concerns within this innovative laboratory environment. Inclusion involves educational reform in many areas of classroom instruction. Parents of all children are concerned about the impact of these changes on their child's development and learning. The identification of common goals stresses the importance of interaction and communication for all children. The

- Even though I am not a professional I feel I "know" my child the best, her personality and her ability. I also like to research all the information given to me by the teachers and then be included in a final decision.

- Yes, as parents we know our children better than anyone, therefore we can load teachers and specialists with information that may take a much longer time to acquire without our input.

- I do not feel that teachers should have equal participation with parents when it comes to making decisions for children. The parental bond is the most important bond. My grammar school teachers did not attend my college graduation—parents are consistent.

- Yes, every step of the way, the parent knows the child best, is aware of the disability, and although does not have the "professional degree," knows what the child needs and if the parent can't do it, will seek the professional who can.

- Yes, parents have basic instincts and parenting skills to assist in making decisions for their own children. The parent has important information that the teachers and specialists would not know, that is, medical background, temperament at home, changes at home, siblings. The parents' involvement is vital for success.

- I believe that the child's parent knows what makes the child "tick." Parents should be able to help teachers understand the temperament and learning style of his child, also the child's interests and frame of reference. Teachers should help parents recognize immediate instructional goals.

Note: Parents at SLCD and in school districts all over Long Island were sent anonymous surveys. These responses are representative samples.

commonality of focus, which is established collaboratively by parents and teachers, creates a social environment that will facilitate the individual and personal growth of each child within the classroom. The important aspect to be highlighted, however, is that parents of regular education students and children with disabilities must collaboratively generate and agree to the classroom concept of "a community of learners." These goals, once operationalized, create the social context of the classroom.

Parent–Teacher Teaming

The inclusion classroom cannot be successfully created without collaborative interaction between parents and teachers. We noted earlier that collaboration requires coequality and coparticipation among members of the team. This suggests that parents have as much to say as teachers about the process of learning, the procedural aspects of instruction, and the academic components of curriculum development. A great deal of parent–teacher planning and programming must occur prior to the establishment and during the implementation of the inclusion classroom. This suggests that parent–teacher teaming requires an ongoing working relationship; the collaborative variables of time and communication must be addressed if the team outcomes are to be successful (see Figure 3.15).

Parent–teacher teams need to delineate their roles, rules, and responsibilities during their meetings. Parent–teacher teams also need to establish specific times and goals for all of their meetings by means of a formalized process. This will obviously have an impact on scheduling, since it is difficult for both teachers and parents to meet during the day. The school should make a clear commitment to flexible hours after school and during the evening in order to facilitate working interactions between administrators and teachers, and teachers and parents. The goals of inclusion will require changes in schedules, working hours, and commitments from all of the collaborators involved with the process. Perhaps the greatest benefit to success can be achieved from a break with traditional ideas and notions about roles, rules, and responsibilities. The more flexibility that parents and teachers have for creative solutions, the greater the probability that the goals of inclusion will be accomplished through the collaborative process. The Opinion Boxes on pp. 98–99 and 100–101 provide honest insights about how parents feel about their contributions to the collaborative process.

- Successful inclusion acknowledges that the classroom is diverse and heterogeneous rather than homogenous—the classroom consists of diverse child learners.
- Successful inclusive classrooms focus on children teaching children:
  - Changing how children interact with one another
  - Changing students' learning relationships
  - Changing students' responsibilities
- In inclusive classrooms, children contribute to their own learning and the learning of peers.
- In inclusive classrooms, children contribute to classroom decision making.
- In successful inclusion, teaching personal responsibility and leadership skills to children are critical aspects of the education curriculum.
- Children are taught to accept diversity and respect differences.
- A curriculum is developed to teach children to provide tutoring and peer facilitation.
- Children with disabilities are taught social skills so they can function in small and large group learning contexts.
- Regular education students are taught to assist peers with special needs to learn in social and academic contexts.
- The instructional role of children in inclusive education is acknowledged.

FIGURE 3.16
Strategies for inclusion: Modifications in child relationships in inclusive classrooms.

Designing the Classroom

Just as teachers need to come to terms with significant changes concerning the structure and function of the inclusion classroom, parents also need to understand how the inclusion classroom will alter educational programming. Learning is influenced by the context of socialization, and it is the social process within the classroom that will ultimately create the inclusion culture (Tiegerman-Farber & Cartusciello-King, 1995). They suggest that children learn in a multidimensional and naturalistic classroom environment that must include experiential interactions with agents (children), actions (events), and objects. These experiences provide children with a social, cultural, and physical knowledge. Parents need to understand that the inclusion classroom presents a different knowledge base for learning than the traditional classroom. As a result, the structure and function of the inclusion classroom is dramatically different. The inclusion classroom has a different organizational structure for the individual child and for the group.

As a member of the collaborative team, the parent of a child with disabilities must understand that the process of learning will include different procedures and experiences within the inclusion classroom. Figure 3.17 demonstrates that parents of children with disabilities must develop an understanding of the inclusion mission, goals, and procedures in order to collaborate effectively on child outcomes. Parents of regular students must also become part of the collaborative process in the inclusion classroom. Inclusion can only succeed if there is an intermingling of all students; children need to work together effectively, just as parents need to work together collaboratively.

If parents of regular students are opposed to the inclusion process, the mission of inclusion can never be achieved. School districts cannot run the risk of having parents remove their children from public schools because of fears and concerns about inclusion programming. It is in the best interests of public schools to address the concerns of parents of regular education students *before* inclusion is implemented within a district. Parents of regular education children often worry about the negative effects that children with disabilities will have on the educational programming within a classroom. Discussion and incorporation of parents into the decision-making process benefits the long-term accomplishment of classroom integration. Parents of regular education students and parents of children with disabilities must be part of the collaborative team; each inclusion classroom must have a working team of parents and teachers. It is critical to understand the perceptions, the feelings, and the expectations of parents before inclusion programming is implemented. In the last analysis, forcing parents to participate in a process which they fear or are philosophically opposed to, accomplishes nothing, particularly if parents remove their children from school. It is better to address these issues during the planning phases of the program; the collaborative process provides a mechanism for doing this. Parents must share in the decision-making process of establishing common classroom goals for all children.

OPINION BOX

Question: How should the system be changed so that you can function as a team member?

- I would like to be given true and accurate information about my daughter as soon as possible. I have been given misleading and vague statements in the past which has made it difficult for me to understand my child's needs.

- All cards should be on the table from both sides. Districts need to think of the child, not the economics of the district. Districts should change their attitudes.

- Parents should become more involved even if they have to take time from their jobs. My priority is my child and I will be there as long as she needs me. Parents should be allowed to participate as educational team members.

- This is my child and I should have an equal say in any decision made for my child. Schools should extend their hours to include working parents.

- I think the parent should be at all the team meetings to hear the different opinions and contribute to the final decision.

- The mentality of all school districts must change toward parents. Parents must be treated as professionals. After all, parents are trying to obtain the best education for their child. Where are the parent education classes?

Curriculum

The inclusion curriculum involves individualized programming for each child. Parents must learn to understand the curriculum that is created for the classroom in relation to the IEP that is generated for their specific child. Figure 3.17 describes the relationship between the parents' perceptions of their child and their expectations concerning the child's ultimate performance. Parents of children with disabilities and teachers must work together to establish an outcome that is specifically appropriate to the child. Although the classroom goal may be math skills, an IEP for a child with a disability may indicate counting from 1 to 15 and/or matching. Another child with a disability may have an IEP performance goal which indicates operational computations such as multiplication or division. Parents must understand that individual goals will vary from child to child because individual abilities will be different. The curriculum establishes academic domains for all children, but each child will have IEP goals that indicate individual skills and levels of functioning within specific domain areas. Parents must acknowledge and accept the child's individual ability within the inclu-

- Parents should be more actively involved in all aspects of their children's education. Parents should be asked their opinions and advice. Schools should invite parents to become active in the decision and review process.

- There should be more meetings communicating ideas between parents and teachers. I think that the so-called "professionals" can intimidate a parent, because the parent may not understand their choices. If the parent does not agree with the professional, the parents become the "neurotic parent." Also if one makes waves, the parent becomes afraid that this will adversely affect the child.

- Parents should be considered as a team member in order for everyone to succeed (the child, teacher, and program). The current system doesn't allow the parents to function as a decision maker, except for *attending* the CSE.

- Schools should have hours that are suitable for working parents.

Note: Parents at SLCD and in school districts all over Long Island were sent anonymous surveys. These responses are representative samples.

sion classroom. Parents must also discuss their hopes and dreams for their children with other parents and teachers.

Teachers

How do parents feel about teachers? Parents often complain that the classroom represents the professional domain of teachers and professionals. Parents indicate that historically, they have been excluded from observing and making decisions about the educational process. There is a strong reality base to the way in which parents feel about teachers and educators. Parents of children with disabilities who have proceeded through the CSE process complain bitterly about the fact that they are relegated to the role of observer. The fact that parents do not vote on the CSE and do not function as decision makers within the present educational system creates a barrier to the development and the success of the inclusion classroom (see Opinion Box on p. 103). Parents need to be acknowledged and recognized, and the only way to do this is by

OPINION BOX

Question: Do you, as a parent, feel that parents know enough about their children to be part of an educational team?

- No one person knows more about a child than his parents. If the child has problems at home (getting homework done, following directions/orders) this will carry into the classroom.

- This is why teachers and parents should make the decisions together—so that neither is left in the dark.

- Absolutely. They follow through with what was taught in school. They help with homework and work with their children to achieve desired goals. They are the parents. Professionals are not the child's parent.

- Yes, with the guidance of professionals working with them.

- Yes, but unless we've had parent training in language and child development we wouldn't get too far.

- Schools need to educate parents.

- Yes, if you take the time to learn and get involved.

- I think parents know their child the very best. Except when the child is in school, we are the ones who know all the background and facts on our child.

- I wanted the help but the school system failed. I fought even though some teachers were against my decision. As a parent, I feel that I can make the best decision.

- In some areas the answer is yes, while in other areas they must rely on the insights of the school specialist. Parent education would teach parents about the child's learning. Knowledgeable parents contribute more to the education of the child.

- It depends on how well versed the parents are in the educational decision-making process. Teach me!

- Yes, parents know the most about their children's personalities in all kinds of situations and circumstances. They also know their development since birth and their capabilities.

- I think that there are parents that can make decisions about their children's education and then again there are some that can't. Parents can be observant and realistic as to the child's needs in education. Parents need training courses at night and on weekends.

- I think that parents should have a part in decision making when it comes to their child. Every parent may not be capable of doing this 100%. So there is a need to educate the parents and explain it in terminology that the layman can understand. Even the simplest of people can still have input and know how their child responds under many situations, (or behaves) or communicates.

- Yes, parents should be part of the collaborative team and make decisions. Parents should be actively involved in their child's life and development and be responsible in aiding their child's development. They should be informed as to their child's progress and the hurdles they need to work on and overcome. If parents aren't active participants in their child's educational process, then who should be? It's a parent's responsibility to be there and to be informed for their children.

- Parents should be part of the collaborative team. After four years of special education, I believe that if not for my decisions and input, my son would not be receiving the services he has.

- All parents *must* get involved and be part of the team. It is not a choice; it is a necessity. Again, parents know the child in every aspect of their being. The parent knows things about their child that others are not aware of, thus bringing valuable information to the team.

- I do feel that the parents should be part of a team. The decisions that are made today will definitely affect my child later. As she changes from class to class and program to program, I am the one with all her information and background.

- Absolutely, the parents are the most important part. Decisions should never be made without them. They must follow through and they are responsible for the child forever. They not only know the child best, they are with him the other hours the child is not in school.

- Parents should help make decisions about their child because teachers need to be informed about the "individual" child in order to help her be more effective in order for the child to succeed and the teacher to succeed. The parent should help make the decisions because the child is her main interest, she knows the child most.

Note: Parents at SLCD and in school districts all over Long Island were sent anonymous surveys. These responses are representative samples.

Match = Consonance   Mismatch = Dissonance

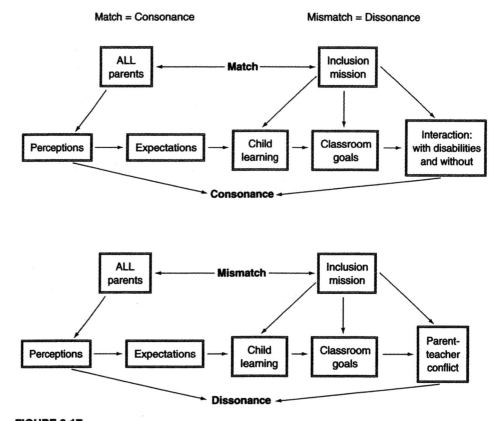

FIGURE 3.17
Parents of general education students and parents of children with developmental disabilities are stakeholders in the successful development of inclusive classrooms.

changing their role. Parents need to participate and contribute to the inclusion process; this does not mean "passive participation." Teachers and administrators must recognize parents as case managers and significant contributors to child-educational change. Parents must be empowered through their changing role and responsibilities as members of the collaborative team. The link, however, between parents and teachers indicates the need for ongoing support, interface, and exchange of information.

Parents need to attend meetings and teachers must provide the reason for them to do so—the education of their children. Just as parents need to provide critical information about the child, the teacher needs to empower parents by educating them about the classroom procedures and content. Parents represent an untapped resource in education that has heretofore been underdeveloped. The requirements of parent education would initially create a significant demand on teacher instruction and time requirements for parent training classes. Flexible schedules for teachers, resources committed to release time, and parent education classes at night must be-

> ### ❧ Opinion Box ❧
>
> **Question:** Do school districts treat you like team members? Does the school district allow you to make educational decisions?
>
> - I have found that the school district thinks they can just tell you what to do and they do not tell you all your options nor do they know the options themselves. I have had to find out information on my own because I am at home and I have the time. But parents who have to work suffer.
>
> - No, not exactly. When you're in this meeting, the professional team members tend to direct themselves to the "chairperson" and really don't care if you are there or not. If you don't show up, they proceed *without you*. How can educational decisions be made without a parent?
>
> - No, school districts don't treat you like a team member. They treat you like a visitor or an observer. The school district allows you limited input and they're not happy if you want to be actively involved.
>
> - My school district has never treated me as a team member. I have been treated as an outsider trying to receive a handout. I was told by a member of the CSE that my child has to wait for services like everyone else. I was also told by the director of CSE that the school I wanted to place him in was lying to me about his problem.
>
> - My district has not treated me as a team member. Decisions had been made prior to my meeting.
>
> - I felt intimidated at first when dealing with the school district. I had to be very assertive and not let anyone push me around. My husband and I are my child's advocate.
>
> - I think parents are caught in an economic war. Any difference in the child's education seems to stem purely from cost. I am not independently wealthy so I understand the concept of settling for what can be afforded.
>
> - *They* informed us of steps along the way. *They* make recommendations or let you know what is available to the child, but they do not let you make the final decision regarding your child. The atmosphere is very intimidating in a CSE.
>
> *Note:* Parents at SLCD and in school districts all over Long Island were sent anonymous surveys. These responses are representative samples.

come viable program components to facilitate interactions between parents and teachers. Attitudes, perceptions, and relationships established between parents and teachers provide an important foundation for educational change within the inclusion classroom.

Administrators

How do parents feel about administrators? Often administrators utilize a top-down decision-making style because they are not comfortable or experienced with collaborative approaches. Parents often comment that their relationships with administrators in the schools are rather distant and impersonal. Generally speaking, parents do not seek the assistance of an administrator unless there is a problem with a teacher or a school policy. This relationship also needs to be changed and recast to reflect a more facilitative relationship between parents and administrators.

ADMINISTRATORS

The role of the administrator should not be hierarchical in nature. Administrators need to present their contribution to the inclusion classroom (Chalmers, 1993). Their responsibilities include providing all of the requirements *outside* of the inclusion classroom that are necessary to the development and ongoing functioning of the classroom:

- Architectural plans
- Building requirements
- Health and safety requirements
- Discipline and security
- Financial resources
- Scheduling
- Staff development

All of these variables, plus others, directly impact the ongoing functioning and ultimate success of the inclusion classroom. Administrators need to share decision making and function as equal contributors to the collaborative team. Inclusion success can only be achieved if the classroom is embedded within a nurturing, supportive environment of a school context and community, which is ready to receive it. The variables of space allocation and financial costs are critically important to the development and implementation of any inclusion classroom (Hixson, 1993). Parents and teachers need to understand some of the pragmatic issues that will impact classroom decision making. As a result, the administrator needs to be a working member of the collaborative classroom team.

The inclusion process involves a significant change in the service delivery system (Laadt-Bruno et al., 1993). It is based on the development of collaborative relationships that establish consensus and commonality in decision making. Administrators should be part of the collaborative team, since they serve an important function in establishing and maintaining the resources required by the inclusion classroom. Administrators must be willing to provide teams with the time to plan, discuss, and implement inclusion programming. This is particularly important when the team is attempting to define its roles, rules, and responsibilities concerning collaborative decision making. Administrators need to assure teachers and parents that there is flexibility in thinking and programming. Administrators must also provide assurances that the needed resources of additional staff and finances will be made available to support recommended changes in organizational and procedural requirements (Roahrig, 1995).

Coequality and Coparticipation

Traditionally, administrative decision making has involved a top-down process. Administrators must now become part of the collaborative team. This means that the administrator cannot act in a unilateral fashion. As a member of the collaborative team, the administrator must work alongside the teacher and the parent to develop and implement inclusion programming. The administrator can contribute to the process by facilitating, supporting, and strengthening the decision-making recommendations of parents and teachers (Hixson, 1993). Administrators may have a difficult time accessing funding, community resources, and board of education support for inclusion programming. However, administrators should not play a different role as a member of the collaborative team. Parents and teachers need to feel that their decisions concerning change will be supported by the administrative team.

Reciprocity

In addition to providing support to facilitate program implementation, administrators must identify alternative means to assess program outcomes. The reciprocal process between the administrator, the teacher, and the parent suggests that the inclusion classroom cannot be cost based or economically driven. The collaborative team must determine alternative means for measuring programmatic success and child development changes. Reciprocal interaction requires ongoing monitoring of classroom problems as the inclusion architecture is planned and implemented. All of the possible difficulties in achieving inclusion cannot be anticipated ahead of time. Rather it is the team's commitment to education reform and to the concept of child diversity that will ultimately resolve pragmatic problems in the inclusion classroom.

As administrators attempt to promote collaborative decision making, the team must identify existing barriers to inclusion. To facilitate the process, administrators should critically analyze the infrastructure of the educational system and identify organizational problems that impede inclusion programming. Administrators must analyze the way in which decisions are made within schools. "It may be the infrastructure of the agency that prohibits movement toward an integrated approach, not the professionals working within that setting. An integrated approach to program development requires communication and decision-making that is both top-down and bottom-up" (Hixson, 1993, p. 56). Malen and his colleagues (1989) highlight several benefits derived from utilizing a collaborative team approach in the schools:

1. Parents and teachers become stakeholders in the school.
2. Teacher morale improves.
3. School-wide planning is strengthened.
4. Instruction improves.
5. Effective school program characteristics emerge.
6. Student success increases.

Common Goals

Administrators must be attuned to the legal ramifications of educational reform. Administrators need to be aware of all of the legal and regulatory requirements that affect changes in educational programming (Huefner, 1994). Administrators often must carefully balance mandated federal and state requirements with the programmatic demands of individual parents and community groups (Evans, Harris, Adeigbola, Houston, & Argott, 1993). What is the relationship between least restrictive environment and free and appropriate public education? As different legal cases come up before the Supreme Court or the circuit courts, how do school districts respond with procedural and programmatic changes? How can the mandate of inclusion programming be balanced with the individual needs of children with disabilities?

Administrators must facilitate a general program policy for parents and teachers. Administrators must consider the number and types of children with disabilities within the community, along with social and cultural issues. The development of a mission statement for the school would include a five-year master plan, which provides a format and a mechanism for dialogue. The collaborative team and the community provide input about the direction for educational reform. Here, the issue of common goals is based on the direction of programming from members of the community. The community represents an ecological environment just as does the school. The school's mission needs to reflect the hopes, dreams, and goals of the cultural community. The role of the school must be clearly articulated for parents and teachers. Community meetings that provide an open forum for parents and teachers to express long-term goals for their children in relation to the school's master plan and mission for the future provide an excellent opportunity for collaborative decision making. The degree to which the mission statement is clear to the school and to the community ensures a working relationship that is defined by mutual respect and based on coequality and coparticipation.

Designing the Classroom

Although administrators may not be directly involved in content and curriculum issues on a daily basis, they certainly contribute to all of the related but necessary factors, such as financial resources. Administrators need to identify creative procedural solutions for parents and teachers to redefine their roles and responsibilities. Obviously, floating teachers, consulting teachers, additional staff for the classroom, and space reallocation all require significant changes in financial resources. It is not going to be easy for many schools to include children with disabilities in existing classrooms. Administrators need to spend a great deal of time identifying the needs of teachers and parents in order to create the new inclusion classroom. Planning with teachers and parents in order to identify the necessary resources requires a significant commitment to the philosophy and ultimate implementation of an inclusion classroom. Figure 3.18 delineates the types of perceptions that need to be shared among parents, teachers, and administrators in order to facilitate a successful inclusion classroom.

We have stated several times within this chapter that inclusion cannot be accomplished all at once. The inclusion classroom requires a commitment to resources, time, preparation, and philosophy; like mainstreaming, inclusion is a final step. Perhaps schools need to think about inclusion as a process of evolution that requires stages of refinement and change. Central administration plays a critical role in this evolutionary process because it can facilitate interactions between parents and teachers that result in collaborative decision making. Administrators can assist parents and teachers to identify their roles, rules, and responsibilities by means of a clearly defined philosophy, a mission statement, a time line, and a detailed program plan (Stahlman, Safford, Pisarchick, Miller, & Dyer, 1990).

- The inclusion classroom is a laboratory for child learning.
- The inclusion classroom is an ecological environment, and it is the role of parents and teachers as a collaborative team to identify the critical learning variables.
- In the inclusion classroom, there are many barriers that interfere with individual achievement and group learning; these barriers must be identified.
- Inclusive classrooms begin with diversity and progressively remove barriers to child learning; this is the path to successful inclusion.
- Successful inclusion involves identifying individual competencies in each child as a diverse learner. Each child's contribution is different.
- Parents and teachers must collaborate as equal partners to decision making.
- Inclusive education extends to the home; parent generalizes classroom learning and instruction.
- The inclusive classroom is open, it is a child-friendly environment. It is responsive to children's needs.
- Educational goals and classroom requirements must be collaboratively determined by parents and teachers. Inclusive classrooms are as diverse as the children in the school.

FIGURE 3.18
Strategies for inclusion: Modifying our perceptions of the classroom.

Teachers

How do administrators feel about teachers? Administrators often complain that teachers do nothing but complain. Teachers take care of their job and do not initiate beyond the absolute requirements of their position. Administrators and teachers need to discuss the changes that must occur within an inclusion environment. Part of educational reform is a change in roles, commitment, and hours. Perhaps schools need to increase the educational calendar from 180 days to 260 days. Perhaps, the hours need to be extended beyond 3:00 P.M. Perhaps schools need to be open during the evenings for parent education and/or on weekends for extended school programming. These changes, however, can only be accomplished if administrators and teachers commit to long-term educational reform, given an understanding of community-based cultural needs. Finally, teachers complain about a lack of respect for their professional contributions. Teachers need to feel that they are not being told to do something but are being facilitated in their decision-making contributions to long-term programmatic goals. Again, decision making must occur between equal partners, with teachers contributing to the direction of change for the school and its mission.

Parents

How do administrators feel about parents? Administrators indicate that the system cannot make decisions in a vacuum; parents are apathetic and do not show up for meetings or for school events. Parent apathy suggests that parents must take a look at themselves and "show up" for their children. Parents complain that administrators, like teachers, treat them as "naughty little children." Parents complain bitterly about a patriarchal system. Administrators must acknowledge parents as decision makers and seek at every level to incorporate parents within the decision-making process. If there is going to be an alliance between the community and the school, parents must play a significant role as catalysts for educational reform and change. Mutual respect and competence require acknowledgement that administrators and parents will work together as equal partners and a common focus to develop culturally sensitive and community-based schools.

CONCLUSION

This chapter discussed the issues underlying collaborative decision making and teaming. Collaboration provides the mechanism for diverse individuals to come together in order to develop inclusion programming. Collaborative teaming involves a learning process for all of the members who embark on the collaborative mission. Parents and professionals who have had the opportunity to be part of a collaborative process have indicated the remarkable changes that have occurred as members of the team work together to develop a mission and a program. Eventually, the team has a life force of its own and proceeds through a series of changes as each member learns about the process and commits to the mission. An in-depth analysis of this transformational process is presented in Chapter 4. The diversity and the difference of each individual contribute to the collective creativity of the team. The resulting creative product reflects a synergy that could not have been achieved by members individually. Perhaps, the process of collaboration itself reflects what inclusion is all about. Differences can be a strength to the creative process when they are collectively focused to accomplish a singular mission or goal. We all learn together and through each other. In time, the "inclusion whole" becomes greater than the sum of its parts. We each contribute to the creation of the inclusion classroom.

Again, it is important to stress that inclusion, although an opportunity for all, remains the *final* step in an educational journey. Parents and teachers must engage in a dialogue process, a collaborative process that allows for child-based decision making which must benefit each and every child within the classroom. Parents and teachers must define what they mean by child benefit. One ongoing concern about inclusion has involved the trade-off between social benefit and academic learning. Does inclusion involve a compromise for children with developmental disabilities? Does inclusion mean that a child with developmental disabilities may benefit socially from the general education classroom but may *not* achieve academically, given the lack of specialized programming? The issue of child benefit becomes a critical factor for parents and teachers to discuss on an individual basis (Fuchs & Fuchs, 1994/1995). The collaborative team must determine who will benefit and how each child will benefit from the general classroom. Clearly, collaborative teaming provides the pathway to the successful achievement of inclusion.

ᴣᴀ A Few Words from Lucy O'Sullivan ᴣᴀ

My name is Lucy O'Sullivan, and my son Kevin received educational services at the School for Language and Communication Development for several years as a preschool and school-age child. The education and peer support received at SLCD was invaluable to me in helping Kevin. I was able to come home and teach Kevin, his siblings, and my husband how to help our son with language and behavior. Kevin is very lucky. We have an older child with learning disabilities, so we were very aware of Kevin's problems. A successful special needs child needs a strong, caring, and committed family, as well as a sensitive school district. The child's emotional and behavioral problems must be addressed on an individual basis if mainstreaming is going to be successful.

All children with disabilities cannot be placed in a general or regular education classroom. Only children who can benefit from the experience should be placed within the mainstream. I see several factors as being important in identifying the child who should be placed in a regular classroom:

1. The child who is ready for the regular education challenge
2. The child who can learn from other children, participate in group activities, and whose social behavior is acceptable
3. The child who is aware of himself and other children

Parents must be a part of the decision-making process. However, parents need to listen to the input from professionals and be aware of the functioning of their school district; this means that parents have a responsibility to be involved.

In placing a child with a disability in a regular classroom, there is a real risk that the child may change for the worse. He may develop aggressive behaviors, he may withdraw, and/or he may have a negative impact on the learning and social interactions of his peers. My greatest fear involved the burden of academic work. I was concerned that Kevin would act differently than the other children. I was also concerned that Kevin presented with behavior problems at home that related to his pressures at school.

The regular teacher needs to be educated about the child with disabilities and have an ongoing professional relationship with a special education teacher. Serious problems can occur because the child requires different academic techniques and procedures; the child with disabilities also has different behavioral and emotional problems that must be addressed. Inclusion requires the cooperation of a regular education teacher, a special education teacher, and parents.

I do not think that parents of nondisabled children understand what it means to have a child with special needs. The PTA has a responsibility to educate parents about inclusion and the needs of children with disabilities. Parents need to be concerned that education is educating *all* children. I have found success by working with other parents and becoming involved. I am one of the founders of the parents' association for special education in my district.

Dr. Tiegerman, it is important for you to know that Kevin was voted into the student council in the sixth grade and has become president of the student council. He told his class that he has learning disabilities and that means that he can do the work, but it takes longer and he has to work harder than other children. He graduated from elementary school and enters the middle school in September. He will take an advanced math class. The last ten years have been an emotional drain on Kevin and his family, but all the time we believed that he could be successful, and we see that now we were right.

Lucy O'Sullivan

QUESTIONS FOR CLASSROOM DISCUSSION

1. Why do parents have to become part of the collaborative decision-making process?
2. Why does inclusion take so long to develop?
3. What are some of the barriers to inclusive classrooms?
4. What kinds of decisions should be made by collaborative teams in schools?
5. Discuss the makeup of the collaborative team and the role that it plays.
6. Collaborative teaming requires that parents and teachers change their roles and responsibilities; discuss the implications for change.

BIBLIOGRAPHY

Adams, L., & Cessna, K. (1991). Designing systems to facilitate collaboration: Collective wisdom from Colorado. *Preventing School Failure, 35*(4), 37–42.

Behrmann, J. (1993). Including everyone. *The Executive Educator, 15*(12), 16–20.

Beninghof, A. M. (1993). Ideas for inclusion: *The classroom teacher's guide to integrating students with severe disabilities.* Longmont, CO: Sopris West.

Chalmers, L. (1993). Successful inclusion in rural school settings: How one rural Minnesota school district made it work. *Rural Educator, 14*(3), 31–32.

Chess, S. (1986). Early childhood development and its implications for analytical theory and practice. *American Journal of Psychoanalysis, 46,* 122–148.

Coufal, K. (1993). Collaborative consultation for speech/language pathologists. *Topics in Language Disorders, 14*(1), 1–14.

Crais, E. (1993). Families and professionals as collaborators in assessment. *Topics in Language Disorders, 14*(1), 29–40.

Denton, M., & Foley, D. J. (1994). The marriage of special and regular education through inclusion. *Teaching and Change, 1,* 349–368.

Dettmer, P., Thurston, L. P., & Dyck, N. (1993). *Consultation, collaboration, and teamwork for students with special needs.* Boston: Allyn & Bacon.

Evans, D. W., Harris, D. M. Adeigbola, M., Houston, D., & Argott, L. (1993). Restructuring special education services. *Teacher Education and Special Education, 16*(2), 137–145.

Farlow, L. (1996). A quartet of success stories: How to make inclusion work. *Educational Leadership, 53*(5), 56–59.

Friend, M. & Bursuck, W. D. (1996). *Including students with special needs.* Needham Heights, MA: Allyn & Bacon.

Friend, M., & Cook, L. (1992) *Interactions: Collaboration skills for school professionals.* White Plains, NY: Longman.

Fuchs, D., & Fuchs, L. S. (1994/1995). Sometimes separate is better. *Educational Leadership, 52*(4), 22–26.

Gutkin, T. (1993). Demonstrating the efficacy of collaborative consultation services: Theoretical and practical prospectives. *Topics in Language Disorders, 14*(1), 81–90.

Hines, R. A. (1994). The best of both worlds? Collaborative teaching for effective inclusion. *Schools in the Middle, 3,* 3–6.

Hixson, P. (1993). The integrated approach to program development. *Topics in Language Disorders, 14*(1), 41–57.

Huefner, D. S. (1994). The mainstreaming cases: Tensions and trends for school administrators. *Educational Administration Quarterly, 3*(1), 27–55.

Idol, L., Paolucci-Whitcomb, P., & Nevin, A. (1986). *Collaborative consultation.* Rockville, MD: Aspen.

Jayanthi, M., & Friend, M. (1992). Interpersonal problem solving: A selected literature review to guide practice. *Journal of Educational and Psychological Consultation 3,* 147–152.

Johnson, L. J., Pugach, M. C., & Hammittee, D. J. (1988). Barriers to effective special education consultation. *Remedial and Special Education, 9*(6), 41–47.

Laadt-Bruno, G., Lilley, P., & Westby, C. (1993). Collaborative approach to developmental care continuity with infants born at risk and their families. *Topics in Language Disorders, 14*(1), 15–28.

Leister, C., Koonce, D., & Nisbet, S. (1993). Best practices for preschool programs: An update on inclusive settings. *Day Care and Early Education,* 9–12.

MacLachlan, P. (1985). *Sarah, Plain, and Tall.* New York: Harper Trophy.

Malen, B., Ogawa, R. T., & Kranz, J. (1989 July). An analysis of site-based management as an educational reform strategy. An Occasional Policy Paper. Department of Educational Administration, The University of Utah.

Marston, D., & Heistad, D. (1994). Assessing collaborative inclusion as an effective model for the delivery of special education services. *Diagnostique, 19*(4), 51–67.

Oberti, C. (1993). Inclusion: A parent's perspective. *Exceptional Parent, 23*(7), 18–21.

Peck, C. A., Carlson, P., & Helmstetter, E. (1992). Parent and teacher expectations of outcomes for typically developing children enrolled in integrated early childhood programs: A statewide survey. *Journal of Early Intervention, 16,* 53–63.

Peck, C. A., Donaldson, J., & Pezzoli, M. (1990). Some benefits adolescents perceive for themselves from their social relationships with peers who have severe handicaps. *Journal of the Association for Persons with Severe Handicaps, 15*(4), 141–149.

Peltier, G. L. (1993). The regular education initiative teacher: The research results and recommended practice. *Education, 1,* 54–60.

Pogorzelski, G., & Kelly, B. (1993). *Inclusion: The collaborative process.* Buffalo, NY: United Educational Services.

Roahrig, P. L. (1995). Fiscal analysis of a special education inclusion program. *ERS Spectrum, 13*(1), 18–24.

Rowan, L., McCollum, J., & Thorp, E. (1993). *Topics in Language Disorders, 14*(1), 72–80.

Salisbury, C. L., Palombaro, M. M., & Hollowood, T. M. (1993). On the nature and change of an inclusive elementary school. *Journal of the Association for Persons with Severe Handicaps, 18,* 75–84.

Sardo-Brown, D., & Hinson, S. (1995). Classroom teachers' perceptions of the implementation and effects of full inclusion. *ERS Spectrum, 13*(2), 18–24.

Shanker, A. (1995). Full inclusion is neither free nor appropriate. *Educational Leadership, 52*(4), 18–21.

Silliman, E., Wilkinson, L., & Hoffman, L. (1993). *Topics in Language Disorders, 14*(1), 58–71.

Stahlman, J. I., Safford, P. L., Pisarchick, S. E., Miller, C. A., & Dyer, D. B. (1990). *Preschool personnel preparation model project: Research/evaluation report.* Cleveland, OH: Cuyahoga Special Education Service Center.

Tiegerman-Farber, E. (1995). *Language and communication intervention in preschool children,* Needham Heights, MA: Allyn & Bacon.

Tiegerman-Farber, E., & Cartusciello-King, R. (1995). The classroom as language laboratory. In E. Tiegerman-Farber, (Ed.), *Language and communication intervention in preschool children* (pp. 185–213). Newton, MA: Allyn & Bacon.

Tiegerman-Farber, E., & Radziewicz, C. (1995). Match–mismatch: A clinical intervention model. In E. Tiegerman-Farber, (Ed.), *Language and communication intervention in preschool children* (pp. 129–153). Newton, MA: Allyn & Bacon.

Van Gunday, A. B. (1988). *Techniques of structured problem solving* (2nd ed.). New York: Van Nostrand Reinhold.

Volk, D., & Stahlman, J. I. (1994). "I think everybody is afraid of the unknown": Early childhood teachers prepare for mainstreaming. *Day Care and Early Education, 21,* 13–17.

White, A. E., & White, L. L. (1993). A collaborative model for students with mild disabilities in middle schools. In *Challenges of facing special education.* Denver, CO: Love Publishing Company.

Wilczenski, F. L. (1992). Measuring attitudes toward inclusion education. *Psychology in the Schools, 29* (4), 306–312.

Yell, M. (1995). Least restrictive environments, inclusion, and students with disabilities: A legal analysis. *Journal of Special Education, 28* (4), 389–404.

4

Collaboration for Inclusion

LEARNING OBJECTIVES

After you have read this chapter, you should be able to:

1. Discuss the need for a cultural curriculum.

2. Describe various issues related to collaborative levels of decision making.

3. Explain the relationship between child diversity and individualized programming.

4. Describe various classroom adaptations that need to be considered in order to include children with disabilities.

5. Discuss the attitudes and concerns described by teachers and parents about inclusive education.

6. Discuss the two case studies presented in terms of the realities of inclusive education.

In the last chapter, we discussed collaborative decision making and the factors that might affect members of a collaborative team. The collaborative team begins with the assumption of child benefit and, therefore, the placement of the child with developmental disabilities within a general education classroom. In defining *benefit*, schools must begin the process of reorganizing educational learning and instruction within the classroom.

The purpose of this chapter is to discuss some of the factors that should be considered in the development of an inclusion classroom. Current literature discusses the philosophy of inclusion, the collaborative process, and the needs of children with disabilities within the inclusion classroom. However, the underlying "boilerplate" for decision making in the development of an inclusion classroom is not clearly described. If a prototype inclusion classroom were to be developed by a collaborative team, which variables should be discussed and resolved by parents, teachers, and administrators? Again, we are assuming that all of the children within the general education classroom will benefit from the inclusion experience. The challenge of this chapter involves the removal of barriers—concerns and attitudes—that interfere with the successful creation of an integrated setting for diverse learners.

COLLABORATIVE TEAMING AND DECISION MAKING

The collaborative team within the school must reflect the concerns and issues of the community in order to plan and implement effectively the multicultural goals of the community. Members of the team must develop a process of decision making that is responsive to the community. Part of the collaborative challenge in the development of any community-based program involves supportive networking before, during, and after a project has been developed. The collaborative team, consisting of administrators, teachers, and parents, must engage in extensive discussions with community leaders before inclusion programming is formulated. The collaborative team must develop a clear mission statement about inclusion that is discussed, negotiated, and agreed on through committee and community meetings. The community itself must make a clear commitment to educational reform during the planning phase; otherwise, programming will never be accomplished in a timely or efficient manner. Members of the community must be clear about the costs related to educational reform and the implications to educational programming when children with disabilities are integrated with children who are nondisabled. The mission statement and the inclusion programming must be linked before the school invests in procedural and programmatic changes. If the community does not support the mission and goals of inclusion programming, schools will have a difficult time achieving physical, social, and instructional interaction between regular students and children with disabilities. The collaborative team must consider (1) the development of a mission statement mandate for parents, teachers, and administrators inside and outside the school setting; (2) a time line for programmatic development that includes community update on progress;

(3) a proposal for procedural changes reflecting the educational reforms that are necessary to meet the mandate of inclusion; (4) the process of change, and how change will be accomplished by collaborative teams that will be established within the school; and (5) the process of resolving differences in philosophy, beliefs, and, ultimately, conflicts. Figure 4.1 lists those modifications that the community, teachers, and administrators must make in order to achieve inclusive schools.

In discussing the decision-making process, in the remainder of this chapter we focus on a process that can be utilized by the collaborative team. Decision making can include the following steps:

1. Identify the problem.
2. Identify ways to deal with the problem.
3. Think about the possible results of each recommendation and action.
4. Generate a responsible proactive decision.
5. Evaluate the decision and its results.
6. Do not be concerned about reconsidering the decision; always be flexible.

Identify the Problem

The collaborative team will be faced with many problems that must be discussed, reviewed, and resolved. Part of the difficulty involves the fact that members of the team have different degrees of training and past experiences concerning collaboration. The team will need many weeks to coalesce and understand the individual needs of

---

- For inclusion to be successful, the school must become a supportive learning environment.
- For successful inclusion, there must be a partnership between school and community:
  - Each community must define the role of the school.
  - Each community must define learning goals for the school.
  - The role of a school within a given community will be as diverse and unique as each of the children within the inclusion classroom.
- Successful inclusion requires that administrators become facilitators and work outside of the classroom to support the inclusion process within the classroom.
- For successful inclusion, administrators must support creative changes in:
  - How parents and teachers function
  - How educational decisions are made within the classroom
  - Scheduling, teaching assignments, supportive staff, and staff development.
- Successful inclusion requires that schools redefine their role in each community.
- Successful inclusion requires a change in our perception of education.

FIGURE 4.1
Strategies for inclusion: Modifying our expectations of schools.

members, as well as the combined mission of the team itself. The development of group thinking or team processing represents an ongoing learning experience for the individual members of the team. The collaborative process and collaborative decision making involve a learning experience for all of the members who contribute their time, knowledge, and expertise. At times, collaborative teaming is frustrating and all too human in its problems and decisions. Over time, however, the team develops its own personality and style; no two collaborative teams are the same—nor should they be.

The team must consider a range of problems that involve the development and implementation of inclusion programming:

1. Financial costs, underlying programming change
2. Hiring new staff
3. The number of children with disabilities and those without in the inclusion classroom
4. Organizational changes within the classroom
5. Space allocation problems
6. Necessary classroom resources, such as supplies and materials
7. Fears and concerns of parents and teachers

The collaborative team needs to discuss all of these issues in order to facilitate the inclusion process and the interactional work that must be accomplished by parents, teachers, and administrators who are working to design the inclusion classroom.

Identify Ways to Solve the Problem

The collaborative team may decide that they can generate recommendations to resolve each of the problems, or they can identify specialists and consultants who can address these problems. Given the time frame established by the community to implement an inclusion program, the team may not have the schedule or the resources to investigate minutely each and every issue. The amount of time spent in preplanning is obviously a critical factor in the ability of parents, teachers, and administrators to implement a program. The amount of discussion related to problems and concerns may short circuit a whole host of later difficulties. It is important for the team to attempt to anticipate obstacles that will arise later, but it may not always be feasible to do this, given the time constraints. The purpose here should be to attempt to identify as many problems as possible and then discuss implications and personnel that will be necessary to address these issues on a long-term basis.

Possible Results and Recommendations

In the process of generating recommendations for program implementation, it is important for the team to discuss the results of such recommendations. What are the implications for introducing children with mild disabilities into the regular classroom? What are the implications for introducing children with physical disabilities into the regular classroom? What are the implications for introducing children with behavioral difficulties into the regular classroom? With each one of these decisions, what kinds of resource services and personnel can be identified to meet the challenge of the committee's goals and recommendations? What are the prerequisites to inclusion? What are the barriers to inclusion? Each change in educational programming that moves a step closer to inclusion programming will create dramatic results for parents, teachers, and children. Children will be grouped differently; they will have different classroom experiences and peers. The educational curriculum within the classroom will be different. Educational outcomes and child performance will reflect a different philosophy in instruction. The number and types of children, along with their teachers, will be different. The very nature of classroom interaction and procedural instruction will change. The team needs to consider how parents, teachers, and administrators will respond to each and every one of these necessary changes. How can members of the staff and leaders within the community assist the collaborative team to support these changes through open discussions and consciousness raising?

Responsible Decision Making

The collaborative team's decisions need to reflect the needs of its community, its children, and its teachers. Although the mission and goals to achieve inclusion programming may be quite similar across communities, the process and the programs may be quite different. Inclusion can be achieved in many different ways. The mission, however, is the same. It is important for the collaborative team to take into consideration the community context and the multicultural diversity of the educational environment. The attitudes of parents and teachers must be taken into consideration by the team when it generates its recommendations. Responsible decision making requires a sensitivity to the cultural diversity of the community and the classroom. Responsible decision making requires the collaborative team to link planning and programming implementation to the needs of the community. The generation of a decision that is not going to be accepted by community leaders and parents will only serve to create a confrontational division between the school and the community. During the process of decision making, the collaborative team should report on a regular basis to the key participants and players: parents, teachers, and administrators. It may also be important to consider discussions with children as classroom programs and procedures begin to change. Because it is the child's environment that will be changed within the classroom, incorporating children may be as important to success as empowering parents within the process. Children make decisions about their partners and peers, just as parents make decisions about whether or not they will allow their children to remain within specific school settings. Making responsible decisions suggests a process of open discussion and inclusion of ideas. The classroom is a community. Inclusion requires a foundation of commitment from all of the stakeholders.

Evaluating the Decision

The collaborative team has the opportunity to observe the impact of their procedural and programmatic recommendations. Is the recommendation workable? Is the decision appropriate? Can the goal be achieved in a reasonable period of time with the proposed staff and resources? It is important for the collaborative team to evaluate its own recommendations and decisions through observation, discussion, and professional reports. Feedback from the classroom, the teacher, the parent, the child, and the administrator completes a critical loop in the decision-making process. Feedback also allows the collaborative team to reconsider its recommendation or its decision. The ability to generate an appropriate decision involves assumptions concerning the reality of data and the way in which critical variables will interact within a context. If there is a problem in any one of these areas, the recommended decision may not be appropriate. The team needs to know as much as possible about the school environment and about its own decisions within the environment in order to develop an insight about itself and its decision-making skills. Part of the decision-making process involves the consequence of the decision; that consequence needs to be reflected back and evaluated by the team. The team should learn on an ongoing basis how to make culturally sensitive decisions. This involves a process—a process of learning and of self-inquiry, self-investigation, and self-modification. Members of the collaborative team need to be connected to the community and to the mission; it is this connection that ultimately facilitates the development of inclusion programming.

CULTURAL AND LINGUISTIC DIVERSITY

Today most schools within metropolitan environments have a multicultural and multilinguistic diversity of children. These differences *already* exist within classrooms. The major problems in education do not involve the infusion of children with disabilities into regular classrooms. The existing problems in education relate to multicultural and multilinguistic diversity, to the development of educational programming for stylistically different learners (Brown et al., 1994). The introduction of a child with a disability just adds an additional difference. The problem of diversity within regular classrooms is a preexisting condition. Cultural differences and linguistic diversity create a stress and strain on schools struggling to deal with the demands of parents and teachers who are clamoring for educational excellence, safe schools, and outcome-based instruction.

Parents of general education students want change as much as parents of children with disabilities. Parents are parents, and they do not realize at this point how similar their issues are. The educational reforms related to inclusion may infuse the entire educational system with new ideas, energy, and evaluative procedures. Educational reform must include a creative process for *all* children. The collaborative team for the community (macro level of decision making) should consider changing general education programming along with special education programming (see Figure 4.2). It is

Level 1: Macro-level decision making —— School and community leaders
District Collaborative Team —— Development of a
  • Mission statement
  • Plan for implementation

Level 2: Building-Level Collaborative —— Parents, teachers, administrators
Team —— Identification of problems related to district plan

Interpretation of district mission for the school

Development of a
  • Building Plan
  • Time Plan

Identification of
  • Space issues
  • Cost issues
  • Resource issues
  • Teacher issues
  • Child issues

Level 3: Micro-level decision making —— Inclusion pre-planning
Classroom Collaborative
Team RET, SET, SLP, parent,
and administrator
  • Which children are appropriate for inclusion?
  • What resource materials are necessary?
  • How must the curriculum be changed?
  • How should the classroom be redesigned?
  • How should teachers' schedules be changed?
  • Redesigning teacher relationships to create an inclusion teacher
  • Redesigning the curriculum to create cultural, academic, and participatory goals appropriate for facilitating interaction between children with disabilities and children without disabilities
  • Instructional modifications necessary to meet individual learning needs
  • Parent involvement, education, and networking

Implementing inclusion programming
  • Profiling individual learners
  • Developing a classroom cultural society
  • Individualizing classroom instruction
  • Developing peer partners
  • Resolving inclusion conflicts

Evaluating inclusion programming
  • Assessing individual child development
  • Evaluating group cultural experiences
  • Assessing changes in attitudes and barriers to inclusion
  • Removing children with disabilities and children without disabilities from inclusion

FIGURE 4.2
Collaborative levels of decision making.

not going to be possible to include children with disabilities in regular education classrooms without addressing resources, equipment, curriculum, instructional techniques, teacher competency skills, attitudes, and individualized programming for all children.

THE DEVELOPMENT OF AN INCLUSIVE CURRICULUM

The process of including children with disabilities in the regular classroom requires an innovative curriculum that provides for instructional and academic adaptations given the educational diversity of children. In the last chapter, the development of common goals was introduced as a variable to be considered by the collaborative team. The conceptual model of the inclusion classroom must be based on a transdisciplinary curriculum that will provide educational goals for children with and without disabilities. As a result, instructional teams consisting of a regular education teacher, a special education teacher, and a number of developmental specialists should work collaboratively to develop the domain areas within the curriculum and the developmental milestones or criteria for achievement within each domain area. In addition, it may be important to separate the domain areas into classroom cultural goals and academic instructional goals.

Classroom Cultural Goals

As described earlier, classroom cultural goals should relate to areas of achievement that reflect social and interpersonal aspects of classroom interaction. Goals such as self-esteem, friendship, communication, personal achievement, leadership, and peer facilitation are all important components of cultural life and success within the classroom. These are goals that all of the children—regular children and children with disabilities—strive to achieve as individuals and as group members. Every child in the inclusion classroom should receive an Individualized Education Plan (IEP) that is collaboratively developed by parents and teachers. Each child's IEP should reflect goals within the classroom domain area. Children may be at different levels of achievement but certainly all children can contribute to the development of a community of learners. Figure 4.3 describes some of the goals related to the development of a classroom–social society and consciousness. Inherent to the success of the inclusion culture is the process of children teaching children. Children learn about stylistic differences and acquire a respect for the contributions of other children as well as their own. A fellowship of learning recognizes and respects the individual abilities and skills of each child. As you look at the classroom goals in Figure 4.3, notice that the focus is on development of respect, responsibility, and interaction between children with special needs and their peers.

In contrast to this approach of including children with disabilities in regular education classrooms, many child advocates and associations for people with disabilities

- Will show personal initiative in contributing to classroom routines and activities.
- Will develop a supportive relationship with the child with disabilities.
- Will show sensitivity for cultural and learning style differences in other children.
- Will help other children to learn and grow in class.
- Will tutor another child in class.
- Will develop an awareness of personal goals and accomplishments.
- Will show concern for the personal feelings of classmates.
- Will socially include classmates during work and play.
- Will develop an identification with classroom cultural and community problems.
- Will contribute to problem-solving solutions when classroom conflicts interfere with learning.

FIGURE 4.3
Transdisciplinary curriculum classroom cultural goals: A child society of learners.

are adamantly opposed to inclusion for *all* children. "Any given learning environment may be restrictive for an individual student if a continuum of options is not available" (Council for Learning Disabilities, 1993). Perhaps even more challenging to the concept of inclusion is the following: "There is no validated body of evidence to support large-scale adoption of inclusion as the service delivery model for all students" (Kaufman, 1991). Parents, teachers, and administrators echo these concerns as they grapple with balancing social policies and the realities of classroom education.

Academic Goals

The academic goals reflect traditional domain areas such as math, social studies, reading, and science. Although the academic areas may not be unique to the inclusion classroom, the fact that each child (special education *and* regular education) has an IEP is an innovative component. Preparing an IEP for the regular education student is unusual, given the history of IEP programming and individualized instruction, specifically for children with disabilities. The inclusion classroom should provide individualized instruction for all children. The regular education student receives an individualized education plan at the beginning of the school year with goals and criteria determined collaboratively by teachers and parents.

This shared decision making ensures the support of both stakeholders to the success of the inclusion classroom. Joint decision making will create a climate of mutual respect and shared problem solving between parents and teachers.

The IEP includes academic and classroom goals that have been tailored to meet the individual learning needs of the *regular education* student (see Figure 4.4). The IEP generalizes the individual program planning process that has existed for the children with disabilities to the regular education student. In addition, the IEP serves as a contractual agreement between the family and the school. It formalizes a collaborative

Classroom Cultural Goals	Academic Goals
Long-Term Goal 1. Bryan will develop a peer relationship with with a child with a disability, Alex, in class during math instruction. **Short-Term Goals** 1a. Bryan will assist Alex as he transitions from the classroom to the lunchroom 1b. Bryan will meet with the other peer tutors and the teacher to discuss Alex's learning needs during math and other classes.	*Math* **Long-Term Goal** Bryan will develop grade-level math skills in . . . *Social Studies* **Long-Term Goal** Bryan will complete the experiential analysis of a culture in South America. *English* **Long-Term Goal** Bryan will develop grade-level writing and grammatical skills by . . . *Science* **Long-Term Goal** Bryan will complete all science laboratory experiments and projects. *Computer Science* **Long-Term Goal** Bryan will develop computer literacy skills by completing workbooks 1–4. *Reading* **Long-Term Goal** Bryan will develop grade-level reading skills by completing Macmillan readers 1–6 . . .

FIGURE 4.4
Bryan Smith: Individual Education Plan.

working relationship that should be extended to all families whose children participate in inclusion classrooms. Parents and teachers can work together to develop an understanding of each child's learning style in order to detail through the IEP a program that meets the needs of all children in the inclusion classroom. The regular education student and his family must be an integral part of the inclusion decision-making process. In order for this to occur, the regular education student's individual profile must be incorporated into the learning dynamics of this classroom. The IEP provides a profile of each child and ensures that her individuality is factored into the group learning process.

The IEP has historically been utilized for children with disabilities. The aspect that is novel here for all children involves cultural contributions to classroom achievement, as well as academic domain areas that can be facilitated by peers and individualized by level (see Figure 4.5). The child with a disability is provided with an extraordinary opportunity for observation and exposure to peer instruction that is much more complex and advanced. He has the opportunity to receive instruction at his level, and exposure to a learning environment that may facilitate his academic and social learning.

Classroom Cultural Goals	**Academic Goals**
Long-Term Goal 1. Alex will develop appropriate social behaviors.	*Math* Long-Term Goals Alex will develop number recognition skills from 1–100.
Short-Term Goals 1a. Alex will be included in all academic and nonacademic activities.	Alex will develop primary computation skills.
1b. Alex will develop participatory skills in all activities.	Alex will hand out materials to classmates and count all the materials.
1c. Alex's negative and aggressive behaviors will decrease as a function of a behavior modification program.	Alex will be assigned an aide and a peer tutor: Bryan Smith.
1d. Alex will learn to sit and attend during . . .	*Social Studies* Long-Term Goals Alex will assist the other children during their cultural presentation. Alex will be assigned a peer tutor: Susan Pierponte.
1e. Alex will learn to transition . . .	*Science* Long-Term Goals Alex will participate in the laboratory projects by handing out materials and following directions.
	Alex will be assigned a peer tutor: Mary Brown.
	Reading Long-Term Goals Alex will listen to narratives and follow directions after each story.
	Alex will appropriately identify words and phrases.
	Alex will be assigned a peer tutor: Carl Adams.

FIGURE 4.5
Alex Court: Individual Education Plan.

CURRICULUM MODIFICATION

Levels of Development

Child diversity already exists within the general education classroom. The regular education classroom incorporates a population of heterogeneous learners so, as noted earlier, it is important to start with the concept of general diversity and modify instruction for each child. Teachers need to focus on common areas of learning for all of the children in the classroom. To achieve inclusive instruction, it is also important to accept the fact that there is going to be a shift in generalized instruction that focuses on group learning dynamics and skills. Diversity in learning as a consideration requires that common abilities in children need to be identified. The identification of common needs across all of the children facilitates the process of children teaching children and educational experiences that focus on group learning dynamics. It does not mean that teachers will not provide individual instruction. Rather, group goals will provide a mechanism to understand the needs of each child's individual potential, given the common curriculum. Child diversity provides a format for understanding stylistic differences in all children in the classroom. Developing a curriculum beginning with the basic concept of child difference allows parents and teachers to develop program content that has built-in levels of academic complexity. Just as the development of the curriculum requires a prerequisite assumption of child diversity, the programming created by parents and teachers assumes that each child will be at different levels of the academic curriculum.

Each domain area and each goal reflects a series of developmental steps. The IEP for each child indicates a specific goal, as well as the child's developmental level of functioning. This would allow for the possibility that two children would have the same IEP goal in reading, but be at two different developmental levels of functioning. This underscores the fact that children at different developmental levels of ability could receive instruction together with all of their individual needs being met; the group goal could be individualized within a learning activity to meet each child's learning needs.

Curriculum Development

How can a transdisciplinary curriculum be created by the teaching staff? Teacher teams, consisting of multidisciplinary professionals can work collaboratively to translate their domain areas into inclusion goals. The inclusion curriculum needs to reflect the diversity of the learning experience for children with and without disabilities. Within each goal area, the team takes into consideration the developmental steps that must occur in order to achieve the goal. Consideration is given to the heterogeneity of classroom instruction, rather than the homogeneity of the group. A transdisciplinary curriculum provides for the diversity of group instruction. Each child is seen as a multilevel learner, which means that each child functions at different levels across the curriculum. Michael may be better at math and, therefore, functioning at a higher level than he is in reading or social studies or science. The transdisciplinary team should approach the development of a curriculum with the viewpoint of capturing and reinforcing multilevel instruction and individualized programming as a cornerstone to the curriculum. Rather than comparing the child to the group or to some concept of the group standard, the IEP allows the instructional staff to compare each child to himself or herself over time. Each child serves as his or her own learning assessment. Each child provides his or her own baseline for instructional learning. Academic success can be evaluated by comparing individual child achievement from one time period to another.

A group comparison takes place in terms of cultural aspects of the classroom. This means that each child's individual accomplishment can be viewed in terms of quality of life issues within the classroom. Identifying and determining how each child contributes to the socialization process and to interactional exchange becomes a group outcome and measure of inclusion success. Each child contributes to the social culture of the classroom. Each child has a personal responsibility to the development of a group process. However, goal achievement within the academic domain areas should remain an individual accomplishment and a determination of how each child progresses over time.

Through the transdisciplinary curriculum, the inclusion classroom provides a mechanism with which to uniquely assess individual and group outcomes. Group outcomes reflect the sociocultural society of the classroom. Each child contributes to cultural quality and group learning. Each child must participate in social exchange and function as a communication member. The inclusion classroom, however, acknowledges and establishes the individuality and personal achievement of each child. Individual accomplishments are achieved within the academic domain area. This would suggest that children enter the inclusion classroom as diverse learners and that individual diversity is maintained over the course of the year. Individual goals can be generated by understanding the learning style of each child in the classroom. Each child's IEP reflects her level of functioning across each academic domain area. The teacher team, consisting of the special education teacher and the regular education teacher, understands each child's individual group learning needs. The IEP reflects the fact that each child has individual as well as social needs—learning for oneself and learning to contribute to others' learning create the synergy of the inclusion curriculum.

PROGRAM MODIFICATIONS

Designing the Inclusion Classroom: A Prototype

How large is the standard classroom—600 or 700 square feet? Is the classroom large enough to meet the needs of a group of diverse learners? Does the classroom provide enough space for large group instruction, as well as small group academic instruction? Does the design of the classroom facilitate creative programming such as learning centers? The collaborative team must consider the kind of instructional goals needed in the inclusion classroom and then look carefully to evaluate the space that is necessary to accomplish the instructional needs of inclusion interaction space. Clearly, the organizational design of the classroom can either facilitate or interfere with the interactional process. Physical structural accommodations in classroom design must be considered. Space should not be a barrier to learning (see Figures 4.6 and 4.7), but rather it must enhance learning. Therefore, the classroom needs to provide a flow for children to move from one learning area to another. The classroom needs to be carefully designed with academic groupings in mind: class activities, small group interactions, and individual instructional contexts (Pierce, Rasdall, & Ferguson, 1993). The organization of classroom space will influence how children learn and socialize within an inclusion classroom. A comprehensive analysis of the diverse learning needs of children sharing the classroom should be considered once the group profile has been identified. The organizational design of the classroom should be an environmental accommodation to maximize children's educational and instructional development.

Equipment

Technology is an important aspect of individualized instructional programming. To individualize learning within the inclusion classroom, the equipment needs of children must be taken into consideration. Is there enough space for computers, wheelchairs,

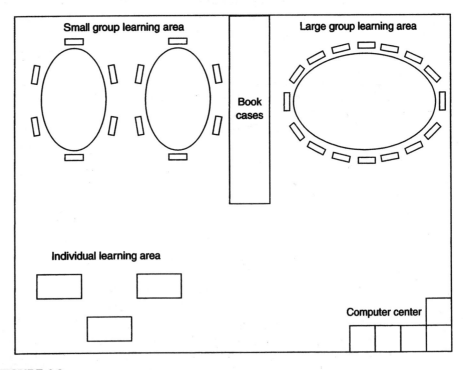

FIGURE 4.6
Design of an inclusion classroom.

and adaptive devices? Can wheelchairs be maneuvered through the classroom door and around the room? How will the wheelchair or classroom chairs be situated within the classroom? Is the classroom large enough for 25 or 30 nondisabled children and children with disabilities? Are resources available to provide computers and computer-based instruction to the classroom? Since children are functioning at divergently different academic and instructional levels, are there enough supplies and materials to meet each child's individual educational needs? The collaborative team must carefully develop a profile of each proposed classroom, based on the children being grouped. The classroom design, equipment, supplies, and materials must reflect the individual and group learning needs of all of the children; organizational structure should provide children with an interactional flow (see Figures 4.6 and 4.7). Classrooms should be designed with the inclusion experience in mind (McCormick & First, 1994).

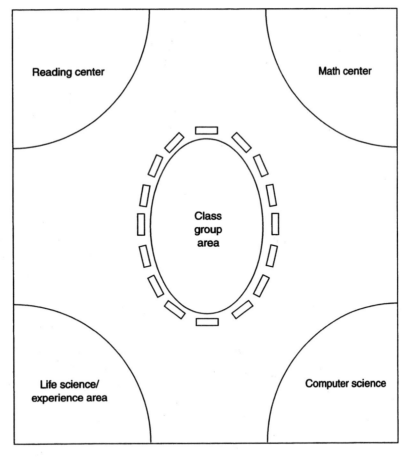

FIGURE 4.7
Design of an inclusion classroom.

CLASSROOM MODIFICATIONS: BUILDING ON DIVERSITY

The inclusion classroom consists of highly diverse learners (Behrmann, 1993). Who are these children and what are their educational needs? The collaborative team needs to profile the individual learning needs of all of the children entering the classroom. Children should be analyzed at the beginning of the school year in terms of their cognitive, social, communicative, academic, cultural, and instructional needs (see Figure 4.2). The classroom as a dynamic group or society of child contributors is a collective compilation of individual children. To develop the classroom goals and establish the cultural dimensions of the classroom society, each child's learning level must be assessed. A profile of each child's needs contributes to the classroom montage; the inclusion classroom maintains the individuality of each child while contributing to the creation of a unique cultural society. As each child's needs are developed, his contributions to the culture of the classroom can be developed. How can each child share, network and teach his peers? Linking children together as peer facilitators empowers them to learn about each other through friendship, mutual respect, and stylistic differences (Stainback & Stainback, 1992). It is important for collaborative teams to begin classroom programming accepting the concept of child diversity. The inclusion classroom begins with child differences and develops an educational program for each child based on group differences and diversity. Teachers and parents need to understand the learning process within the classroom in terms of group versus individual goals. It is each child's diversity that stimulates the potential creativity for inclusive instruction.

Type of Disability

To create the inclusion classroom and achieve a collective synergy, teachers must understand the individual needs of each child. In the case of children with disabilities, the type of developmental disability is important for the teaching team to understand (Brockett, 1994; Brown et al., 1994). What are the individual, behavioral, and social differences of the child with learning disabilities versus the child with mental retardation versus the child with cerebral palsy? What are the similarities? Part of the profile includes levels of functioning within academic and social domain areas. To bring children together and facilitate a process of interaction, it is important to understand how each child learns and how the environment must be organized to facilitate the instructional and social learning process. Children within the classroom must also be taught to understand that all children-peers possess learning differences; the learning difference provides the diversity of instruction. The diversity of instruction allows children to achieve at their own level and in their own unique way. Each child requires facilitation and each child provides facilitation of peers.

Number of Children with Disabilities

Just as it is important to take into consideration the individual differences of children, it is also important to consider the number of children within the inclusion classroom. The absolute number may be a function of (1) the individual needs of all children and (2) the collective needs of the group. Collaborative teams determine class size based on the children's abilities to achieve an inclusion social interaction. In the process of integrating more children, collaborative teams may decide that the inclusion classroom should be smaller at the beginning of the school year. This would provide a mechanism for teacher teams to work more closely with individual children and facilitate interaction between children. Class size may be a variable but critical factor in inclusive classrooms. Schools may have to adapt class size requirements based on instructional and child dynamics. This will impact policy, planning, and budgetary concerns for schools. One concern expressed has been that to remove inclusive barriers to classrooms major modifications will have to be considered in space, teacher scheduling, cooperative teaming, and parent–teacher decision making. Just as inclusive classrooms must begin with the concept of child diversity, inclusive schools will have to include other stakeholders. A shared problem-solving process may create greater costs and nontraditional solutions to classrooms (Shanker, 1995).

As the number of special needs children in the classroom increases, the class size should be regulated to ensure classroom cohesion. In creating the inclusion classroom, the type of disability, the number of disabled children, and the social–behavioral needs of children must be factored into the decision-making process. The greater the ability of children to function independently and socialize with peers, the larger the inclusion classroom. Teacher teams may consider starting the school year with fewer children and incorporating additional students into the inclusion room as the school year continues. Adding new members to the classroom cultural society introduces new opportunities for learning and greater challenges to social interaction. Here, programming flexibility becomes significant to classroom inclusion goals. It is important for teacher teams to feel comfortable about child diversity; it is a factor that requires a higher degree of instructional attention. Children's differences must be understood so that they can be creatively facilitated and directed.

Level of Disability

Some proponents of inclusion discuss the placement of all children with disabilities in regular classrooms. Others admit that the least restrictive environment (LRE) continuum must be safeguarded by ensuring that educational decisions will be based on the individual needs of the child with a disability. In generating placement decisions based on the levels of disability (mild, moderate, and severe), several factors must be taken into consideration (Kauffman, 1995). First, there are no standard definitions for mild, moderate, and severe disabilities. The assumption is that children with mild disabilities

present with social interactional skills that allow them to maintain appropriate inter-actional behaviors in a regular classroom, but these children require instructional modifications to meet their academic learning needs. Often, children with learning disabilities are described as being mildly disabled, and therefore most easily pro-grammed for inclusive educational classrooms. Carr (1993) argues that children with learning disabilities do not represent a uniform population of children with educa-tional and developmental needs. Students with learning disabilities can present with severe and pervasive learning needs, and as a group includes as much diversity in in-dividual styles of learning as a normal population; children with learning disabilities are not all the same.

Interestingly enough, whereas most of the literature describes the placement of children with learning disabilities in regular classrooms, the population that is most of-ten excluded from the regular classroom is the autistic child with severe behavioral deficits. Most of the proponents who support inclusion programming are quite pointed in their descriptions of inclusion for "nondisruptive learners." The level of disability seems to suggest that the critical developmental criteria that seem to vary from mild to moderate to severe involve the following abilities: social skills, pragmatic language skills, behavioral skills, social regulation, and social judgment. Evans, Harris, Adeigbola, Houston, and Argott (1993) indicate that including students with mild disabilities in the regular classroom reduces the use of pull-out services, and underlies the focus of educational reform. Who is the child with a mild disability? What are the characteristics related to mild disability? Burton and Hirschoren (1979) argue against the placement of the severely handicapped child in proximity to non-handicapped peers. They argue that "mildly handicapped children are socially excluded by their non-handicapped peers, and as the severity of the handicapped increases, so will non-handicapped peers' rejection" (Gerrard, 1994). Who is the child with a severe handicap? What characteristics relate specifically to severe disability? If the primary factor for placement relates to the *level* of disability, then collaborative teams must define the specific characteristics for the levels of functioning—mild, moderate, and severe. Rimland (1993) states that if a child is not appropriately labeled, "it deprives the handicapped of their most valuable asset—the recognition of their disability. . . ." The issue of recognition may not just relate to the aspect of categorical labeling; it may also include the aspect of appropriate description in terms of disability characteristics and level of functioning. The inclusion classroom builds on the concept of child diversity—levels *not* labels within the classroom. Inclusion requires a different set of organizational and instructional assumptions for the classroom.

Age versus Stage of Children with Disabilities

Many proponents of inclusion programming discuss the fact that children with disabilities need to be placed in settings that are *age* appropriate rather than stage appropriate (York, Doyle, & Kronberg, 1992). The controversy centers around the fact that there is going to be a marked discrepancy between the physical age of the child with a disability and her level of functioning. Polansky (1994) notes "all children have ranges of education needs and that all students require an educational program which addresses their unique talents." Matching the child with a disability to his nondisabled peers by age creates a significant difference between his academic skills and the abilities of his nondisabled partners. Michael, age 8, may be functioning at a prereading level, a first grade math level, 48-month language level, 36-month social level, and 48-month cognitive level. The collaborative team must determine Michael's age and stage of development within an inclusion classroom as a factor for immersing the child within the larger context of other nondisabled children and the appropriate peers who can meet his needs.

Some collaborative teams may consider other alternatives such as type of disability as a more primary consideration; age and stage may not be as important as type of disability within a larger equation for decision making. Children with communication and social abilities may be more easily placed in inclusive settings with instructional modifications. The team, however, must develop some kind of decision-making formula in which these variables are factored into the ultimate decision. The decision-making process should be based on what will work best within a classroom to achieve a coalition of children.

Classroom Modifications

To include children with disabilities within the general education classroom, parents, teachers, and administrators must discuss modifications in all of the variables that influence classroom decision making. The child diversity will require adaptations in physical space, equipment arrangement, child seating, class size, teacher relationships, and teacher–parent partnerships. Classroom instructional changes involving children with disabilities within the general education classroom require that parents, teachers, and administrators discuss modifications in all of the variables that influence classroom decision making. Classroom instructional changes involving teaching procedures and the kinds of techniques that teachers utilize will also have to be considered, given individual as well as group learning needs. The success of the inclusive classroom will be based on peer instruction and teaching children to facilitate learning in their peers. Academic achievements in various instructional areas will be based on the teachers' understanding of each child's group versus the individual learning profile. The partnership between the regular education and special education teachers will require the use of various coteaching techniques and problem-solving solutions to the various diversity issues that arise on a daily basis. Teachers must develop an attitude that the classroom is a learning laboratory for all of the stakeholders involved with inclusive instruction. Parents, teachers, and children must share in the decision-making process so that each child as an individual learner achieves her potential and contributes to the learning of others. The greatest contribution to the teaching partnership is the very diversity that each teacher contributes to the classroom. Therefore, academic and training differences will create a new learning environment for all children. The learning partnership requires an openness and a willingness to explore different types of instructional techniques within the inclusive classroom. The use of compensatory learning strategies, a creative setting, large versus small group instruction, direct and indirect teaching techniques, and peer facilitation all provide instructional support for diverse learners.

TEACHERS

The regular education teacher and the special education teacher serve as members of the collaborative team. There should be a number of collaborative teams within the school district that are at the macro and micro levels of decision making (see Figure 4.2). One collaborative team would serve to develop the mission statement of the community and the school. Another collaborative team would preplan the creation, development, and implementation of a specific inclusion classroom. In the process of collaborating on the development of an inclusion classroom, the regular education and special education teachers must evaluate their own attitudes about the entire interactional process with colleagues and children.

Regular Education Teacher: Attitudes

The regular education teacher must share the inclusion classroom with a special education teacher. Figure 4.8 highlights the attitudes of regular education teachers regarding this. These comments were taken from questionnaires distributed to regular education teachers in local school districts. Coteaching is not easy to accomplish or even to think about without confronting one's own personal attitudes about the process. Coteaching involves a true collaborative relationship between two divergently different professionals. In a sense, the regular education teacher is proceeding through

---

- I do not have the education or the training to deal with children with disabilities.
- The quality of education is going to be affected by having children with disabilities in the regular classroom.
- Too much of my time is going to be taken up with managing the behavior and instructional needs of children with disabilities.
- I would not know where to begin. I do not know what is educationally or instructionally appropriate for children with disabilities.
- I really resent being told that I will have children with disabilities in my classroom. I was not part of the process, but I will have to deal with the problems in my classroom.
- Dealing with parents of regular education students is difficult enough.
- There are not enough personnel, resources, supplies, materials, and aides to go around.
- What do I know about children with autism or mental retardation? This is a frightening nightmare!
- We cannot deal with normal diversity in education. Bilingual education has failed. What are we going to be able to do for a child with a disability in regular education?
- After all these years, I really do not like having another teacher in my classroom.
- What does inclusion mean in a classroom? How can a teacher educate everyone individually? Children have to learn to learn together. I have 25 children in my classroom next year! Now I am expected to teach a child with disabilities as well?
- Consultants give advice. I do not want advice, I want someone in the classroom helping me deal with behavior problems and instructional difficulties.
- Are we changing educational goals to social goals? Are we going to replace individual achievement with group achievement?

FIGURE 4.8
Attitudes and feelings described by regular education teachers about inclusion programming.

a process that the children within his classroom will ultimately learn about (Sardo-Brown & Hinson, 1995). The regular education teacher must consider his own attitudes, concerns, and fears about working with another teacher, sharing ideas, decisions, and consequences. Who decides? How are decisions made? How do we resolve conflict? How do we work together in the same space? How do we talk to one another? How do we share ideas, materials and children?

The regular education teacher must also evaluate his attitudes about the interaction between regular education students and children with disabilities (Wilczenski, 1992). What kind of child with disabilities can be included? Is it only the child with mild disabilities? Is it only the child with learning disabilities? How many children with learning disabilities can be included in the classroom? How can the child with a learning disability be linked instructionally with a regular education peer? Perhaps, one of the most important issues concerning children with disabilities involves expectations. What can the regular education teacher expect from children with disabilities in a regular classroom? The management of children becomes an issue related to teacher perceptions and expectations. Ultimately, the regular education teacher needs to see herself in a different role with different responsibilities changing into a different type of teacher. Change can be perceived as a negative force, but it can also be a catalyst for a highly creative process. The regular education teacher can utilize this catalyst to serve her own creative synergy to ultimately develop a new teacher and recreate herself into the inclusion teacher.

Special Education Teacher: Attitudes

The special education teacher may be faced with many of the same issues about collaboration and decision-making (Rock, Rosenberg, & Carran, 1995). Figure 4.9 lists some of the concerns of special education teachers which they stated on questionnaires distributed to them in their local school district. One significant issue for the special education teacher relates to filling and playing a secondary role in the inclusion classroom (Dougherty, 1994). The reality is that special education stands to contribute equally to the development of the inclusion classroom. The special education teacher need not feel that she has been relegated to a supportive position or a secondary classroom role. The academic training and expertise of the special education teacher provide an important cornerstone to the development of the transdisciplinary curriculum, given the diversity of learners in the inclusion classroom. The key to success in inclusion programming relates to individual instruction for each and every child. Special education teachers are uniquely trained in just this instructional respect. The special education teacher can contribute to instructional programming by utilizing his skills in individualizing all aspects of the curriculum; child diversity must be viewed in terms of individual strengths and skills.

The success of the classroom will ultimately be based on the ability of the regular education teacher and the special education teacher to collaborate on instructional, programmatic, and interpersonal aspects (Crowe, 1994). The collaborative relationship will

- I do not want to work as an aide in a regular classroom, I am a certified special education teacher.
- Regular education teachers do not want us in their classrooms. I feel like an intruder.
- Children with special needs will not get the individual attention or services they need in a regular class.
- Children tutoring children cannot replace an occupational therapist or psychologist working with a child.
- If you think that inclusion is the answer for a child with a disability, then you also think that nothing works. How can the *lack* of treatment and services help a person with a disability? Can the lack of medicine help a sick child?
- I think teachers are afraid to express their true feelings because inclusion is presented as a segregation–integration issue.

FIGURE 4.9
Attitudes and feelings described by special education teachers about inclusion programming.

define the classroom and the nature of the experience provided to the children within the inclusion classroom. As the two teachers learn to work together more effectively and share their differences, the classroom will develop its own unique educational personality. No two inclusion classrooms will be exactly the same because no two teacher team relationships will be the same. The more unique the teaching relationship, the more unique the inclusion classroom. Collaboration provides a mechanism for teachers to develop a working relationship. The synergy of that working relationship establishes the pathway to inclusion. The children within the classroom will walk that path.

Professional Modifications

The success of the teaching partnership will be based on the belief that inclusive education will benefit all children within the general education classroom. Regular education and special education teachers must engage in shared problem solving in order to develop creative solutions to instructional problems. Teachers clearly have access to a range of strategic tools from team teaching to classroom modifications to academic modifications and compensatory learning strategies. So, the instructional possibilities are as diverse as the child learners in the classroom. The success of the partnership, however, is based on the teachers' belief system and their willingness to attempt a new educational venture. The negative attitudes must be addressed by schools before inclusive classrooms are implemented. To require teachers to accept an inclusion program when they are not willing establishes a self-fulfilling prophesy of classroom failure. The NYSUT Policy on Inclusion states the following: "Inclusion is based on the information that all students, regardless of the nature or severity of their disability, should be educated in the general education classroom. In its pure form, inclusion would dismantle the present special education system and replace it with one education system, the general education classroom, for all students. There is no underlying assumption in the inclusion philosophy that the disabled student can and will benefit academically from placement in the general education classroom" (New York State United Teachers Information Bulletin, *Special Education—Inclusion: An Update*, 1993).

With this statement, schools need to take into consideration that teachers will express their concerns about the inclusion process. Schools cannot form a policy perspective and mandate a belief system for teachers and professionals. Because inclusion involves a way of thinking about education, it is important for the school to engage in an ongoing discussion with community stakeholders to develop a policy that all can agree on and commit to.

THE INCLUSION EXPERIENCE: DETERMINING CHILD BENEFIT

We now present two profiles of children who have divergently different educational needs. The issues of decision making and inclusion programming are discussed in terms of each of these children. Catherine is deaf and Alex has autism. This is an exercise in decision making. There is not necessarily a single solution to the program problems that are presented. The purpose of the exercise is to stimulate discussion about the problems and issues related to inclusion decision making (Somoza, 1993). We have discussed many factors that must be taken into consideration by members of the collaborative team. How would you decide about the placement of these children? Should they be in an inclusion classroom, given their individual educational needs? What is the LRE? What kinds of accommodations must be made within the classroom to meet the needs of each child? What are the possible responses to the parents who support the decision versus the parents who are opposed to an inclusion placement? There may never be a single solution because the decision-making process is an individualized one—a collaborative decision between parent and teacher.

Catherine

CATHERINE AND LEAST RESTRICTIVE ENVIRONMENT

As noted earlier, Catherine is deaf. She has very little residual hearing and has very poor speech intelligibility, even at the age of 6 years. She is now being considered by her Committee on Special Education for placement along a mainstreaming continuum. What is the LRE for Catherine? The principle of normalization discussed in one of the earlier chapters seems to suggest that all children who are deaf could be and should be educated in an environment with hearing peers. Many members of the deaf community object to a definition of culturally *normal* for deaf children. The issue of normalization suggests a definition of normal, which provides an important educational reference standard. Within the normalized environment, the child has access to a cultural experience, a common language, a social process, and an opportunity to achieve a potential.

The deaf community argues that the LRE is not the regular classroom and normalization for the *deaf* cannot be achieved in the hearing environment. The deaf child's potential must be understood given the backdrop of deaf education, specialized training, and deaf models and peers. Members of the deaf community object to the notion of normalcy based on the hearing environment; they do not perceive themselves as being abnormal. The deaf have a commitment to their community, a sense of self-respect and self-esteem, and they do not strive to be like "hearing peers." They share a deaf culture. In fact, members of the deaf community find it quite offensive that politicians, legislators, and educators argue the issue of inclusion, given the principle of social justice.

The deaf community feels that social justice involves the process of decision making and that they have a right to decide what is best for their own children and for themselves. Their accomplishments and achievements are closely tied to a separate cultural community and determinism. This separate community has historically established a separate school system that utilizes a distinctive language, curricula, teachers, models, and goals. Many deaf educators do not see inclusion as a mechanism to achieve educational equity, normalization, personal opportunity, or academic development. The American Deaf Association has taken a strong position against inclusion for all students; decisions must be made based on the individual needs of the child and family. The reality for most deaf children must include access to a separate and distinctively different approach to mainstream education.

Parents of the deaf advocate for special schools and special programs because they perceive the fundamental need for deaf teachers and deaf peers. Innes (1994) states, "The Least Restrictive Environment provision may just as easily be used to deny a child access to otherwise appropriate services that can best be obtained or are only available in alternative placements sites" (p. 154). It is also interesting to note that Public Law 94-142 emphasizes the need to educate children with disabilities to the maximum extent appropriate with regular education peers. Most parents of the deaf argue that their unique human experience relates to their identification with their own cultural community. Inclusion for the deaf involves an identification with the deaf community; a full inclusion model would be anything but inclusive for the deaf child. To include a deaf child in a regular classroom would in fact deny the child a basic cultural identification and the human experience of social communicative development.

CATHERINE AND LANGUAGE DEVELOPMENT

In order for Catherine to communicate effectively with other members of the deaf community, it is important for her to develop a facility with American Sign Language (ASL), since this is the preferred mode of communication. ASL represents the language for the deaf and provides Catherine with access to a world of interactional communication and socialization. To deny Catherine the development of a formalized system of language isolates her from other deaf communicators. ASL represents the mechanism for Catherine to "talk" to other members of the deaf community. To deny

Catherine instruction in ASL limits her ability to interact, limits her education, and limits her potential for learning. Catherine must be taught the language of the deaf community—ASL. The ability to use the language of her community opens up a world of opportunities.

In understanding the needs of the deaf population, one must understand the very basic need for the development of ASL as the primary language for instructional learning. The key question then becomes: Can regular programs and public schools provide Catherine with the same degree of proficient-efficient instruction in ASL as a school for the deaf? Are there enough teachers of the deaf who can provide such individualized instruction to a deaf child in a public school? Most of the research statistics indicate that there are not enough quality teachers of the deaf or sign interpreters to teach in schools for the deaf, let alone in public schools. "Inclusion settings are particularly hostile to teachers of the deaf who are themselves deaf. Policies of inclusion have all but wiped out the field's modest gains in hiring teachers who are deaf role models or models for minority deaf students. These professionals still work primarily in self contained settings" (Polowe-Aldersley, 1994, p. 162).

To place Catherine in a regular classroom with hearing children involves a complex process; an intermediary between the deaf child and the hearing children must be identified. Most hearing children do not know sign language. Regular teachers do not have the facility to mediate between the deaf child and hearing peers. Certainly, the regular education teacher is not going to become a teacher of the deaf. For normal development to occur, a child must acquire a standardized language; for the deaf child, that language is ASL. ASL is the deaf child's preferred mode of communication. Where can the deaf child best acquire his or her own language? This would be similar to trying to teach English to a child placed in a French class with an interpreter who speaks fluent French but limited English; consider the complexities of bilingual instruction and the related social peer problems.

Catherine can acquire ASL, her dominant language, in a setting in which there is a teacher of the deaf, who is teaching language to children who are deaf. Education should not be impeded by the communication process. Language and communication must be utilized to facilitate education and instructional learning. For the deaf child, it becomes important to identify peers in a setting that will provide a shared base for language learning. Language cannot be learned in a vacuum, since it is a social process. A community of peers becomes pivotal to language development and communicative interaction. What does inclusion provide for the deaf child when there is no means or mode to facilitate the language exchange between teacher and child, and deaf child and hearing child? "In a fully inclusive environment, the deaf student would not need the services of an interpreter. The presence of a sufficient number of language-model peers is an important factor in determining if a setting is fully inclusive" (Innes, 1994, p. 139).

CATHERINE AND SOCIALIZATION

Since the peer experience is so critical to the inclusion process, it becomes important to consider how Catherine will socialize with her hearing peers. Basic to the inclusion philosophy is the principle that children will be better off in classrooms with regular

education peers. Some educators take the position that normalized learning is beneficial to the child with disabilities. Members of the deaf community object to this claim
since they do not see an inequity within their own community and their own school
settings. "Normal is better" suggests that there is something abnormal about deaf
people; this is a highly discriminatory viewpoint.

For some deaf children, socialization may be enhanced and facilitated by interaction with hearing peers. The child's level of hearing loss, type of hearing loss, language
ability, mode of communication, and social emotional needs should be taken into consideration in determining the individual placement of the deaf child. For most parents
of deaf children, the needs of the deaf child can be appropriately met only within a setting that provides the degree of specialization that is necessary to instructional learning and that may be a school for the deaf.

One criticism of the regular classroom involves the fact that the deaf child may be
the only child in a regular classroom with a hearing impairment. Who does Catherine
socialize with? How does Catherine socialize with hearing peers? Can a deaf child and
a hearing child socialize without the shared language system of communication? If
they do socialize, can the interaction simulate what educators refer to as "normal" social and emotional interaction? Can Catherine be included in an environment where
no one understands her language? How can Catherine socialize, develop normal relationships, play, tease, attend parties, and make TTY telephone calls if no one uses ASL?
Innes (1994) notes that "placing a child, any child, in an environment where he or she
requires constant intervention in order to engage in basic social activities actually may
obstruct normal development" (p. 155). In placing Catherine within an inclusive environment, accommodations must be made to bridge the language barrier in order to
integrate her as a deaf child into the hearing mainstream. Providing a sign interpreter
or teacher of the deaf may be a necessary prerequisite accommodation; personnel costs
and resources become a significant factor in including the deaf into regular education
classrooms. However, the question remains: How can Catherine tell a hearing peer a
secret that is just shared between her and her peer?

CATHERINE AND CULTURAL NEEDS
In understanding Catherine as an individual, it is important to determine her cultural
needs. Cultural identification is important to all of us. It establishes our framework for
who we are and who we aspire to be. We all need to have social models, people whom
we look up to and that we identify with. As a deaf child in a hearing world, can
Catherine define herself as an individual? Does an inclusion classroom with hearing
children provide Catherine with the appropriate identification for cultural imagery?
Most deaf educators argue that the deaf community provides appropriate peers and
models to facilitate peer interaction, self-identification, and positive role models
(Stinson & Lang, 1994).

Deaf culture cannot be taught in a hearing environment by hearing teachers with
hearing peers. Cultural issues and dynamics must be presented within the context of
the community itself. The values, social ideas, and aspirations of any cultural community must be presented by representative leaders of that community. In order for

Catherine to learn to be a member of the deaf community, she must be educated with deaf peers, network with deaf role models, and instructed by means of a process that uniquely reflects the values of the deaf community. Can a hearing teacher or hearing peers appropriately teach Catherine about who she is as a deaf child? Members of the deaf community express strong concerns about the deaf child's identification with deaf society. Reich, Hambelton, and Houldin (1977) describe the fact that students who are fully integrated have significantly more personal and social problems than those who were in specialized educational classes. What are the implications for Catherine in an inclusion classroom?

CATHERINE AND PARTICIPATION

To what extent can Catherine contribute to the ongoing learning and educational exchange within the regular classroom? If the classroom teacher and general education students within the classroom do not have a facility for sign language, then an interpreter is of primary importance. The sign language interpreter is going to bridge the gap between the deaf child and the other members of the social context. Clearly, without the sign interpreter, communication and social interaction are severely limited and limiting. Catherine's ability to contribute and participate then becomes dependent on her interpreter; she cannot travel anywhere without her interpreter. Catherine's interactions with other children, her movement from class to class, her ability to function on the playground and get involved with a whole range of nonacademic activities involve this third person. What kinds of social interactions and relationships can be established between child peers, given this triad of communication? It certainly is not a normal means of exchange, since there is always a delay in understanding and responding. Where are the childhood secrets—the whispers? How is participation facilitated by the interpreter? How is socialization facilitated by the interpreter? How is the inclusion classroom the natural environment for Catherine as the only deaf child? Is the regular classroom the LRE? Or is it the most restrictive? The purpose of inclusion is to promote to the maximum extent possible interaction with normal peers. For a deaf child such as Catherine, would this facilitate or inhibit her learning?

Alex

ALEX AND LEAST RESTRICTIVE ENVIRONMENT

Alex is autistic. He is now being considered by his Committee on Special Education for placement along a mainstreaming continuum. What is the LRE for Alex? As a child with autism, Alex presents with a constellation of behavioral and developmental disabilities that provide a challenge for the regular classroom. Teachers and peers must make academic, instructional, and social accommodations to meet Alex's individual learning needs.

Alex has severe language and communication deficits, social relational problems, and behavioral management needs. The principle of normalization discussed in one of the earlier chapters suggests that Alex would benefit from the normalized learning experience provided by nondisabled peers. Within an inclusive environment, Alex may initially need an individual paraprofessional or aide to provide behavior management and transition into the formalized instruction of a regular classroom. To address Alex's language and social problems, a speech–language pathologist and special education teacher could provide individual push-in instruction within the confines of the classroom. Teacher consultants provide a mechanism for a specialized professional to facilitate the interaction between Alex and his peers, modify instruction to meet Alex's individual needs, and maintain Alex's behavior during ongoing academic activities within the classroom. Since Alex has very limited language abilities, it is important for the speech–language pathologist to provide ongoing instructional support for Alex and the regular education teacher. All academic instruction must be modified to Alex's level of functioning. Although there is an attempt to maintain Alex within the framework of all of the ongoing academic activities such as reading, math, social studies, and science, the difference in learning requires individualized goals within each of these academic areas. Academic instruction must be translated by the speech–language pathologist into specific language and communication goals so that the regular education teacher and classroom peers know what to expect from Alex's behavior.

A special education teacher functioning as a classroom consultant can also provide educational support in individualizing Alex's instructional needs. Because Alex also has severe behavior problems, management concerns must be addressed by means of a behavior modification program. To maintain Alex within the classroom, the paraprofessional and regular education teacher must utilize a token economy to maintain Alex's appropriate social behavior. Although Alex cannot communicate, perform, or interact in the same way as all of the other children within the classroom, it is important to highlight for all of the children in the classroom Alex's abilities and strengths within each one of the academic activities. In a reading assignment, when the class is engaged in individualized reading or small group instruction, Alex may be involved with listening to a story or organizing workbook materials in relation to a story. In the case of a math lesson, Alex's abilities must also be analyzed in terms of his potential to contribute to the organization of the lesson, the learning of others, and his own acquisition of new knowledge. He may be involved in handing materials out and counting each item as he distributes them to his peers. His lesson may also include sorting and coding different math materials. The regular education teacher and special education teacher must work together to identify appropriate instructional modifications for Alex, given each academic area of the curriculum. The important issue is to keep Alex engaged, learning, and involved with ongoing classroom activities.

Part of the decision making concerning the appropriateness of a regular classroom for a child with autism involves the issue of resources in personnel and instructional time. Can an individual aide be assigned to the child? Will a speech–language pathologist, a special education teacher, and/or other specialists be available for IEP planning and programming? Can appropriate modifications be made in classroom instruction to meet the individual learning needs of the autistic child?

ALEX AND LANGUAGE DEVELOPMENT

In order for Alex to communicate effectively he needs to be provided with highly individualized instruction to facilitate language and communication development. If Alex is nonverbal, several alternative systems of communication may be considered within the classroom: a communication board, facilitative communication, or sign language. Each of these systems of communication requires the technology, the time, and the expertise of a speech–language pathologist who can work in the classroom to provide training for the regular education teacher, the special education teacher, and the teaching assistant/paraprofessionals. Communicative interaction and social success will be based on the child's use of the alternative system and everyone else's facility with the child's mode of communication. Part of the dynamic issue then becomes involving the entire class in this alternative system of communication; it becomes important for everyone to support Alex's communicative initiations and interactions.

If Alex presents with some verbal language abilities such as echolalia, then everyone within the social context must be supportive of Alex's communication attempts. It is important for all members of the social community to understand the uniqueness of Alex's behavior. He may engage in some self-stimulatory behaviors or some catastrophic temper tantrums during transitions when he becomes frustrated. At times, Alex may become quite disruptive to the ongoing educational instruction within the classroom. As Alex becomes more familiar with the routines and classroom transitions, these individualized characteristics will present less of a problem. The regular education peers must be prepared for these behavioral outbursts.

ALEX AND SOCIALIZATION

Because the peer experience is so critical to the inclusion process, it becomes important to consider how Alex will socialize with his peers. The collaborative team must establish socialization goals that will provide a mechanism for Alex to interact with nondisabled peers during academic and nonacademic activities. Teaching nondisabled peers about the child with a disability provides one mechanism for support and understanding. Peer facilitation which establishes a buddy system and tutoring is another means of creating links between regular learners and learners with special needs. Regular education children can show leadership skills tutoring Alex and assisting him from one activity to another. It is important for all of the regular education children in the classroom to share in this responsibility as Alex attempts to move through the complex sequence of events during the course of the school day. It is important for regular education children to learn that Alex can learn. Alex may have a different style or means of interacting but he can be responsive—in his own way—to the interactions of others. The process of integrating children with disabilities into the regular classroom requires the support of nondisabled children and their parents. Programming must be provided to peers in order to address their fears and concerns about children with disabilities. A peer facilitation curriculum must be developed by the collaborative team so that peer partners and tutors will understand their new role and responsibilities with regard to the child with a disability. The teasing and rejection responses are due to the lack of teacher instruction and classroom discussion about the child with a disability. When issues deteriorate to "getting the kid on the playground," the mission of inclusion has failed (Westby, 1994). Linking children together in classroom instruction is a key to maintaining interaction between regular education peers and children with disabilities.

ALEX AND INSTRUCTION

One criticism of the regular classroom involves the fact that a child with autism may not receive the individualized instruction that he requires. Alex has been placed in a classroom with 20 children. What is the nature and quality of the individualized programming that he is to receive? One issue of placement within the inclusive setting involves the benefit to the child. It is important for teachers to document how the regular classroom benefits Alex's learning. Specifically, how will Alex's behavior change as a function of inclusion within a regular classroom? Will his reading scores increase? Will his language improve? Will he be able to sit in his seat for a longer period of time? Will he have tantrums less frequently? If benefit is defined for the child with autism in terms of socialization learning, then the quantity and quality of social behavior must be defined and measured by parents, teachers, and peers. To understand the relationship between the child with a disability and his impact on classroom learning, it is important to understand the reactions and attitudes of teachers and peers over time. How has everyone's perception of Alex changed? As Hehir (1994) notes, "disability is just one form of diversity. We have to restructure the classroom environment to handle that diversity." Hehir goes on to discuss that the inclusive classroom provides a framework to view and to understand differences in child diversity. The reality of what we learn from the inclusion classroom is our perception of disability. The disability has not changed—what has changed is our view of the disability. Perceptual attitudes represent barriers to learning. Parents, children, and teachers need to address these attitudes over time.

In placing Alex within an inclusive environment, accommodations must be made to bridge the language and social barriers that interfere with academic instruction and social interaction. Providing a behavior modification program, ongoing specialty services, and individual aide and peer facilitation may represent prerequisite instructional accommodations in order to maintain the child with autism within the regular classroom. Polowe-Aldersley (1994) indicates that the primary concern in education involves the identification of an educational placement that will be in the best interest of the *child*. In the two examples presented, best interest, benefit, and readiness are issues that must be discussed and defined by members of the collaborative team. The inclusion of a child with a disability within a regular education classroom requires a great deal of time, negotiation, and commitment from the school and the community. Inclusion is a mission that must be accomplished collaboratively—all members must agree to participate if the realities of the classroom are going to be resolved. Is the LRE the regular classroom for all children with disabilities? Can all children with disabilities benefit? Who should decide and how should the decision be made? How would you have decided about the two children described here?

BEGINNING THE INCLUSION PROCESS

The past several chapters have addressed theoretical issues underlying inclusion programming. We discussed the "whys" of inclusion in Chapter 2. We also discussed in Chapter 3 the development of the components necessary to implement inclusion programming within a school, which lends itself to the "hows" of inclusion programming. In reaching this point within the present chapter, perhaps it is important to focus on the "when" of inclusion programming. Specifically, when should inclusion begin for children in various communities throughout the United States? Most researchers and parents take a strong position about beginning the inclusion process during the preschool years (Odom & McEvoy, 1988; Tingey, 1989). Preschool education should be formalized nationally to address the divergent needs of multicultural families, socially at-risk children, economically deprived children, and children with disabilities. This organized focus on early intervention integrative programming would provide communities with an opportunity to address the issues of peer interaction, early identification–intervention, and the LRE.

Early Intervention

Since the passage of P.L. 94-142 in 1975, there has been a growing awareness of the need for early identification and early intervention services for children with disabilities. As a result, over the years special education programs have progressively become more specialized and focused to meet the developmental needs of the divergently different populations of children with disabilities. As special education flourished, services were provided to younger children and there developed an awareness that the earlier a developmental problem was identified, the greater the probability that the disability could be addressed and remediated. Early intervention is cost efficient and educationally effective. Long-term research highlights the fact that children with disabilities receiving early intervention services:

1. Are mainstreamed more frequently during school-age years
2. Present with less severe developmental problems long term
3. Are placed in mainstreamed environments more easily
4. Are institutionalized less frequently

Legislators, communities, and schools that "invest" in early intervention programs receive the greatest long-term educational and social benefits to the integration of children and families within mainstream society (McEvoy, Shores, Wehby, Johnson, & Fox, 1990).

Diversity of Needs

The nature and structure of the traditional family has been changing for many years. Today there are many more single-parent families and working families that require extended child care services. Nationally, there is also a dramatic need for quality child care programming. Most of the child care programs are either small private programs or social welfare and charitable programs supported through county and state departments of social services. Few state-operated or government-organized preschool programs exist that provide a regional network of services to all infants and preschool children. Given the Individuals with Disabilities Education Act and P.L. 99-457, most communities have a range of programs and services for infants and preschoolers with disabilities.

The time to begin inclusive programming may be during the early preschool years (birth to age 5) when inclusion can be achieved with parent choice. The mission for local governments is the development and organization of a network system of regional preschool programs that comprehensively serve children with disabilities *and* nondisabled children within local communities by means of an extended child care day model. Figure 4.10 presents a model for a comprehensive child care program. The development of such comprehensive regional preschools would bring together the diverse needs of children and families:

- Nondisabled children → Head Start/extended day child care
- Infants and preschoolers with disabilities → educational services *and* child care
- Nondisabled multicultural children → extended day child care
- At-risk children → Head Start/extended child care

The diverse needs of families with infants and preschoolers have not been formally addressed by local governments and legislators through community programs. There is an LRE issue that can be addressed by bringing together all preschoolers in state-sponsored early intervention programs. Cultural diversity within urban communities presents many challenges to twenty-first century schools and educational reform. The sweeping changes projected for American education will never be achieved without the development of inclusive early intervention preschools. Education involves a life cycle vision for children. The most critical period of child development—preschool (birth to 5 years)—must be incorporated into the educational reform process. Education does not begin at age 6. Parents must be provided with educational options and opportunities for their infants and preschoolers. The plight of the working poor and the nonworking family can be more effectively addressed through a network system of inclusive preschool programs. A parent receiving state aid can more easily search for and maintain a job if the child is enrolled in an extended child care day program. Community social service programs can be linked—adult rehabilitation/training and child care services—if state and local governments make a commitment to early intervention.

Most of the public schools throughout the United States are not organized or interested in extending or expanding programming below the age of 5. The educational

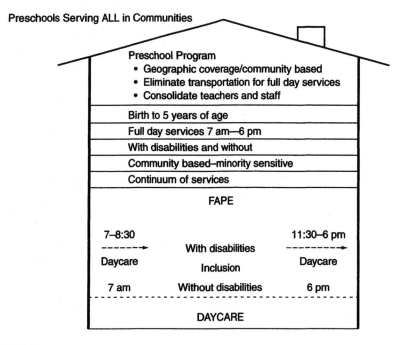

Preschools Serving ALL in Communities

Preschool Program
- Geographic coverage/community based
- Eliminate transportation for full day services
- Consolidate teachers and staff

Birth to 5 years of age

Full day services 7 am—6 pm

With disabilities and without

Community based—minority sensitive

Continuum of services

FAPE

7–8:30   11:30–6 pm
------>   With disabilities   --------->
Daycare   Inclusion   Daycare

7 am   Without disabilities   6 pm

DAYCARE

FIGURE 4.10
A comprehensive inclusive model providing community-based services to children birth to 5 years of age. A model must be developed as a national commitment to early childhood and child care.

expertise required to address the needs of infants and preschoolers is dramatically different than programming required for school-age children. The family with the 3-year-old is not the family with the 8-year-old. For the preschool child, a family-centered approach is critical to educational programming and the integration of goals from the school to the home context. Preschool programs focus on socialization, readiness, self-esteem, language development and learning, and affective–emotional independence—all of the prerequisites to academic education. The family-centered approach and educational curricula shift as the child enters school-age programming. Legislators and educators need to recognize the difference between early childhood and elementary school experiences.

Twenty-First Century Vision

Regional preschool programs also provide an opportunity to address multicultural issues that are becoming much more demanding in most communities. Integrating children from multicultural backgrounds, addressing issues related to economic and social poverty, and the early intervention needs of children with disabilities can be synergistically addressed by formalizing and centralizing early childhood programming and planning. The preschool years provide an optimal learning experience for developing "a child mix" of inclusion learners. The preschool curriculum creates an opportunity to facilitate child learning, heighten integrative social awareness among children and parents, maximize learning potential in at-risk children and families, address social learning deficits during the formative years, empower parents to function as advocates and teacher partners, and link children to teach children (Odom, Hoyson, Jamieson, & Strain, 1985; Odom and McEvoy, 1988; Peck, Hayden, Wandschneider, Peterson, & Richarz, 1989; Reichart, Lynch, Anderson, Svobodny, DiCola, & Mercury, 1989; Tiegerman-Farber, 1995). Preschool provides the greatest hope and the greatest opportunity for educational reform in American schools. Begin the inclusion process early by bringing together those populations who are most at risk in our society: the young, those with disabilities, the multicultural, and the poor. In addressing the needs of these populations during the critical period of learning—early childhood—communities make a strong commitment to the future and an investment in educational success.

Early identification and early intervention work. Parent training works. Preschool education works. Good child care works. Parent empowerment works. Parent–teacher partnerships work. Family-centered programs and family–school partnerships work. These component pieces need to be brought together in regional preschools. State and local governments need to fund early intervention programming for all children. Special education is most effective during the preschool/early childhood years. Prevention and early intervention services for families are always less costly and more effective in terms of long-term benefit than school-age or adult programming. Governments must focus their funding on the creation of national preschool programs that collectively bring together the needs of children with and those without disabilities.

Inclusion requires commitment and collaboration at many levels of government and community. Like many social ideas that underlie legislative and educational policy, the idea may be wonderful but the implementation issues are real. The problems expressed by parents, teachers, and administrators may not be as insurmountable if the process begins during the preschool years and the system focuses on developing community-based, multiculturally attuned inclusive preschool programs. This issue is explored further in later chapters.

❧   *A Few Words From Millie Alpert*   ❧

My name is Millie Alpert. I have twin boys who were diagnosed as having severe handicaps. I had the extraordinary opportunity of placing both of my boys at the School for Language and Communication Development in a preschool program for children with severe language disorders. Let me start out by saying that I believe strongly in early intervention programming for children with disabilities. I have also had the opportunity to transition my two boys from special education into mainstream programming and now inclusion. My early training and years at SLCD provided me with the knowledge and advocacy skills to support and represent my children as they developed and changed. I have been through a great deal with my sons, and I remain their staunchest advocate and primary teacher.

Inclusion is going to work only if parents are trained to work with the children at home in order to supplement classroom programming. I also believe that early intervention and preschool services provide the foundation for later inclusion. My sons would never be in a regular classroom if they had not received early special education programming. My sons have made it in the system, but only because I was able to bring together my children's needs with the necessary teacher resources. I would like to share my feelings about special education and inclusion.

If the parents and professionals concur that the child's needs can be met successfully in a regular education class, then he or she can be included. The teacher and support staff must be trained *prior* to the child's entry into the mainstream. Services *should* be provided in the regular education class. If the child's disability is so severe that high levels of academics are frustrating and inappropriate, the core academic subjects such as language arts, reading, and math could be taught by a special educator in a separate setting. Other curriculum areas such as science and social studies should be modified and rewritten. Tests also need to be rewritten and modified.

If the behavior of a child is so disturbing that it interferes with the general education of mainstream students, and that behavior cannot be modified, then that child should not be included. Children can be placed in a regular classroom if the parents and educators can successfully identify the services the children need to meet IEP goals, and then *provide* them. The child only benefits from the experience if he or she is not overwhelmed and is receiving the services needed to grow and learn.

All too often, services are provided but they are not the appropriate services and/or the specialists are not sufficiently trained in the child's disability area; as a result, the child will inevitably fail. For example, a boy with dyslexia was included this year in a regular fourth grade class. Even with ten periods of special education per week (five push-ins and five pull-outs, two periods of speech, two sessions of occupational therapy, and an aide for one hour per day) the child did not make academic gains. The teacher reported excellent social growth, but little or no academic growth. The problems that were identified at CSE were as follows: the instructional day was too fragmented, and the child was deficient in reading and writing skills and parents could not assist the child with homework assignments. In addition, the classroom teacher was not trained to handle a student with such severe learning disabilities. The special educator had little training in teaching children with dyslexia to read. Districts may give inclusion their best shot, but it takes a great deal of time and *highly* trained professionals to make it work.

A different child with dyslexia, mainstreamed in the fourth grade in the same school, made substantial gains in most areas. Why? This child had a classroom teacher who was sensitive to his needs. He trained the aide to fulfill certain responsibilities such as helping the child spell words for written language activities or helping him with small manipulatives in a science class. The parents argued that there should not be more than one pull-out service a day. Speech and resource room were alternated, and occupational therapy was given during one recreation period and one library period. The child's conceptual ability was above average; therefore he very much understood what was going on in the classroom. The parent is a teacher and did lots of reteaching at home. The child's academic deficits were not as severe as those of the first child mentioned. This youngster had reading and math skills that were close to grade level. This child did not, however, make the social gains the other boy made. He became frustrated at times and suffered a great deal. His only real friend in the class was the teacher. Parents have a key role in choice of programming if and only if a parent wants a child included in a regular class; special education options do not represent choices.

Socialization depends on the child being included. Nondisabled children will usually shy away from a child with a disability. Initially, they may be mean and intolerant. However, if the teacher accepts the child, eventually the nondisabled children will learn to accept him. They may reach out and become friendly, but more often they seem to accept the child in school but not invite him to parties or for play dates. Sometimes it seems more like tolerance than acceptance. It is interesting to note that if the teacher is persistent in trying to help an immature somewhat socially inappropriate child find a buddy, a connection can be made. Remember that the first dyslexic boy I described was very socially appropriate and made his own friends; the second child, although higher functioning academically, was tolerated by classmates and not totally ostracized.

My children did not progress through programming to mainstreaming. I decided, after having them tested by outside professionals, to include them in a less restrictive environment. At the time, they were close to grade level in reading and math. Was I afraid? Yes I was, and I still am afraid. I included two children with moderate impairments in regular education classes in a district that has a population of mostly bright average, nondisabled children. The teachers are biased toward a very high functioning population. They are used to teaching on a very high level and fight against inclusion because of the challenges and difficulties it presents. Sometimes my children become nervous or anxious in the mainstream. Sometimes, they become overwhelmed and frustrated. Do the benefits then outweigh the problems? I would say yes, my children have grown emotionally, socially, and academically in the regular class.

With whole-language approaches to subjects, traditional mainstreaming will become increasingly difficult. A student could not be mainstreamed for just reading because reading goes on all day long, and the other subjects may relate to literature read that day. The other drawback to mainstreaming is that it represents another pull-out, in addition to the therapies received by the child. This fragmented the child's day.

As the material and demands of the curriculum increase in intermediate grades, I do not know how successful the children will be. It is a constant challenge to determine how to give them the tools and services to meet with success. Parents must be persistent, committed, and believe in their children unconditionally for inclusion to work. They must also be prepared to work consistently with that child at home and communicate often with the professionals in school.

The regular education teacher today is asked to use new approaches to learning, such as integrated language arts, hands on math and science, technology, portfolio assessments, etc. Now she is also being asked to teach heterogeneous groups that include children with disabilities. This is a lot to ask. While some teachers are intuitive, some are not. Most haven't got a clue as to how to teach a moderately or severely impaired child. Intensive in-service by highly trained individuals is necessary. Consultants should also be available as problems come up during the school year. School districts also need to provide more in-depth diagnoses for each child. The parents and professionals must have a clear picture of what types of specialists the child needs, if he is to be successful in school. A child with a hearing impairment may need a consultant teacher from the School for the Deaf, a child with dyslexia may need an Orton-Gillingham specialist, or a child with motor impairments may need a highly trained occupational or physical therapist. *Any* consultant teacher is not the answer. The consultant teacher giving advice or service should be a specialist with knowledge and expertise in the child's area of disability.

The parents of nondisabled students do not always welcome the idea of having handicapped students in their children's classes. Although I have to admit, when the topic was brought up at PTA meetings, not one parent commented. It was as if they only knew of one type of child in the community—the bright normal child—and no other child existed.

After a while, with some explanation by an administrator, a few parents expressed concerns about behavioral issues. The principal assured the parents that children with severe emotional or behavioral problems would not be included. I strongly believe parent education classes should be implemented in order to educate regular education parents about children with special needs.

The administrators know what inclusion means. They explain it to the teachers and support staff, but the regular staff will not always accept it. They complain that they want aides for a full day. The support staff worry they will no longer be needed, if regular education teachers learn how to educate children with special needs. New teachers inevitably accept the students in their classrooms. The teachers make every effort to accommodate the classified student and the child does progress. If a veteran teacher takes an "inclusion" student, the parent usually has to communicate with that teacher quite often to work out problems.

My district has not yet rewritten curriculum and tests for students with disabilities. In a few isolated cases, special education and one consultant teacher have worked on modifying curriculum and tests. This has not been done "across the board." My district has tried to provide in-service for staff and administrators but it is expensive and time consuming.

The parents must take an extremely active role in advocating for their children. In my particular case, both of my sons would never have been mainstreamed or included in a regular class. My sons have learned so much by being in this setting. They are reading the literature other children are reading, being exposed to the same science, math, and social studies. They have been given the same New York State tests and standardized tests. They have been communicating with nonhandicapped peers and working in larger groups. Is it worth it? Yes, but it is difficult. Professionals can sometimes intimidate parents, even make them feel guilty for what they have done. Regular teachers do not want to be accountable for the education of a child with a disability. For example, the regular education teacher feels it is difficult to evaluate pupil progress on a report card with respect to the curriculum and age-appropriate peers.

It is the parents that must have the strength, courage, and belief that what they are doing is the right thing *for their children*. They must be secure, determined, persistent, and know how to follow through. If there are problems, they must try to work with the professionals on solutions. No one wants to see a child suffer or fail. The answer is not to place all children in any one setting, but to decide what problems exist and how they can be solved, that is, to be solution focused, rather than problem focused. Parents must be ready for an incredibly bumpy, sometimes heartbreaking roller coaster ride.

In the following box [p. 153], I have listed 16 points that demonstrate what can go wrong when schools try to implement inclusion programs.

Millie Alpert

QUESTIONS FOR CLASSROOM DISCUSSION

1. How would you define inclusion?

2. Discuss issues related to child diversity in an inclusion classroom.

3. What kind of physical adaptations can be made in a general education classroom?

4. What kind of instructional adaptation can be made in a general education classroom?

5. What kind of concerns do parents express about inclusion?

6. What kind of concerns do teachers express about collaborative relationships?

7. What do you feel are the major barriers to implementing an inclusive classroom?

SOME SCHOOLS HAVE AN INCLUSION PROGRAM—
WHAT GOES WRONG?

1. There is no district definition of inclusion and no formalized mission statement about process, procedures, and protocol.
2. There is no input from teachers, administrators, classroom aides, or the general education students about the definition of inclusion.
3. Inclusion placement decisions are made without consulting teachers and are usually done during the summer vacation break.
4. A classroom paraprofessional is promised to teachers who accept an inclusion child in September, but the aide does not show up until February. In addition, none of the aides receives any training about the management of the child with a disability.
5. Consultant teacher and specialty service providers are not available until January or February of the school year.
6. Teacher schedules are not prepared with common collaboration periods so that teachers can meet together.
7. Classes are much too large to give children with disabilities and those without the individual attention they need.
8. Push-in services, as well as other specialty services, are difficult to schedule and often conflict with ongoing academic activities.
9. Many children with disabilities are resistant to push-in help.
10. No curriculum modification is done prior to the placement of a child with a disability in a general education classroom. Instructional changes are made as problems arise with the child.
11. The goals generated for included children are not realistically defined because regular education teachers are poorly prepared.
12. Instructional modifications are not determined until the child with a disability is actually present within the general education classroom.
13. The selection of students for the inclusion classroom is often based on the needs of the parents or the school district, rather than on the needs of the child. There is no consideration given to the nondisabled children in the classroom.
14. Introducing inclusion programming without appropriate training for parents and teachers creates a great deal of stress and results in inappropriate placement decisions.
15. Most models of inclusion have involved children with mild disabilities or physical challenges who come to school with their own aide.
16. When the achievement of inclusion is more important than the education of the child, it is obvious that inclusion is not right for that child.

Note: These comments were provided by Mrs. Millie Alpert, based on her experiences and networking with parents from other school districts.

BIBLIOGRAPHY

Behrmann, J. (1993). Including everyone. *The Executive Educator, 36,* 16–20.

Brockett, D. (1994). Disruptive disabled kids: Inclusion confusion. *Education Digest, 60*(2), 4–7.

Brown, L., Long, E., Udvari-Solner, A., Schwarz, P., VanDeventer, P., Ahlgren, C., Johnson, F., & Bunch, G. (1994). The interpretation of full inclusion. *American Annals of the Deaf, 139,* 150–152.

Burton, T., & Hirshoren, A. (1979). The education of severely and profoundly retarded children: Are we sacrificing the child to the concept? *Exceptional Children, 45,* 598–602.

Carr, M. (1993). A mother's thoughts on inclusion. *Journal of Learning Disabilities, 26*(9), 590–592.

Council for Learning Disabilities (1993). Concerns about the full inclusion of students with disabilities in regular education classroom. *Journal of Learning Disabilities, 26*(9), 595.

Crowe, L. K. (1994, November). *Inclusion plus collaborative teaming equals success in early childhood education.* Paper presented at the annual meeting of the American Speech-Language-Hearing Association, New Orleans, LA. (ERIC Document Reproduction Service No. ED 382 335)

Dougherty, J. W. (1994). Inclusion and teaming: It's a natural collaboration. *Schools in the Middle, 36,* 7–8.

Evans, D. W., Harris, D. M., Adeigbola, M., Houston, D., & Argott, L. (1993). Restructuring special education services. *Teacher Education and Special Education, 16*(2), 137–145.

Gerrard, L. (1994). Inclusive education: An issue of social justice. *Equity and Excellence in Education, 27*(1), 58–67.

Gruenwald, L., & Jorgensen, J. (1989). Should students with severe disabilities be based in regular or in special education classrooms in home schools? *The Associations for Persons with Severe Handicaps, 14*(1), 8–12.

Hehir, T. (1994). Changing the way we think about kids with disabilities: A conversation with Tom Hehir. *Harvard Education Letter, 10*(4), 5–7.

Innes, J. (1994). Full inclusion and the deaf student: A deaf consumer's review of the issue of *American Annals of the Deaf, 139,* 152–156.

Kauffman, J. M. (1995). Inclusion of all students with emotional or behavioral disorders? Let's think again. *Phi Delta Kappan, 76*(7), 542–546.

Kaufman, J. (1991). Restructuring in social political context: Restructuring of the effects of current reform proposals on students with disabilities. In J. W. Lloyd, N. N. Singh, and A. C. Repp (Eds.), *The Regular Education Initiative:*

Alternative Prospective on Concepts, Issues and Models (pp. 57–66). Sycamore, IL: Sycamore.

McCormick C., & First, P. (1994). The cost of inclusion. Educating students with special needs. *School Business Affairs, 30,* 34–36.

McEvoy, M., Shores, R., Wehby, J., Johnson, S., & Fox, J. (1990, September). Special education teachers' implementation of procedures to promote social interaction among children in integrated settings. *Education and Training in Mental Retardation.*

New York State United Teachers. (1993). *Special education—Inclusion: An update.* NYSUT Information Bulletin. Albany, NY: Author.

Odom, S., Hoyson, M., Jamieson, B., & Strain, P. (1985). Increasing handicapped preschoolers peer social interactions: Cross setting and component analysis. *Journal of Applied Behavior Analysis, 18,* 3–16.

Odom, S., & McEvoy, M. (1988). Integration of young children with handicaps and normally developing children. In S. Odom and M. Karnes (Eds.), *Early intervention for infants and children with handicaps: An empirical base.* Baltimore: Paul Brooks.

Peck, C., Hayden, L., Wandschneider, M., Peterson, K., & Richarz, S. (1989). Development of integrated preschools: A qualitative inquiry into sources of resistance among parents, administrators and teachers. *Journal of Early Intervention, 13,* 353–364.

Pierce, J., Rasdall, J., & Ferguson, J. (1993). A bridge over troubled water: Facility needs for inclusive classrooms. *Educational Facility Planner,* 10–15.

Polansky, H. B. (1994). The meaning of inclusion. Is it an option or a mandate? *School Business Affairs, 60,* 27–29.

Polowe-Aldersley, S. (1994). Human resources and full inclusion of students who are deaf. *American Annals of the Deaf, 138*(2), 162–163.

Reich, C., Hambleton, D., & Houldin, B. (1977). The integration of learning impaired children in regular classrooms. *American Annals of the Deaf, 122,* 534–543.

Reichart, D., Lynch, E., Anderson, B., Svobodny, L., DiCola, J., & Mercury, M. (1989). Parental perspectives on integrated preschool opportunities for children with handicaps and children without handicaps. *Journal of Early Intervention, 13,* 6–13.

Rimland, B. (1993). Beware the advo zealots: Mindless good intentions injure the handicapped. *Autistic Research Review International, 7,* 4.

Rock, E. E., Rosenberg, M. S., & Carran, D. T. (1995). Variables affecting the reintegration rate of students with serious emotional disturbance. *Exceptional Children, 61*(3), 254–268.

Sardo-Brown, D., & Hinson, S. (1995). Classroom teachers' perceptions of the implementation and effects of full inclusion. *ERS Spectrum, 13*(2), 18–24.

Shanker, A. (1995). Full inclusion is neither free nor appropriate. *Educational Leadership, 52*(4), 18–21.

Somoza, A. (1993). Inclusion: A child's perspective. *Exceptional Parent,*
    23(7), 17.

Stainback, W., & Stainback, S. (1993). Resources on inclusion. *The Executive*
    Educator, 52, 18–20.

Stinson, M., & Lang, H. (1994). Full inclusion: A path for integration or isolation.
    American Annals of the Deaf, 139 (2), 256–258.

Tiegerman-Farber, E. (1995). *Language and communication intervention in*
    preschool children. Boston: Allyn & Bacon.

Tingey, C. (1989). *Implementing early intervention.* Baltimore: Paul H. Brookes.

Voeltz, L. (1980). Children's attitude towards handicapped peers. *American*
    Journal of Mental Deficiency, 84(5), 455–464.

Westby, C. (1994). The vision of full inclusion: Don't exclude kids by including
    them. *Journal of Childhood Communication Disorders, 16*(1), 13–22.

Wilczenski, F. L. (1992). Measuring attitudes toward inclusion education. *Psychology*
    in the Schools, 29(4), 306–312.

York, J., Doyle, M., & Kronberg, R. (1992). A curriculum development process for
    inclusive classrooms. *Focus on Exceptional Children, 25*(4), 1–16.

5

The Role of the Family
in the Collaborative Process

LEARNING OBJECTIVES

After you have read this chapter, you should be able to:

1. Describe the changing role of parents in education. Why do parents need to be advocates for their children?

2. Explain how the family functions as an ecological system. Discuss various factors that contextually influence the quality of family relationships.

3. Discuss the variables that may present learning barriers for families within schools.

4. Describe how parents and teachers need to reformulate their thinking about educational decision making.

5. Elaborate on the kinds of techniques and tools that can be used by parents and teachers to develop classroom partnerships.

6. Discuss how conflicts can be identified and resolved.

As we discussed in earlier chapters, it is important for parents and teachers to collaborate and make decisions about pragmatic classroom issues: instruction, classroom organization, adaptive equipment, learning expectations, and child outcomes. Successful inclusion will never be achieved unless parents and teachers work together with a common focus and vision about basic classroom realities. The purpose of this chapter is to discuss some of the issues related to the changing role of parents and families in multiculturally diverse communities. The organizational changes that have occurred in families are reflected within the diverse aspects of inclusive classrooms. Social and economic factors that affect families also often affect children's behaviors, attitudes, and educational achievements. In order for schools to change, parents and teachers need to change their thinking about the educational process. One of the first questions that must be addressed collaboratively between communities and schools involves the necessity for reorganizing or reforming the educational process. The reality is that inclusion represents one small aspect of educational reform in American schools; many other issues are facing schools that would also benefit from collaborative decision making—special education represents only one issue. Schools and communities must collaboratively address a range of social problems that have come to the forefront of our attention in the past decade: Drugs, drinking, teen pregnancy, violence, truancy, and academic failure are all significant problems that require ongoing discussion and pragmatic solutions.

Just as the structure of the family has changed during the past several decades, schools too have changed. The traditional American family no longer consists of a mother, father, two children, and a puppy. The percentage of single-parent families and alternative families is much higher. The influx of immigrants from all over the world has created a multicultural diversity of students within large metropolitan areas in the United States. The impact of family values, languages, religions, and cultural expectations has influenced the ecology of schools and classroom instruction. Today, there are more working mothers and more children in day care programs than ever before. The demand for extended day care and quality child care raises many questions about our commitment as a society to the changing organization of families and their ecological needs.

What is the role of the school within any given community? What do parents want from their community school? The history of the educational process during the past several decades has created a dramatic separation between schools and communities, parents and teachers. The social problems that many communities face emphasize the fact that the process for decision making must change as well. Inclusion provides an opportunity to create a framework and a mechanism for decision making that will positively affect many other areas in education that need to be addressed. Many researchers describe inclusion as an issue of social justice. If it is, then the process by which educational decisions are made must reflect a collaborative structure that includes parents and teachers.

Children with disabilities should not be placed in general education classrooms without the consent and support of *all* parents. If schools take the position that educators can make child and educational decisions *independent* of the feelings and perceptions of parents, inclusion will never be successful. Inclusive classrooms require a collaborative process that involves parents and teachers making decisions with a common focus, vision, and goal. Communities and schools must develop collaborative teams that can be organized to develop and implement inclusive changes. Inclusion is a *final* step; it can only be achieved successfully if there is agreement about the social mission and the pragmatic process of decision making.

Classroom and instructional procedures are different in the inclusion classroom; parents and teachers must agree about the difference. Inclusion requires that parents and teachers think about the ecology of the classroom with new ideas, expectations, and goals. Traditional procedures, viewpoints, and perceptions are not helpful when reorganizing classrooms and schools. Certainly inclusion can be accomplished, not, however, without the support of parents. The purpose of this chapter is to discuss family issues and provide personal insights from parents about the inclusion classroom.

THE ROLE OF PARENTS

Historically, parents have been described as heroines or villains depending on the success of the child in school. In the case of a child with a behavioral and/or emotional disorder, parents may be viewed as contributors to the child's learning problems. Family dynamics and adult parenting skills are often factored into the evaluation process. One problem for parents involves the fact that they have been relegated to a secondary role in education. Parents are entitled to an annual open house and a semi-annual parent–teacher meeting. It is rare for parents to be involved in ongoing classroom instruction or provided with formal educational instruction or included within curricula programming.

Parents of children with special needs are relegated by education law to a role of participation; the *definition* of that term varies from school district to school district. The *reality* of the term *participation* indicates that parents have a voice but no vote. Parents are not viewed as teachers of their children and are not accepted as advocates. Parents who express an opinion and attempt to become more involved in classroom instruction are often faced with procedural barriers. In fact, the very design of schools in terms of hours of instruction presents a barrier for working parents. There is very little opportunity for schools to provide evening or weekend programs for parents and children. Teaching must be left to the educators; parents are on their own. Most of the social problems experienced in the schools can be traced back to the schism between parents and teachers. The fact that American schools today do not include parents in educational decision making should indicate that this is the very first problem that needs to be addressed. The two significant individuals in the life of a child are his parent and his teacher.

The problems occurring in education highlight broader social issues. The classroom represents a microcosm of diversity problems that impact on learning. These problems must be addressed collaboratively by parents and teachers. Clearly, education cannot succeed without parent support. If teachers are not supported by parents, children will not behave, will not achieve, and will not learn. The very mission of the school as an institution of moral, social, and academic learning will be undermined by the match–mismatch in values and attitudes between teachers and parents. The following Opinion Box presents a range of concerns expressed by the collaborative "stakeholders" about the placement of a child with disabilities in a general education classroom. The successful achievement of inclusion requires that these concerns be addressed by means of a collaborative model. In this chapter we discuss the concerns of parents and the need to incorporate, to empower, and to educate parents in collaborative decision making. The first adaptation for education is the recognition of parents within the collaborative process. To understand parent concerns, factors that influence

---

❧   OPINION BOX   ❧

Question: Describe the most significant problems encountered in attempting to place the child with disabilities within a regular classroom.

- Do you place the child with disabilities in an age-appropriate class, or do you place the child in a class according to his academic skills? How large should the class be? How many children with disabilities and nondisabled children should be mixed together? What types of children with disabilities can be placed in a regular education classroom?

- If inclusion represents an issue of social justice, then the key issue is the *benefit* to the child. How do teachers decide whether the regular education classroom will provide a benefit in learning? Do we take a risk with children with disabilities just to see if the experiment works?

- The most significant problems include appropriate personnel, sufficient resources to the classroom, learning devices, and flexibility in scheduling for teachers. I also feel that there is a great deal of negativity that must be addressed; parents, teachers, and administrators must talk to each other about making a commitment to this entire process.

- Large class sizes and unqualified professionals pose serious threats to the child with special needs in a regular education classroom. There are no instructional guidelines for inclusion programming.

- There must be an alignment between the school and the community. Teachers and parents must agree on a mission statement and work toward inclusion programming. Forcing parents to place their children in regular classes will never work. Forcing teachers to accept children with disabilities in their classrooms will never work. Parents and teachers need to work together to develop the inclusion classroom.

Note: Regular education teachers and parents in the local community were sent anonymous surveys. These responses are representative samples.

family life should be discussed in schools by parents and teachers. The family environment in today's society heightens a complex set of issues for parents.

The family represents an ecological system that shapes and modifies the fears, the concerns, the attitudes, and the values of all of its members. It is in the best interest of schools and educational professionals to make time to formalize the educational procedures that will highlight the needs of parents. Schools must begin the process of developing programming and curriculum for parents. By teaching parents and empowering them through knowledge and shared decision making, parents will become invested in their child's education and in classrooms.

The first step in the process, however, is to understand parents and their needs in schools; an assessment of family variables requires careful and ongoing analysis. Clearly, part of the process of collaboration involves communication; in this case, listening to the voices of parents. We must answer some questions as educators. What do parents want for their children? What do parents expect from schools? What do parents need to know about classroom instruction and educational learning? What do we need to teach parents? How do we teach parents, given our existing resources within the schools? In essence, we must engage in an outcome assessment process with parents just as we have with students within the classroom.

PARENT AND FAMILY ISSUES

An ecological approach provides a mechanism for understanding family issues in terms of a systems theory. The family functions as a social system whose members are interrelated and interdependent. Parents and children affect each other within the framework of an ecological environment (Szapocznik & Kurtines, 1993). The affective influences explain that the child's behavior is inextricably related to the interdependent factors occurring within her family. The parents' behavior can also be understood by identifying the critical variables that influence the ecosystem of the family. These variables include internal as well as external factors that impact the social, emotional, cultural, economic, and personal accomplishments of family members. Each family is unique; family members create a highly idiosyncratic microsystem (Bronfenbrenner, 1989; see Figure 5.1).

Special education research has described the fact that a child with disabilities influences members of his family just as he impacts significantly on the quantitative and qualitative aspects of the family ecosystem. Parents of children with disabilities often describe an emotional transition process that involves a series of steps and stages related to the acceptance of the child (Murray & Cornell, 1981). The initial recognition and acknowledgment by parents that they have a child with disabilities often create a tremendous amount of stress within a family. Parents describe a sense of unreality, shock, and disbelief. This numbness often changes to anger and frustration, which is sometimes displaced and externalized to the spouse, to other children, and to members of the extended family. Some parents turn their anger inward and blame themselves for the child's disability.

Over time, parents describe a sense of peace that comes with acceptance of the child. Parents reflect on the fact that having a child with disabilities shatters the

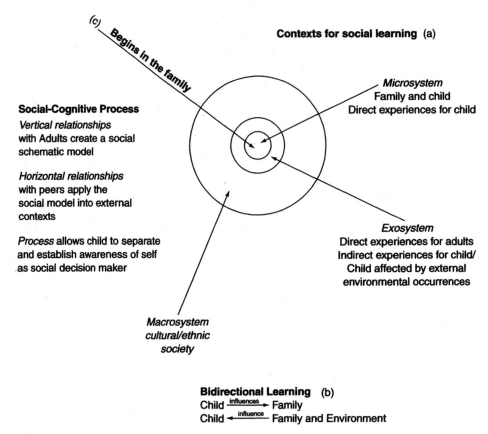

FIGURE 5.1
Ecological systems approach to child development.

expectations of normalcy and life cycle transitions. Many things that parents take for granted—such as my child will go to college, my child will get married, my child will be a professional and I will be a grandparent—are all shattered by the realization that the child has a disability. Parents of children with disabilities need emotional support from their partners, their children, their extended families, and professionals to read-just their expectations of life cycle issues (Turnbull, Barber, Behr, & Kerns, 1988). Disability is only one factor that can affect the interdependent relationships within the family ecosystem. There are many other factors.

Cultural Determinism

American society is often described by its multicultural pluralism. Schools have always been the recipient of a wide variety of immigrant populations (Edwards, 1990). The role and function of schools have always involved educating diverse populations of children having differences in language, economic backgrounds, and social beliefs. Historically, schools have functioned as normalizers and equalizers for *all* children. The various cultural values and differences in perception impact classroom learning, peer interaction, and English language instruction. Cultural differences may create educational barriers that must be identified and removed. Families from different communities will send their children to school with viewpoints and values that may compete with the educational goals and principles presented by teachers and school curricula (Edwards, 1990).

It is important to understand cultural differences so that effective learning can be achieved. If particular cultures perceive the role of women as secondary, then the female teacher in the classroom may have significant problems in providing instruction to male children. If particular cultures do not recognize the needs of children with disabilities, then those issues must be identified and addressed by professional teams. If particular cultures accept specific types or levels of behavior that schools find inappropriate, then parents and teachers are going to have to discuss appropriate levels of classroom behaviors. Inclusive classrooms will have to identify cultural barriers and adapt to the needs of multicultural families.

Linguistic Differences

Multicultural diversity also presents language variations and differences that affect classroom instruction (Alper, Schloss, & Schloss, 1994). In some cases, parents when they arrive as immigrants from other countries do not speak English and the barrier created by the communication problem may create further problems for the child and the teacher within the classroom. It is of critical importance for parents and teachers to be able to understand each other's needs, goals, and concerns about educational programming. It is also important for parents and teachers to communicate on a regular basis about child progress, learning, and any developmental differences that may arise as a function of academic instruction. When linguistic differences interfere with parent–teacher communication, educational programming may be compromised.

In addition, the parent cannot function as a facilitator of classroom instruction if she or he cannot understand instructional techniques and procedures (Correa, 1989). In order for the parent to complement classroom programming, she or he must be in a position to network on a regular basis with school professionals. Language interpreters are not always available in schools to facilitate the communication exchange.

Just as language may present as a learning barrier for families, it clearly presents controversial issues for children. Bilingual education represents an important aspect of regular education programming in most metropolitan school districts. In the past several decades, large city schools have utilized various forms of bilingual instruction—English as a second language (ESL) (Fradd, Weismantel, Correa, & Algozzine, 1990). Within this category of children who are struggling to learn a second language is a small subgroup of children with developments disabilities. It is always difficult to identify a child with a disability given standardized assessments, multidisciplinary evaluations, and observational investigations. The younger the child in question, the more tenuous the evaluation process. Imagine how much more complicated all of this becomes when the child does not speak English (as a primary language), and a bilingual evaluator is difficult to identify and/or standardized assessments are not available in the native language.

The problem is further complicated by the child's age of entry into the public schools. The younger a child transitions into an English-speaking classroom, the easier the acquisition of the second language. In elementary school, and by the age of 6, bilingual instruction is complicated by the fact that the child is older, and academic learning subjects may be hindered when they are not presented in the child's native language. The history of bilingual education, its efficacy, and its continuation may ultimately be viewed in the same way as special education is being viewed today (Diaz, 1990). The child's ability to socialize, develop new relationships with peers, and acquire competitive academic competencies is based on English proficiency. The language difference can represent a barrier for the child and the family within the inclusion classroom. The language difference is a factor of multicultural diversity that must be taken into consideration by teaching professionals in order to develop an inclusive learning environment. Schools must be prepared to adapt traditional teaching schedules to meet the needs of diverse children and families. Bilingual instruction before, during, and after school must be provided with a family focus. The inclusive classroom must incorporate diverse families. Multicultural diversity is a cornerstone of inclusive classrooms and curricula (Fletcher and Cardona-Morales, 1990).

Economic Pressures

Most of the research on family problems highlights the fact that socioeconomic factors contribute significantly to child development. The economic factors that impinge on a family represent critical issues in defining the child's contextual opportunities. The economic climate, its stresses, its changes, and its demands impact workers, which in turn influences family decisions. The fact that the majority of American families include working mothers and require a second income emphasizes the relationship between the work environment and the home environment. Families are interdependently connected with social factors and issues. Almost 71 percent of all mothers with young children (children below the age of 5) find themselves within the workforce in order to "make ends meet" at home. The need to have two working parents to support the family creates other problems within the home in terms of the management of children, the emotional support between the spouses, child care, and home-related responsibilities. Parents who are better educated provide greater opportunities and more enhanced home experiences for their children.

Poverty creates a generational cycle of social failure that is difficult for children to overcome (Pianta & Reeve, 1990). The barriers of poverty impact on education, behavior, social success, peer networking, self-esteem, marriage, addiction, and lifelong decision making. The struggles of families to overcome economic deprivation have been documented throughout the literature (Turnbull & Turnbull, 1990). Schools have always functioned as mechanisms for children to overcome their social problems and backgrounds. Schools provide an opportunity for social equalization. Education facilitates mobilization in society, allowing children extraordinary opportunities for advancement that they would not achieve in any other way. It is important, therefore, for teachers to work closely with parents so that parents and children see schools as an opportunity for professional learning, personal growth, and economic advancement.

Children from impoverished home environments often fail in school not because of disabilities but because of negative social attitudes about learning (Miranda & Santos de Barona, 1990). Children feel disenfranchised from school environments because they are uncomfortable about the learning contexts and the adults who function as role models and facilitators. The entire social process within school settings is alien to many children from poor families. Children drop out of school because they are not invested in the academic process. Children are violent in school because they are not invested in the social process. Schools fail because children cannot relate to academic learning expectations; children do not see themselves as academically successful.

The background of the family and the child must be taken into consideration as a critical factor to the inclusion classroom. Understanding the family, its issues, and its problems underscores many of the barriers that exist even before the child enters the inclusion classroom. Inclusion success requires committed and engaged parents. The history of many educational initiatives indicates the secondary role of parents in critical decision making; this must change. Classroom barriers must be identified so that parents can serve as role models for their children. The child who invests in the educational process has a parent who is committed to her learning—this is an axiom that must be acknowledged.

Alternative Family Dynamics

The notion of the traditional American family no longer exists as a reality in today's complex multicultural society (Levitan, Belous, & Gallo, 1988). Most families involve a working single parent or a melded family situation. The learning dynamics of single-parent families and melded families must be considered by teachers and schools, given the impact on child learning. The single parent is usually a working parent who is highly stressed, has scheduling problems, and cannot meet during the day. Child care becomes a critical issue with single-parent families. This child may be left at home alone, may be taken to a day care program before and after school, or may be taken care of at home by a non-English-speaking babysitter or relative. In the melded family, divorced parents remarry and sibling relationships become further complicated by step siblings. Children raised in melded families often complain about differences in child-rearing practices between the adults. Stepchildren and melded families create additional difficulties as children struggle with realignment within the family and individuation issues in development.

Single parents and stepparents complain about child care problems, relationship conflicts, and extraordinary feelings of guilt. Parents struggle with the aftermath of divorce, the loss of an earlier relationship, and all of the problems related to creating new relationships in today's complex adult society (Ihinger-Tallman, 1986). Adult values have changed, and as a result the models provided to young children, given these new adult relationships, create additional questions for children and schools. Teachers need to understand the organization of the family, as well as the values presented by parents within the home. The home represents a cultural community just as the classroom does. The relationship between family members will contribute to the learning determinism of the child within the inclusive classroom. Family goals and values need to be reflected within the curriculum of the inclusive classroom. Schools need to be more closely connected to and attuned to specific communities.

Gender and Ethnicity

Although traditional families have changed in terms of their organizational structures, women in the workforce complain vociferously about the fact that some things have not changed. The demands on women working outside the home have created a degree of stress in mothers who must also play a significant role with children and home care responsibilities. Most marital relationships, cultures, and social institutions continue to focus on mothers as primary facilitators of their children. It is still the mother who comes to school to pick up the child when he is ill. It is still the mother who has the primary responsibility for organizing chores and children in the home. It is still the mother of a child with special needs who deals with discipline, management, and educational issues. Women often complain that working responsibilities outside of the home have not liberated them from the responsibilities within the home. The outside employment only adds another job and set of responsibilities. The ongoing demands of work responsibilities inside and outside of the home create additional stress in women who must also function as parents of children with disabilities (Wikler, 1986).

Managing the home, the work setting, and children often creates serious interpersonal problems between the spouses. Whose job is it? Is it always the mother's responsibility when there is a child-related issue? Whose salary and income are more important to the management of the household? To what degree can a woman continue working when her husband feels that it is not expedient or convenient to his perception of his household and his children? Women within the workforce complain as well about the difficulties related to professional growth and advancement. There are very few women mentors within any given discipline area, especially at the administrative and upper levels of business and corporate employment. Most women do not function in decision-making positions to assist other women who are attempting to progress and to achieve in the business world. This is very obvious in education as well. Although education has historically employed a much larger number of women than men, an inordinate number of men are in administrative positions. Most principals are men. Most superintendents are men. Most assistant commissioners are men. Most commissioners are men. Although women work in education and mothers advocate for their children in education, decision making remains within the hands of men in our society. This dual difficulty for women and mothers suggests that when mothers appear in school to advocate for their children, they tend to feel much less effective than their husbands, given the perception that men in general are primary decision makers—in school, at work, and at home. One problem, therefore, for parents who are attempting to advocate for children with disabilities is that the parent who is attempting to advocate is perceived as being the "weaker" of the two genders.

Ethnicity also plays a role in the perception of judgment and decision making. Minorities are often ignored or perceived as being uneducated about educational procedures and issues. Minorities are stereotyped as being less involved with their children, less able to manage home-based problems, and not as committed to educational issues. There is obviously a heightened synergy when a child with disabilities is represented by a minority parent who happens to be a woman. Gender and ethnicity issues clearly impact the ability of parents to function in schools as collaborators and decision makers (Edwards, 1990).

Educational Expectations

It is important to determine how parents perceive schools, educational procedures, and the role of education within their culture. Effective communication plays a key element in understanding multicultural families, their issues, their goals, their dreams, and their children. School professionals need to learn how to take into consideration the perceptions of families of culturally diverse children—some of whom are developmentally disabled (Fradd *et al.*, 1990). Part of the collaboration process will involve developing a family profile that will identify not only the risk factors that will clearly impact the inclusive classroom, but the issues that are educationally significant to multicultural families. What do parents expect from teachers and schools? Schools need to identify common goals with parents as well as areas of perceptual mismatch (see Figure 5.2). This profile provides some insights about how parents perceive their children. Teachers need to take into consideration the feelings, concerns, and perspectives of parents. How parents perceive their children can provide teachers with information about family, organization, management, child rearing, and beliefs. Cultural beliefs may create different barriers than educational beliefs.

The reason that so many parents have absented themselves from parent–teacher meetings, school participation, and educational integration relates specifically to the school's primacy in decision making. Schools are going to have to initiate the development of parent–teacher partnerships in order to facilitate collaborative decision making in inclusive classrooms. Inclusive programming will never succeed without the participation of multicultural families and the direct input of parents whose children will participate in inclusive classrooms. Schools will have to develop a philosophy of respect and mutual understanding before inclusive classrooms are developed. The collaboration process is the "hinge pin" to inclusive education. Without parents, there will be no

1. I would describe my child as

___ sensitive	___ impulsive	___ plays with peers	___ team worker
___ moody	___ serious	___ leader	___ completes
___ overly active	___ listens	___ follower	activities
___ follows directions	___ strong willed	___ expresses ideas	___ pays
___ hits	___ distractible	___ concerned about others	attention
___ expresses feelings	___ quiet	___ friendly	___ shy

List other characteristics: _____ _____ _____ _____

2. I would like my child to learn:

___ social skills	___ reading skills	___ to complete activities
___ language skills	___ writing	___ to work independently
___ to make friends	___ to work in a group	___ to show initiative
___ to be more confident	___ to play with peers	___ to be motivated

List other classroom skills: _____ _____ _____

3. What kind of values should be taught in our classroom?

___ honesty	___ sharing	___ caring	___ expressing feelings
___ respect for others	___ self-esteem		

4. What kind of learning problems does your child have?

_____

_____

_____

_____

FIGURE 5.2
Parent/family expectations.

partnership. Without collaboration, there will be no inclusion. Schools will never be able to successfully "mandate" a forced inclusion process. Inclusion is based on child diversity. The diversity of the classroom reflects not only a range of regular education students, a range of children with developmental disabilities, but also a range of cultural values. The inclusive classroom provides a belief that education can bridge cultural differences by collaborating with parents from various cultural backgrounds. The following Opinion Box discusses some of the challenges faced by schools attempting to develop inclusion classrooms. Parents must be part of the educational team.

UNDERSTANDING THE NEEDS OF PARENTS

Historically, parents have not played a significant role in formal education. The reason for this is quite simple: Parents have not been part of the decision-making process. Inclusion provides the mechanism and the reality for parents to be more involved in their children's education. The collaborative team should include the parent. Again, there must be many different collaborative teams. In the formulation of the mission statement for the school district and the community, a collaborative team should be formed consisting of administrators, parents, and teachers. The decision making at this point is at a macro level, a broad-based statement for the whole district. The contributions of parents, teachers, and administrators will involve the philosophy of inclusion for the school and the implementation of that philosophical approach to the development of the curriculum.

❧ OPINION BOX ❧

Public Law 94-142 clearly states that its purpose is to provide a free and appropriate education for students with disabilities in the least restrictive environment with children who are not disabled and, to the extent possible, in the school or program the child would attend if he/she did not have a disability. The term "inclusion" is not part of the language of 94-142, but the philosophy of inclusion and participation in public education are the driving force of the law.

The inclusion of students with disabilities in public school provides many challenges. The challenges are similar to those encountered by business and society. It requires a "can-do philosophy," a creative approach to education, a willingness to change and grow, and a belief that all people have valuable contributions to make to one another. It requires good planning and crossing new bridges as they suddenly appear. Teamwork is essential, and the child's parents must be part of the team.

School districts should begin to address the training needs of staff. Regular education teachers have realistic concerns about the impact of a student with a disability on the delivery of instruction. The district must also provide the ancillary supports that are required by teachers and students.

Students with more severe disabilities have traditionally been educated at special schools and centers. School districts did not need to address wheelchairs, elevators, space for OT and PT, and the nursing services necessary for medically involved students.

Additional supervision is often necessary at lunch and on the playground. Adaptive equipment for the classroom and the gym will be required. Students with visual disabilities need materials in braille and students with hearing impairments require sign language interpreters. The necessary adaptations must be provided for instruction, for class trips, and for extracurricular events.

There are costs associated with providing these services. There are greater costs associated with ignoring the needs.

Eileen Fitzgerald
Director, Pupil Personnel
Garden City Public Schools, New York

Another collaborative team may be formed within the school consisting of parents, teachers, and administrators who will work to address building problems and develop a particular transdisciplinary curriculum. Here, pragmatic issues related to classroom design, resources, school reorganization, and teacher schedules are discussed. Financial costs and long-range planning may all be considerations for a pilot program. Still another collaborative team may be generated to address specific classroom issues once a pilot program has started consisting of a regular education teacher, a special education teacher, an administrator, and a parent. Here, specific children requiring placement will be considered by the team. Decisions will be made about the number of children with disabilities in each classroom, the type of disability, the individual goals, the instructional procedures, classroom organization, etc. The decision making at this micro level will involve implementing the programming to meet the mission of inclusion—collaborating to actually *do it*. Through this entire process with all of these teams, parents must be involved as decision makers.

Parents of Children with Disabilities: Attitudes

Parents of children with disabilities must address their anger and fear that their children will be isolated and ostracized. They need to feel comfortable that *they* have made the right decision about placing their child in a regular classroom. Obviously, the child with a disability is different socially, communicatively, academically, and sometimes physically. Many parents of children with disabilities feel strongly about the fact that only in a special education setting will there be a high degree of individualized and specialized programming, services, attention, intervention, and resources. Parents of children with disabilities are not generally supportive of inclusion, let alone full inclusion (Behrmann, 1993). What will inclusion mean in terms of social and academic instruction? Will the child's individual needs be addressed? Can the child with a disability make progress in the inclusion classroom? It is important for the parent of a child with a disability to be clear about the individual goals, the learning accommodations, and the cultural aspects of the classroom.

At times, the path may be difficult; children will have to learn to be sensitive and supportive of each other. At times, parents will have to change their expectations, their perceptions, and their fears about the classroom. Inclusion will be a learning experience for all concerned—the parent, the teacher, and the child. Negative attitudes provide the greatest barriers to social interaction and self-actualization.

Parents of Regular Education Children: Attitudes

Inclusion cannot succeed without regular children. If parents of regular education children are frightened of the inclusion process, they may seek private school placements. The greatest challenge to inclusion involves the public relations problems that have traditionally surrounded inclusive learning. Parents of regular education children must be convinced that there is benefit to *all* children involved in the inclusion class-room. General education will be different; the regular education child is going to be affected and *educational* outcomes will be different. The regular education student will learn a great deal about cultural and individual diversity. Children can learn from children, and children can learn by teaching children. The goals of self-esteem, self-actualization, mutual respect, altruism, and friendship are just as important as acade-mic achievement; each community will have to decide about educational "trade-offs." The ideal of social justice will have to be balanced against the realities of educational programming. Educational goals and outcomes will have to be redefined for all chil-dren. Kirchner (1994) speaks about including students with hearing impairments and notes that academic instruction in inclusion classrooms proceeds at a slower pace as information is presented to divergently different learners. "Communication does re-quire more time for any topic to be taught or discussed. Full inclusion can be a detri-ment to all if the hearing impaired student is not capable of the academic work" (p. 164). Parents of regular education children will want to know how educational changes—instructional and academic—will affect child learning and development. Communities and collaborative teams must engage in active discourse to address these sensitive issues and underlying attitudes.

Support Groups

Part of the collaborative process should include support groups consisting of parents of children with disabilities and regular education students. Parents do not realize that they are a significant untapped resource; their combined effort can reform educational programming within any community. Parents need to realize that they can change ed-ucation and that they really have the same goals. All parents want safety in the schools. All parents strive for educational excellence. All parents want their children to achieve. Parents must learn to talk to other parents. Support groups for parents to deal with their feelings and concerns, so that they can constructively support each other, create a powerful force underlying inclusion success. Parents working with each other require a great deal of rapport building. The relationship between parents must be as strong as the relationship between parents and teachers.

Parent Network Groups

Parent partners provide a mentorship experience for parents. Parents need to be men-tored and coached as they enter the inclusion classroom. Parents who have been through the process and have children in the upper grades can function as volunteers in a district-wide parent mentor program. Parents helping parents to deal with diffi-cult child-based issues creates a network of support. The parent partnership fosters a generation of parent giving; parents have a great deal to offer each other (Tiegerman-Farber, 1995).

Parents in the Classroom

Parents should be allowed to observe and volunteer their time in the inclusion class-room. Parents have historically been excluded from the classroom except for a day of observation. This denies parents an ongoing learning experience. Parents need to understand the problems of teachers and children and contribute to the learning process by being a partner to the classroom. The only way that parents can learn about educational problems is through direction and observation, particularly in daily experiences. There should be some rotating mechanism for parents to observe and participate in daily classroom learning.

Parent Education Classes

Providing parents with an opportunity to observe in the classroom should be coordinated with parent education classes that can be offered either during the day or at night. The intent here is to train parents to function as teacher collaborators in the home. Parents need to learn about academic curricula, teaching techniques and procedures, and the needs of their own children. Parents need to be provided with formal coursework in educational and developmental issues (Tiegerman-Farber, 1995).

Teaching parents to teach their children supports the entire educational process and bolsters educational success. Parents need to learn that they have a role in and a responsibility to their children's education. It is, however, the responsibility of the educational system to educate parents on how to do this. Parents are not educators, so they need to be trained about the form and function of educating their children. Extending educational programming into the home expands learning beyond the hours of 9:00 A.M. to 3:00 P.M. Extending learning into the home ensures a collaboration of ideas and goals. It is important for the school and the home to agree on educational philosophy and programming. Inclusion programming creates community schools and the coalition between parents and teachers.

Listening to the Concerns of Parents

"No one knows my child better than I do." There is no one more effective as an advocate than a parent of a child with disabilities. Parents have a wealth of developmental experiences that can be shared with teachers. Parents have insight about their child's learning that can be included within the instructional curriculum (Wiese, 1992). Parents can act as facilitators and teachers when schools are closed and classes have ended. Parents must be viewed as educational missionaries.

A review of legal and political challenges underscores the fact that parents of children with disabilities have been actively involved in the courts for several decades. With the intent of challenging the political system and educational decision making, parents of children with disabilities have organized to change laws, create programs, and ensure the provision of services. Many of the cases filed by parents of children with disabilities have attempted to guarantee to children with disabilities access to public schools and educational services. The development of parent organizations describes an educational history that has denied children with disabilities access to society and opportunities for learning prior to 1975. The passage of P.L. 94-142, the Education for All Handicapped Children Act of 1975, can be attributed to parent advocacy and their commitment to social change. The legal victories and achievements of parents of children with disabilities have been financially costly, time consuming, and emotionally draining. The due process procedure has not been an easy road for parents of children with special needs.

It is also important to be aware of the fact that the majority of parents do not get involved on a daily basis with educational issues. The majority of parents of children with disabilities do not challenge the educational decisions made by Committees on Special Education (CSEs). Relatively few parents can afford financially and emotionally to proceed through due process procedures, impartial hearings, and then the courts. The majority of parents who request impartial hearings lose at the state level. The system is so organized against parents that the impartial hearing officer is paid by the school district in New York State. A parent's viewpoint on that single issue invoked the following comment from a parent: "When the impartial hearing officer is paid by the school district, is it surprising that parents lose most of their legal cases?" There has been a complaint that when parents win, school districts are required to pay for the legal expenses. There are so many parents who lose that the criticism is hollow. Legal fees engendered by school districts are part of the taxes collected from the community on an annual basis. Parents pay directly from family savings to defend and to protect the rights of their children. Families face a much greater risk and have much more to lose—their child's rights and future.

The greatest advances in programming for children with disabilities have occurred as a function of parent organizations and the collaboration between parents and national professional organizations. Parents of children with disabilities have organized as a function of educational need. The strides in education would not have been possible if parents had not become actively involved in the political process. Parents of general education students have not been as actively involved in parent advocacy or educational reform. Parents of general education students can learn a great deal about political advocacy from parents of children with special needs. Inclusion requires that all parents become an integral part of school reform.

Parent Advocacy and Empowerment

The educated parent is the parent who advocates on a long-term basis for the needs of her child; the educated parent is the empowered parent. Historically, advocacy has been an issue confined to parents of children with disabilities. The inclusion process, however, expands the philosophy of advocacy to all parents. Each child within the inclusion classroom has an Individualized Education Plan; the foundation of inclusion programming is individualized instruction. The process of individualization in education incorporates the parent as an advocate. The educational system works more effectively and efficiently when the parent plays a role as decision maker and contributor. The parent advocate provides a safeguard that the system will do its best to meet the needs of the child. Part of parent education must include advocacy training for parents. The parent as advocate will serve as a collaborator, teacher facilitator, and educational supporter if he has been trained to understand the needs of his child. It is in the best interest of education, its reform, and its success to educate parents and focus their skills as child advocates (Tiegerman-Farber, 1995).

Parent Choice and Educational Coercion

Parents of children with disabilities have experienced a history of legislative programming that has described participation without decision making. Parents of children with disabilities have never been able to vote on the CSE. There has never been parental choice in educational decision making or program placement. The introduction of inclusion as a program option to mainstreaming opens a potential Pandora's box. Most legal cases support the choice of parents when they fight for an inclusion option (Behrmann, 1993). Inclusion, however, cannot be forced on parents of regular education children.

It may be the case that for a limited period of time, parents of children with disabilities will find themselves coerced into placing their children into regular classes. This cannot last very long if educational reform is going to proceed collaboratively in public schools. Parents, teachers, and administrators are going to have to come to terms with two key issues. In an educational system striving for change, schools will have to balance parental choice and child placement. Successful inclusion requires a choice for parents of all children. Bunch (1994) indicates: "The essence of the struggle for full inclusion is the desire for the right of choice of placement within the educational system, a choice which remains denied for too many children" (p. 151).

Parents of regular education children will not tolerate for very long the coercion of child placement that parents of children with special needs have experienced for years. The reality is that inclusion will fail if parents of regular education children are not clear about the benefits and mission of this process. They will simply remove their children from the public schools and place them in private settings. The public schools will not be able to survive or sustain the economic flight of families nationwide. Polansky (1994) comments: ". . . the bottom line is make sure the student is ready to be included, the staff is trained and the program is appropriate." This may be easier said than done! Part of educational reform will require recognition of parental decision making and the acknowledgment that inclusion can only succeed if parents *choose* inclusive programming. Inclusion cannot be forced, and parents cannot be coerced; the stakes are too high given the present demand for reform.

Collaboration Modifications

In considering the adaptations that need to be made to include children with disabilities in the general education classroom, this section has discussed parent concerns and attitudes. Parents must be included as members of the collaborative team if schools are going to achieve successful inclusion classrooms. Parents must assist and contribute to the development of a school-wide policy concerning inclusive education (Ayres, 1988). Parents must also be part of the inclusive classroom once programming is implemented within the school. As stakeholders, when resources become limited, programs will be cut and parents will fight among themselves for educational excellence and services. Historically, parents of general education students have viewed themselves quite *differently* from parents of children with disabilities. It has often been noted that special education programs are much more costly than general education. With the advent of inclusive instruction the quality of education and the removal of special education services will have to be addressed so that both sets of parents contribute to classroom success. If the needs of either are not adequately considered, parents will not contribute to the long-term success of inclusive instruction. Schools cannot afford to have parents fighting with parents or parents fighting with teachers about educational instruction. It is in the best interest of all concerned, whether the viewpoint is social justice or educational achievement, for the stakeholders to be identified and a collaborative approach utilized for educational decision making.

OVERCOMING DIFFERENCES

Developing a Family Profile

Parents and teachers, as they discuss and develop an inclusion policy for a school, need to identify the barriers that interfere with inclusive programming. It might be helpful for teachers and parents to develop a profile that reflects attitudinal barriers and concerns about inclusive instruction. Parents of regular students and children with developmental disabilities should provide a profile that highlights cultural, religious, economic, communicative, and linguistic determinance characteristics that might affect child performance and educational interactions (see Figure 5.3). Part of the survey should include issues that are most important to the family. What are the hopes and dreams of the family in terms of the child's long-range education? What kind of problems do parents have attending meetings and visiting the classroom? What are the parents' specific fears or concerns about the child within the inclusive classroom? Parents also should be asked directly how teachers and school personnel could assist families and children with their goals.

At the beginning of every school year, part of the development of an inclusive classroom would involve a family profile of all of the children participating in inclusive classrooms. It is important for parents of all children to contribute to the dynamics of the classroom. More importantly, however, is the *perception* of the school, the teacher, and the classroom. Many times the family's perceptions are based on educational philosophy, cultural determinism, and ethnic factors. Teachers need to identify these issues in order to facilitate interactions with families. Cultural values and beliefs are unique and diverse; the recognition of these factors provides a starting point for conversational exchange and understanding of child-based learning issues.

To understand your child's learning needs, it is important for his/her teachers to know about family issues.

1. Family members/parents/children/extended family: Tell us about the people who live in your home.
2. How would you describe your home environment? Is it quiet? noisy? Is there a place for your child to do his/her homework? Is there someone home when he/she gets home from school?
3. Do all of the adults work? What kinds of jobs do members of the family have?

   mother _____ grandfather _____ siblings _____
   father _____ grandmother _____

4. What would you like your child to be? What are your goals for your family?
5. Is there anyone in your household who is not working? lost a job? looking for employment? Does this create any tension in the family? How do you think your child is affected?
6. Is anyone in your family ill? Do you think your child is aware? Do you think he is affected or his behavior has changed?
7. Is there any problem in the family which could affect your child's learning and/or behavior in school?
8. Is there another language spoken in the home? Does your child speak or understand this language? Would you feel comfortable discussing school issues in English? Do you need an interpreter?
9. What family and social values are important at home? Which values should be stressed in school?
10. What time of day is it best to meet in school?

    _____ day time   _____ night time

FIGURE 5.3
Questions to develop a family profile.

The Perceptual Report Card

Often, perceptual differences contribute to communication barriers and misunderstanding. Although the diversity in families contributes to multicultural education in inclusion, conflicts may arise when the expectations differ between teachers and parents. One significant problem involves child performance; whether or not children have benefitted from inclusive instruction in classrooms. One procedure that may be helpful as a tool in understanding differences and perceptions involves the develoment of a parent–teacher–child report card. This report card lists a number of child performances that translate into social learning behaviors that are critical to academic development (see Figure 5.4).

The classroom context can be operationalized by parents and teachers to determine which behaviors are important to classroom success: attending, task completion, helping others, socialization, leadership, independent skills, etc. A written scale can be

11. If we need to call you for a meeting, what time is convenient?

_____time   _____telephone

12. When can you attend parent–teacher meetings in school on a weekly basis?

Day		Evening	
Monday	_____	Monday	_____
Tuesday	_____	Tuesday	_____
Wednesday	_____	Wednesday	_____
Thursday	_____	Thursday	_____
Friday	_____	Friday	_____

13. How do you discipline your child?
14. What responsibilities does your child have at home?
15. What is the best way to talk to your child?
16. Do we need to be aware of any cultural, social, or religious beliefs that may influence your child's learning in a multicultural inclusion classroom?
17. What are your feelings and concerns about your child learning in a multicultural inclusion classroom?
18. How do you feel about having children with disabilities in the regular classroom?
19. If your child has a disability, describe your fears about the quality of education in the regular class, the regular peers, and how your child may be affected.
20. If your child is a regular learner, describe your fears about the quality of education in the regular class, the peers with disabilities, and how your child may be affected.
21. Would you like to serve on a parent–teacher collaborative team?

used that allows parents, teachers, and children to rate these behaviors on a sliding scale. Parents, teachers, and children are asked to measure the degree of ability or success for each behavior listed on the report card. Differences in perception between parents and teachers should stimulate a great deal of discussion and conversation. Perceptual differences can be identified but need to be resolved since conflicts may arise as a result of disappointments and expectations.

Parents must be encouraged to express their opinions and play an active role in classroom decision making. Cultural differences may create frustrating and anxiety-provoking situations for both parents and teachers. Initially, the ongoing process of communicative dialogue will clear up many misunderstandings, given the opportunity to overtly rather than covertly express negativity. Inclusion classrooms cannot succeed without parent collaborators. Schools fail when parents remain uninvolved, unresponsive, and apathetic. Conflicts need to be viewed as a mechanism for understanding, with the ultimate goal being a positive partnership between school and home. The

REPORT CARD

Development is indicated on the sliding scale as shown:

1 ————→ 5

Developing ability   Exceptional ability

*P = Parent Rating
T = Teacher Rating
C = Child Rating

Learning skills and traits	1st Report Period			2nd Report Period		
	P	C	T	P	C	T
Curiosity						
Masters facts						
Applications of facts						
Sustains involvement						
Socially aware						
Enjoys reading						
Verbal reasoning						
Personal responsibility						
Critical thinking						
Creativity/imagination						
Conceptual integration and association						
Generalizes learning						
Moral reasoning						
Problem solving						
Introspection						
Projects consequences						
Heightened perceptions						
Shows initiative						
Productivity						
Motivation						

Learning skills and traits	1st Report Period			2nd Report Period		
	P	C	T	P	C	T
Independence						
Leadership						
Peer sensitivity						
Self-esteem						
Accepts criticisms						
Open to new challenges and skills						
Personal awareness and self-concept						
Academic skills						
Reading						
Math						
Writing						
Science						
Foreign language						
Social studies						
Computer science						
Art						
Music						
Physical education						
Special abilities listed _____						

FIGURE 5.4 The inclusive report card.

classroom report card should be filled out several times a year to identify areas of difference and potential conflicts.

One unique aspect of the classroom report card involves children rating themselves in a number of learning areas. Part of the classroom cultural society requires that the child contribute to her own learning and to the learning of others. The child learner needs to develop an awareness of this cultural society; she needs to see herself in relation to other children. Children should be asked to contribute to this process by expressing their own concerns about the classroom and their educational needs in order to achieve. Often, children express concerns and issues that are quite different from those of parents and teachers. Because the child is the primary beneficiary of the educational process and the parent–teacher collaboration, her perceptions need to be factored into the inclusion formula.

Resolving Conflicts

Parents are not grownup children. Conflicts are created when schools do not recognize and acknowledge multicultural diversity and the significance of parent collaboration (Comer, 1986). Schools need to invest a great deal of time and energy in parent–teacher training and development (see Figure 5.5). Teachers and professionals need to develop an understanding of multicultural diversity and the needs of culturally diverse families (Cornelius, 1990). Within and across the diversity issues will be an even more fragmented subgroup—parents of children with developmental disabilities.

Schools need to develop strategies that will assist teachers in identifying attitudinal factors that conflict with parent–teacher interactions. Some of the factors may relate to differences in communication style, language barriers, parental expectations, family limitations, discipline differences, financial problems at home, time constraints, and family stress. Some or all of these factors need to be discussed by teachers and professionals in order to identify early warning signs in parents; proactive strategies can then be created to establish a process of ongoing dialogue and discussion.

Communication Feedback

Parents and teachers need to schedule regular meetings to assess the progress of children and the outcome of educational instruction within the inclusion classroom. Ongoing communication is an essential element to maintaining the commitment of inclusive classrooms. Parents need to feel that they play a significant role within the inclusion classroom and that there is a direct relationship between their educational input and the educational decisions that are generated. Communication feedback will provide critical information before issues become problems and problems become conflicts. The interaction between parent and teacher can be accomplished through a variety of procedural tools: meetings, classroom visits, home visits, home notebooks, etc. Parents and teachers can use different kinds of communication strategies to facilitate an ongoing dialogue. The process, however, must be to establish and maintain a communication dialogue over the course of the academic year; parents and teachers cannot lose contact with each other. The ease of the process will facilitate the content and relevance of the information exchanged. One interesting procedure might be for teachers to develop a questionnaire that is filled out by parents on a weekly basis. The use of such a technique would serve to minimize cultural linguistic and social barriers that interfere with effective communication.

Another tool might involve an evaluation procedure that is utilized after parent and teacher meetings. With this technique, parents and teachers could use a common evaluation form which highlights the effectiveness of the meeting, the content of the information exchanged, and recommendations for issues to be discussed at the next meeting. Clearly, differences in opinion and, hence, conflicts can arise. Conflicts must be addressed expeditiously and parents must be left with the feeling that there is concern as well as support from school personnel. Teachers must develop strategies that are multiculturally sensitive to the needs of specific families.

- Are parents collaborating at the district level to generate school mission and policy?
- Are parents collaborating at the school level to generate decisions about inclusion in specific classrooms?
- Are there collaborative teams for each inclusion classroom? Parents and teachers need to be directly involved.
- Did the collaborative team decide about
  1. Classroom community goals?
  2. Classroom organization?
  3. Profile for children in the classroom?
  4. Adaptations in curriculum?
  5. Individual goals for each child?
  6. Special equipment needs?
  7. Additional staff-instructional supports?
  8. Staffing ratios?
  9. Learning profiles of children with special needs?
- Are parents of general education students committed to the goals of inclusion in this classroom? If not, what strategies can be used to change the negative attitudes expressed by parents?
- Are parents of children with disabilities committed?

FIGURE 5.5
Checklist for inclusion success.

Parent Meeting Room

The school needs to formalize various contextual settings for parents to function *on* collaborative teams, *within* peer support groups, and *as* parent facilitators for other parents in crisis. The aspect that is critical relates to formalizing the role of parents in education. Parents can no longer be relegated to bake sales and open house fund-raisers once a year. Parents need to have their own place and space. Where can parents meet? The parents meeting room should be a place with ongoing scheduled activities for parents. Parent training classes, peer support groups, educational conferences, and parent networking must be formalized as part of the school's curriculum. Parents "in the building" must become the usual and the expected rather than "by appointment only."

Communication Problems: Confusing Messages

Obviously, many difficulties will arise as schools begin the process of developing an inclusion policy. As indicated earlier, the "hinge pin" to success for inclusion will ultimately relate to the collaborative process that is established. Administrators must identify times, places, and procedural techniques to facilitate meetings between parents and teachers. There cannot be too much time set aside for this groundbreaking process. The development of collaborative teaming and the framework that establishes the interactional guidelines for parents and teachers will create the foundation for the inclusive classroom.

Historically, parents and teachers have not functioned as equal partners in decision making; however, schools must seek to identify and to eliminate the communication barriers that will definitely occur.

Parents and teachers must learn *how* to talk to one another. They must learn to function as coequals, copartners, and cocontributors to the decision-making process. Parents and teachers should meet together and separately in a staff development effort to train everyone involved with the process about effective communication techniques and goals. Whereas, teachers have been trained as part of their academic coursework and professional experiences to be consultants and collaborators, parents are at a distinct disadvantage. Teachers need to teach parents about child advocacy and educational instruction. Eventually, trained parent advocates could provide the training and mentoring for newer parents entering the schools. Parent training and advocacy will facilitate and enhance parent collaboration (Wiese, 1992). Schools must be willing to teach parents to function as independent thinkers, contributors, and collaborators. Perhaps one of the first barriers relates to the knowledge difference between parents and teachers; is that knowledge judged to be more or less valuable when information is presented by a parent?

There also needs to be a great deal of discussion concerning multicultural differences that affect communication. Verbal and nonverbal communicative strategies will determine how parents interact with each other and with teachers (deMontfort Supple, 1996). These differences need to be identified so that they can be factored into the communication formula. In understanding parents, it is critical for administrators and teachers to identify the various values, goals, and concerns of parents who are now being asked to advocate and to collaborate. Teachers often ask "How can parents collaborate as partners when they do not have the same degree of expertise?" Schools will have to begin the process of educating parents. Inclusive classrooms establish collaborative responsibilities. Schools will have to think about inclusive education and how to achieve the goals of integrated learning. Diverse learning should be utilized to develop new ideas, procedures, and solutions.

CONCLUSION

If collaboration requires parent partnership, then schools are going to have to educate parents to function as equal partners. This takes time, staff development, and commitment from schools. Teachers will have to build a bridge for parents. Teachers will have to develop parent education and parent training programs. Teachers will also have to change their roles and their functions inside and outside of the classroom. In the inclusion vision for the future, teachers may no longer be specialists; they may be generalists. If schools want inclusion, then teachers are going to have to think about classrooms in a different way. The most important factor to the achievement of inclusion is parent collaboration. Schools need to evaluate on a continuing basis the process for integrating parents into the life of the school and into the educational curricula (see Figure 5.6). Where are parents in the system? Has progress been made about advancing the role of parents in the decision-making process? As parent advocacy pro-

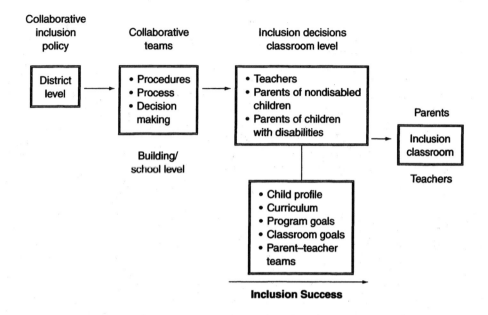

FIGURE 5.6
The parent indicator: Are parents integrated into collaborative decision making?

gresses, so will collaboration. Although teachers may be hesitant about the role of parents in educational decision making, it is in the best interest of teachers to facilitate the parent initiative. Some teachers may think that there is a loss of control with shared decision making. Empowerment, however, has resulted in schools that function more effectively with parents who are knowledgeable and actively involved in classroom-based issues. Although the school may set the policy for inclusion, implementation occurs at the classroom level. It is the parent–teacher partnership that must engage in the process of reorganization to develop the inclusive classroom.

🏵️ *A Philosophical Point of View* 🏵️

Having worked with children at risk for more than 30 years both in public and private schools, I believe I can offer a historical perspective on some of the current issues in special education, especially the inclusion movement.

In my opinion, the inclusion movement could not and should not be institutionally conceptualized as appropriate for all children. To do this, I be-

lieve, is motivated not by a genuine concern for children, but by political concerns and the belief that past legislation has created a system that is out of control, both legally and financially. Inclusion for any individual child should be a decision based on many important factors: the setting, personalities, attitudes, parental support, administrative receptiveness, and the social skills of the student. A successful inclusion experience for a child working within one particular set of variables can be a miserable experience for that same child if even one variable is negative. For a child currently in a more restrictive program who is viewed as capable of a successful transition to a less restrictive program, there must be planning and commitment from everyone involved with the child on the continuum of service delivery.

It would be wonderful, of course, to see people of all races, religions, social strata, and capabilities working together, each individual contributing at optimal potential to the society as a whole. However, social utopia does not exist, nor can it be legislated. The notion of the inclusion of all children into one system suggests this kind of unrealistic ideology. Morality and social harmony derive from within each individual and from that individual's early familial experiences. Besides, pedagogical debates continue to rage regarding the relative benefit and harm of both homogeneous and heterogeneous groupings of children not even identified as having an educational disability.

Having stated this not so encouraging philosophical position, let me add that if we had not put legislation in place, children with disabilities would not have fared as well as they have, in educational settings as well as in society as a whole. Legislation can serve as an important force in modifying opinions, attitudes, and, to some extent, sensitivity of people and institutions that have not autonomously taken the responsibility for "doing the right thing." On the other hand, I believe that the very educational institutions which, historically, have been sensitive and responsible in shaping the education and development of all children, and have committed necessary resources to children with disabilities, have become stalled in their mission by such a leveling process. School districts, in attempting to comply with bureaucratic mandates, are being strangled with paperwork and litigation. What is emerging is political, legal, and financial chaos.

Currently, we see a special education system that is overburdened with litigation (more than any other field of law), experiencing political ambivalence and financial backlash, and drowning in overwhelming amounts of paper work. I do not believe this was the intent of P.L. 94-142 when it was presented in the mid-1970s. At that time, children with disabilities were not receiving an appropriate education in many school districts in this country, and legislation regarding integration, civil rights, human awareness, etc., although directed to all, was intended for those who were not sufficiently responsive to children with disabilities. The intent of P.L. 94-142 was to force such states and institutions to recognize and deal with these children in an educationally responsible manner, and to incorporate parents as partners in the process, recognizing that harmony between school and home is critical for the educational success of a child with a disability. The major components of the law, guaranteeing children with special needs a free and appropriate education at public expense, individualizing the educational program, ensuring parent involvement and placement in the least restrictive environment (LRE), with support and related services, were—and continue to be—righteous and responsible. However, while the federal government promised financial support, it gave only a small fraction of the dollars promised to the states. States and institutions now are questioning priorities, in view of the extraordinary expenses required to support the current state of special education in an environment of finite public financial resources. Also, there must be reform in the due process system. As it stands, millions of dollars are drawn from direct services to children to pay legal costs which stem from the fact that institutions are placed on the defensive no matter what the situation. There is a real danger that confusion may exist between controlling costs and creating one complete, integrated system called "inclusion."

I do not believe there is anything wrong with the intent and purpose of P.L. 94-142 and LRE. I do believe political reform is necessary to give back to the schools professional discretion and responsibility in meeting the needs of all students. Yes, political forces should set standards for the development of human potential and should hold districts accountable for student achievement. However, they should not dictate process through burdensome administrative checks and balances that lead to useless financial burdens and wasted time. If dollars currently used to support legal defense and bureaucratic compliance were redirected to professionals who work directly with the children, I believe the human and technical supports required for the responsible inclusion of children with disabilities in a regular education placement could be significantly increased. To do this right is expensive. It requires additional teacher training in classrooms as well as on the job. It also requires paraprofessionals in the classroom, special education and regular education teachers working side by side, and clinicians and other specialists working directly with the children in and out of the classroom. These specialists need to work with parents as well, and if parents do not come to school, then we should be able to support them at home.

Little of this will occur without sufficient financial support. New public dollars will not be coming to special education in the foreseeable future to support this movement, but I believe new money is not needed. Minimizing legislative and bureaucratic involvement could result in the redistribution of necessary funds.

Vincent Mandato, Ed.D.
Director, Pupil Personnel Services
Syosset Central School District
Syosset, NY 11791

QUESTIONS FOR CLASSROOM DISCUSSION

1. What kinds of problems do parents experience in school?
2. What kinds of changes can schools engender to incorporate parents in programming and decision making?
3. What should be the role of parents in educational decision making?
4. Why is the success of inclusion "tied" to parent collaboration?
5. What can parents contribute to schools and the educational process?
6. What kinds of issues are presented by parents and teachers that need to be resolved?
7. How will education be strengthened by parent–teacher collaboration?

BIBLIOGRAPHY

Alper, S. K., Schloss, P. J., & Schloss, C. N. (1994). *Families of students with disabilities*. Needham Heights, MA: Allyn & Bacon Publishing.

Ayres, C. B. (1988). Integration: A parent's perspective. *Exceptional Parent, 18*(6), 22–25.

Behrmann, J. (1993). Including everyone. *The Executive Educator, 15*(12), 16–20.

Bronfenbrenner, U. (1989). Ecological systems theory. *Annals of Child Development, 6,* 187–249.

Bunch, G. (1994). An interpretation of full inclusion. *American Annals of the Deaf, 139*(2), 150.

Comer, J. P. (1986). Parent participation in the schools. *Phi Delta Kappan, 67*(6), 442—446.

Cornelius, G. (1990). A border issue in teacher training: Respecting the diversity of children. *The Journal of Educational Issues of Language Minority Students, 7,* 111–117.

Correa, V. I. (1989). Involving culturally diverse families in the educational process. In S. H. Fradd & M. J. Weismantel (Eds.), *Meeting the needs of culturally and linguistically different students: A handbook for educators.* Boston, MA: College Hill Press.

deMontfort Supple, M. (1996). Prologue: Beyond bilingualism. *Topics in Language Disorders, 16*(4), 109.

Diaz, R. M. (1990). Bilinguistic and cognitive ability: Theory, research and controversy. In A. Barona & E. Garcia (Eds.), *Children at risk: Poverty, minority status and other issues in educational equity.* Washington, DC: National Association of School Psychologists.

Edwards, P. (1990). Strategies and techniques for establishing home-school partnerships with minority parents. In A. Barona & E. Garcia (Eds.), *Children at risk: Poverty, minority status, and other issues in educational equity.* Washington, DC: National Association of School Psychologists.

Fletcher, T. V., & Cardona-Morales, C. (1990). Implementing effective instructional interventions for minority students. In A. Barona & E. Garcia (Eds.) *Children at risk: Poverty, minority status and other issues in educational equity.* Washington, DC: National Association of School Psychologists.

Fradd, S. H., Weismantel, M. J., Correa, V. I., & Algozzine, B. (1990). Ensuring equity in education: Preparing school personnel, for culturally and linguistically divergent at-risk handicapped students. In A. Barona & E. Garcia (Eds.) *Children at risk: Poverty, minority status and other issues in educational equity.* Washington, DC: National Association of School Psychologists.

Ihinger-Tallman, M. (1986). Member adjustment in single parent families: Theory building. *Family Relations, 35,* 215–221.

Kirchner, C. (1994). Co-enrollment as an inclusion model. *American Annals of the Deaf, 139*(2), 163–164.

Levitan, S., Belous, R., & Gallo, F. (1988). *What's happening to the American Family?* Baltimore, MD: The Johns Hopkins University Press.

Miranda, A. H., & Santos de Barona, M. (1990). A model for introduction with low achieving minority students. In A. Barona & E. Garcia (Eds.) *Children at risk: Poverty, minority status and other issues in educational equity.* Washington, DC: National Association of School Psychologists.

Murray, J. N., & Cornell, C. J. (1981). *Parentalplegia. Psychology in the Schools, 18,* 201–207.

Pianta, R. C., & Reeve, R. E. (1990). Preschool screening of ethnic minority children and children of poverty: Issues for practice and research. In A. Barona & E. Garcia (Eds.) *Children at risk: Poverty, minority status and other issues in educational equity.* Washington, DC: National Association of School Psychologists.

Polansky, H. (1994). The meaning of inclusion: Is it an option or a mandate? *School Business Affairs, 60* (7), 27–29.

Szapocznik, J., & Kurtines, W. M. (1993). Family psychology and cultural diversity: Opportunities for theory, research and application. *American Psychologist, 48,* 400–407.

Tiegerman-Farber, E. (1995). Training the parent as facilitator. In Tiegerman-Farber, E. (Ed.), *Language communication intervention in preschool children.* Newton, MA: Allyn & Bacon.

Turnbull, A. P., Barber, P., Behr, S. K., & Kerns, G. M. (1988). The family of children and youth with exceptionalities. In E. L. Meyen & T. M. Skrtic (Eds.), *Exceptional children and youth* (pp. 81–107). Denver, CO: Love Publishing.

Turnbull, A. P., & Turnbull, H. R. (1990). *Families, professionals, and exceptionality: A special partnership (2nd ed.).* Columbus, OH: Merrill Publishing Co.

Wiese, M. R. (1992). A critical review of parent training research. *Psychology in the Schools, 29,* 229–236.

Wikler, L. (1986). Family stress theory and research on families of children with mental retardation. In Gallagher, J., & Vietze, P. (Eds.), *Families of handicapped persons.* Baltimore, MD: Paul H. Brookes Publishing Company.

6

Formalizing a Collaborative Model: Questions and Answers

LEARNING OBJECTIVES

After you have read this chapter, you should be able to:

1. Discuss some of the factors that contribute to effective collaborative teaming.

2. Describe how various teachers and specialists need to make accommodations in order to collaborate.

3. Describe the barriers that interfere with effective collaboration.

4. Discuss why collaborative decision making represents the cornerstone to successful inclusion.

5. Explain why parents need to be an integral part of the collaborative team.

*I*n beginning this chapter, it is important to note that the theme of this textbook has emphasized an ongoing learning process for the stakeholders of inclusion. Collaboration as a process has been discussed in different forms; the process is further elaborated in this chapter. We feel strongly about the fact that we can share only what we know. Since we were writing a book about inclusion, it was important for us to engage in the process. Since we wanted to experience the process ourselves, we created a collaborative team that would discuss the internal issues related to decision making and then reflect about those decisions by means of self-inquiry and self-investigation. This experiential process allowed us to provide information about an internal schema and framework for the collaborative team.

In this chapter, we present our experiences and the process of collaboration through many voices—the voices of professionals who must ultimately make decisions in schools throughout the nation. We felt it was of critical importance to "walk the walk and then talk the talk," so that other professionals would have a living record of insights, perceptions, and feelings about a process that has been experienced by professional colleagues. It is clear from our experiences with collaborative teaming that educational reform cannot be achieved all at once. It takes a great deal of time, discussion, energy, and negotiation to formulate the educational programming that will reflect the mission of various communities. This would suggest that the process of collaboration is as individualized as the final product—the inclusive classroom. The suggestions and recommendations concerning collaborative relationships discussed within this chapter represent guidelines for professionals as they embark on their own path to educational change.

This chapter provides professionals with insight about an ongoing interactive process. Collaborative decision making will transform individuals in their ability to:

1. Communicate
2. Work together
3. Develop common ideas and goals
4. Design an inclusion program
5. Evaluate resources
6. Redefine their roles and responsibilities

If inclusion is to be achieved within the framework of a school, the collaborative process must be formalized. This suggests that teachers, parents, and administrators must sit down together and discuss the prerequisite issues to the development of the inclusion product. It is true that inclusion is an ideal, and perhaps not an option for every child. The school, however, must define what it means by inclusion and go forward from that point to develop a program that meets the goals and ideals of the school's mission statement. To explore this process of collaborative formulation, two informational techniques were utilized. First, 56 formal surveys were returned by administrators and teachers from 77 school districts on Long Island and New York City (see the Appendix at the end of this chapter). This technique provided a mechanism to analyze general education issues and concerns expressed by a large number of teachers with diverse backgrounds, teaching expertise, and educational skills. The analysis of the survey provided a generalized overview and a macro level of investigation which highlighted broad-based conceptual factors influencing the collaborative process.

Secondly, selected professionals at the School for Language and Communication Development were invited to participate in collaborative ongoing discussions. Teachers and specialists from various professional domain areas were given a series of questions to answer and a number of research articles to read on the topic of collaborative decision making. These professionals were also instructed to research the topic within each of their prospective professional areas by searching journals and associations for position statements and articles about the topic of collaboration. This team approach allowed for a micro level of investigation and inquiry through ongoing discussions with various professionals. This micro laboratory provided a mechanism for reviewing and analyzing specific aspects of a collaborative model. The team approach stimulated a great deal of transdisciplinary dialogue that was not only enlightening but empowering for teachers and specialists. It allowed professionals working within an educational program the opportunity to review the existing system, discuss the operating procedures, and develop recommendations for changes in form and content. This facilitated a strong sense of commitment between professional decision making and the organization of the educational environment within which teachers work. In working through this process of creating a collaborative environment, teachers expressed a commitment to an educational context that they had helped to create. It is also important to understand that we were able to engage teachers and specialists at SLCD in an ongoing process because of our professional relationship with this outstanding group. They gave generously of their time and expertise to an all-consuming but challenging project. If inclusion is to be achieved at any meaningful level, then this chapter should be viewed from the perspective of its realities. Teachers and administrators will have to commit to and engage in a similar process—it was complicated and complex. The process was empowering for all of us.

To stimulate discussion and dialogue, members of the team were provided with the following theoretical information from Coufal (1993):

> Collaboration requires a substantial amount of time, professional effort and interpersonal negotiation. Part of the collaborative process assumes a philosophical change in the decision-making approach to special education. Specifically, no single individual, professional or parent can problem solve the complex issues underlying special education decision-making. Collaborative consultation provides a systematic process of planning and problem solving that stimulates active involvement from diverse individuals.

Collaborative consultation is an interactive process that enables people with diverse expertise to generate creative solutions to mutually defined problems. The outcome is enhanced and altered and produces solutions that are different from those that would be produced independently by individual team members. "The major outcome of collaborative consultation is to provide comprehensive programs for students with special needs within the most appropriate context" (Idol, Paolucci-Whitcomb, & Nevin, 1986).

Collaboration defines how we interact, whereas consultation defines the process. Collaboration includes how we work together in a mutually beneficial manner for the purpose of joint decision making. As a result, collaboration requires a cooperative working relationship among team members, including parents. The underlying assumption of collaboration is that all members of the team are equal and interdependent. The collaborative process must include the following if it is going to be successful: mutual goals, shared participation, shared resources, shared respect, shared competency, and shared accountability. The competencies identified with collaboration are:

- The ability to establish and maintain rapport
- The ability to learn from others
- The ability to be flexible, open, and receptive
- The ability to respect another person's input, opinions, and criticisms
- The ability to communicate clearly
- The ability to incorporate another person's suggestions within one's interpersonal framework
- The ability to support the viewpoints of others
- The ability to manage conflict
- The ability to develop alternative strategies
- The ability to formulate clear ideas, plans, objectives and decisions

Before scheduling a meeting with members of the team we put together, a list of questions was developed and circulated. Team members were provided with the questions given in the following sections for consideration, and were told that these questions would be discussed at the upcoming collaborative meeting. The statements that follow in the chapter reflect the professional insights that were generated by individual team members. In expressing their opinions, team members provided information about themselves, their disciplines, and their professional experiences. This framework for professional interchange and exchange created a process that allowed for individual professionals to reflect on the concept of collaboration. Over time, this personal–professional insight stimulated some thought-provoking questions about the practical concerns relating to the implementation of a collaborative model in a school. The result of this process of self-inquiry and self-investigation is the development of a collaborative model that may *not* work for every school or every professional but does work for us. Perhaps that is the ultimate lesson of this experience for our teachers and this chapter: Collaboration involves an ongoing learning process of equality and shared decision making for parents, teachers, and administrators. There may be great diversity across schools and communities but the result will always be the same— collaboration to develop inclusive classrooms.

Finally, schools do not always have the same types of professional teachers. There is as much teacher diversity in schools as child diversity in classrooms. Certainly, teacher training and professional expertise are contributing factors to collaborative decision making. The most important variable involves the teaming process itself; it requires flexibility and the time to develop a working model—which defines collaboration.

The success of inclusion is based on development of a collaborative model within the schools. All of the teachers and professionals contributing to the present chapter stressed the significance of the relationship between their decisions and the realities of classroom programming. Just as inclusion cannot be imposed as a social system or model, collaboration must be facilitated as a parent–teacher communication process. Parents and teachers must develop an understanding of each other and work toward a concept model that will work within the school as a reflection of the community. Collaboration is a learning process. It cannot be achieved all at once; healthy relationships are partnerships that develop, grow, and change over time. This chapter provides teachers with some insights about factors that contribute to collaborative models. The feelings and concerns of professionals teaching across the curriculum in a variety of programs provided the organizing structure for this chapter. Perhaps we can learn best from our colleagues within the educational system who have been working to achieve collaboration with the mission of inclusion for the future.

QUESTION 1: DO YOU HAVE THE COMPETENCY SKILLS NECESSARY FOR COLLABORATION? HOW ARE THESE SKILLS DEVELOPED WITHIN YOUR DISCIPLINE AREA?

Response: Regular Education Teacher Surveys

We feel that the skills necessary to the collaborative process are part of the human experience. Our academic training and educational experiences have provided the basic required abilities for collaborative interaction. Collaborating with other professionals is quite different than collaborating with parents. Educational history and programming have provided a foundation for teachers to work together to analyze and to solve child-based problems. The basic effectiveness of the school and the success of the classroom also rely on the interactional abilities of teachers to communicate, to share, to listen, and to change. The school represents a network system of teachers who must function interdependently in order for a school to be a place of learning for children. Teachers must learn to put aside their own personal feelings in order to achieve a common goal and long-range vision. With inclusion as a long-term mission for the regular education classroom, parents must be incorporated into the collaborative process.

Response: School Psychologist

HELENE MERMELSTEIN, PSY.D.
I believe psychologists have these skills. In the field of school psychology, the need for consultative services arose due to the onset of the mainstreaming movement in which

regular classroom teachers were dealing with children with mild and moderate disabilities in the 1970s. The model for the school psychologist changed from the medical model to a school-based consultation model. Meacham and Peckham (1978) stated after conducting a survey of school psychologists that "the consultation function is becoming more central, and if practitioners have their way, it will become primary" (p. 205).

I have personally worked under several different models of collaborative consultation. I believe consultation is an inherent part of the school psychologist's role today. The field has recognized this and incorporated it into the field of study. Therefore on the doctoral level at Yeshiva University, I took courses dealing with consultation in the schools. Secondly, as part of becoming certified, one must do an internship, which often provides an introduction to some type of collaboration.

The list of skills previously mentioned can be only partly addressed in a classroom forum. The way a group is managed or handled can certainly support some of these skills; however, many skills are connected to emotional issues on the part of the individual who enters into the collaborative process. For example, I believe the ability to *communicate* clearly can be supported by an organization. It is not simply a transfer of *information* that many people might think it is. As Schein (1988) states "We communicate facts, feelings, perceptions, innuendoes, and various other things all in the same 'simple' message. We communicate not only through the spoken and written word but through facial expressions, gestures, physical posture, tone of voice, timing of when we speak, what we do not say, and so on" (pp. 21–22). As you can see, communication skills can be overtly taught while the finer points are too closely aligned to the personality of the individual. However, even these can be addressed over time through ongoing interactive learning.

Response: Regular Education Teacher

DEBORAH LEVINE, M.S.

These competency skills are an integral part of any creative education program. Although I am a regular education teacher, I am also a trained creative arts educator and therapist; these competency skills are the foundation of my work with children. The ability to learn from others has provided me with a variety of ideas for new art projects to motivate children to create. I work with other colleagues outside my classroom to exchange philosophies and ideas. In addition, I attend art therapy and art education seminars to further my knowledge in these fields. Exposure to new materials and remaining informed about current research keep me on target and enable me to further develop my competency skills.

Flexibility and being open and receptive to new methods and materials help me expand the program. I test a variety of procedures and evaluate the effectiveness to determine whether I have accomplished my instructional goal. The exchange of information and project evaluation extend beyond a given classroom to include other art professionals, teachers on staff, and my immediate supervisor. A great amount of information (i.e., art contests, new art programs) is passed along by my supervisor. I enjoy working on new projects, since this stimulates each child's involvement and enhances individual creativity.

I respect the input and *opinions* of others regarding the work done in my classroom. I constantly receive feedback from other teachers and parents about how excited the children are with the work they produce. It is also quite helpful to get feedback if the child is uncomfortable with some particular art medium. This helps me better understand the child and direct him or her to try another art form or investigate why there might be a problem. Constructive criticism is very helpful for a successful art program. Clear communication with students, teachers, and parents helps to establish individual goals for each child.

Communication and *compromise* are critical strategies in managing conflicts. Flexibility and understanding are important when working with different teachers. Teachers need to appreciate the limits of time and space and plan ways to compensate for programmatic restrictions. When working with special education students, teachers need to develop alternative strategies. The children are constantly and eagerly asking, "What else are we doing?" I'm always ready with something new up my sleeve.

A regular education teacher develops these competency skills in many ways. First, one must have a strong academic background in development, disabilities, and intervention techniques. Knowledge of curriculum materials and learning styles is a must. A solid and strong background in special education and psychology is also necessary so that the educator is comfortable with all aspects of each disability and is equipped to meet the individual needs of each child. The child's needs come first. Classroom projects should fit and enhance child learning. This helps to build a child's positive self-esteem. Personal achievement and success are primary for the student.

Hands-on training should be available throughout the academic life of the professional. Academic learning and working need to occur simultaneously; done separately, they do not make for an effective classroom teacher. Creative inclusion professionals need to be up to date in all areas of special education, psychology, and related fields. Reading current publications, belonging to professional organizations, and taking advanced college courses in related areas are a must. I belong to Women in the Arts, a national organization that provides never-ending information about art and I find it extremely useful in the continual development of my competency skills. These competency skills are acquired on the job by sharing ideas with other professionals. Mini-courses on current information conducted by colleagues or administration would be an excellent medium. Publication of courses and professional seminars should be posted regularly to consider for continuing education.

Working as a member of a transdisciplinary team is the approach that helps to develop many of these skills in a supportive atmosphere. Evaluation and discussion keep communication open for the development of these skills and enhances the specialist's ability to formulate clear ideas, develop strategies, and support and incorporate ideas and suggestions from colleagues. Classroom teachers must use their ability to understand

and use research methodologies in addition to the traditional case study to expand their knowledge and justify educational decision making. Solid research training should be ongoing in all related fields such as psychology, education, speech–language, and parent training. I believe in an integrative approach toward treatment: a combination of solid psychological frames of reference from Freud, Jung, Adler, and other theorists which can be fused together to understand diversity in children's learning needs.

Response: Dance Movement Therapist

DEBRA MCCALL, M.A., A.D.T.R.

Dance movement therapists and movement analysts are trained verbally and nonverbally, through creative means, in the competencies identified with collaboration. The dance movement therapist receives academic and clinical training in interpersonal theories and methodologies, vis-à-vis group dynamics and process classes, experiential workshops and seminars, and extensive fieldwork and internship with on-site and academic supervision playing a critical role. Academic classroom situations often require working in teams on special projects as well as role-playing the difficulties one encounters with clients/students as well as within institutions.

Before one is awarded "professional" status in the field, one must undertake adequate postgraduate supervision—individually or as a member of a group. Within such a context, one's motivations, projections, defenses, transferences, and countertransferences are thoroughly analyzed and "worked through" in the supervision. Consequently, the style and content of one's interactions with clients, students, colleagues, supervisors, institutions, etc., become familiar to the professional. Additionally, it is highly recommended for the dance movement therapist to be engaged in personal/group therapy in order to explore *interpersonal patterns* of behavior.

The dance movement therapist/movement analyst works toward integrating all parts of the client/student's personality and behavior, and toward crafting a safe "holding environment" within which the range of emotional expression and interaction can be explored. From helping a child fortify his or her defenses against a world perceived as terrifying, to redirecting a child's aggressive behavior into a positive motivator for classroom learning, or intervening with a hyperactive child in order to prolong and sustain focus and attending skills, the dance movement therapist utilizes specific techniques for establishing rapport, such as "mirroring" another's style and content of expression, "amplifying" expressive qualities for reinforcement of therapeutic goals, incorporating the child/client's "world view" (modes of verbal and nonverbal expression) into the treatment plan, etc. These few examples illustrate how the competencies identified with collaboration are integral to the training and professional work of the dance movement therapist/movement analyst. On a macro level, these competencies translate into interstaff attitude, relationship, and working protocol. The therapeutic/clinical training of the field is ideally conducive toward adaptation to a collaborative model within the institution and among colleagues.

Response: Special Education Teacher

LINDA CASILLO, M.S.ED.

As part of my graduate studies, I was able to learn a set of interpersonal competency skills. They were, however, presented as individual topics in classroom discussion, and it was not until I actually began to work within the field of education that I was able to integrate these skills. I have learned on the job to function as a more effective teacher and team member; as a result, I have learned to put into practice abilities that were merely abstractions in class. I feel that personality, interpersonal communication, and the ability to *share knowledge* with other professionals are critical components in attaining and maintaining collaborative relationships.

Competency skills are developed over time. Time and experience provide the professional with the ability to integrate the philosophies and perspectives of different disciplines with a focus toward generating a treatment goal that reflects the child as a whole. Specialists, psychologists, and teachers have spent many years acquiring information pertinent to their particular area of expertise. Each professional has valuable information to contribute if she can collaborate and work as a member of a professional team. According to Bricker (1989), several factors affect the functioning of a team. These factors include attitude, accessibility, communication, and transmittal of selected information.

Most of these competency skills are acquired on the job by working as a member of a professional team. Team members are often called on to complete an assessment on a child, generate a treatment plan, and establish goals for an IEP; this involves a collaborative process. I have also found that supervision by a master professional has helped to nourish all aspects of my work and professional development. By seeking and receiving constructive feedback regarding my professional work, I have been able to enhance my own knowledge and integrate valuable perspectives and philosophies. Academic coursework provides only a limited frame for reference about collaboration and the intensive negotiation that must occur among team members. Whether a team consists of two, three, four, or five professionals, the interpersonal exchange of information is always complex and challenging. There is nothing described in a textbook about collaboration that can adequately prepare a novice professional for the rigorous demands of the experience.

Response: Music Therapist

LAUREN STERLING, M.A., CMT

In response to the questions concerning competency skills, I feel strongly about the fact that I presently possess these skills. I would also like to add that I am always developing, integrating, and implementing these skills in my professional work. To develop these competency skills, many factors must be taken into consideration. Aspects such as personality, life experience, clinical training, and professional experiences all play a significant role in the development of these competencies. From my own personal and educational experiences, I do not think that these skills can be taught within an academic classroom. These competencies, which reflect a *process* of hands-on clinical experiences, require an *interface* between the therapist and other professionals within the clinical setting. During my training, these skills were not taught in any of the classes required for academic accreditation; instead, they were presented as a process of self-exploration and learning on the clinical-practicum side of training. I believe that the underlying philosophy of music therapy theoretically supports the development of these competency skills.

I also believe that there is an ongoing process that each new experience brings in developing a greater level of understanding. To further develop and maintain these communication competencies, I must be consistently aware of myself within the communication exchange process. It is critical to speak with teachers and other specialists in order to cross reference clinical insights and develop alternative perspectives on specific educational issues in decision making.

Response: Special Education Teacher

MAUREEN SHAPIRO, M.S.

I believe that I have the competency skills to participate in a collaborative process. Based on my professional history, my personal experiences, and my present working environment, I feel that I have developed these abilities and can support the collaborative approach in theory and practice. I recognize all too well that the success of ongoing collaboration is based on the *interdependence* of the professionals involved. The ability to communicate is the primary facilitative skill that connects team members.

As a professional educator, I have learned that collaboration is not a skill acquired in an academic classroom. As a graduate student, general discussion concerning the theory and significance of collaboration represents the beginning of the process itself. I believe that many of us as teachers possess *most* of the skills necessary for collaboration; we are not, however, cognizant of our own abilities until the situation presents itself. It is at this moment of "creative crisis" that we realize an inner resource of skills and abilities.

It is my opinion that collaboration relies primarily on personality variables. For example, the ability to support the viewpoint of others, the ability to learn from others, and the ability to be flexible are all related to a strong sense of professional *self*. If we have difficulty accepting the viewpoints, feelings, and ideas of colleagues and parents, then collaboration can never be achieved. It is interesting to observe that these competency skills do not play a role in academic success, but do play a significant role in my professional success as a special educator.

Working as a team member by means of a collaborative process has become an important area of interest in general education. Today, a number of textbooks, articles, studies, and workshops discuss and describe this interactional process. There is, however, a tremendous difference between the textbook and the actual working experience. It is my belief that academic courses should develop training experiences that facilitate collaborative learning. Collaboration requires professional discipline and personal sensitivity in order to work effectively with colleagues and parents. Becoming an effective member of the collaborative team requires an understanding of the process and a strong sense of self as a professional.

At this point in time, the required competency skills must be acquired on the job, under the direction of key administrative personnel. Schools need to develop a collaboration model that should then be demonstrated to members of the staff. Collaboration cannot be achieved unless the staff is committed to the mission and the model for educational programming. To identify something, we must be aware of what we are looking for. Once collaborative goals are established by the professional team, the process of collaboration is negotiated to its logical result.

Response: Speech–Language Pathologist

ANGELINA DeNOIA, M.A., C.C.C.

I believe that I fundamentally possess these competency skills. In addition, I also believe that flexibility, *respect,* and support determine the success of the collaborative team. We can continue to grow as individuals and professionals as long as we are willing to keep our minds open to new ideas.

I think professionals within all of the discipline areas can develop these skills if there is a strong desire to learn about the team process. Taking control is easy; it is sharing the responsibility that takes ongoing *negotiation* and work. On a basic level, each professional must be willing to make a personal commitment to the concept of collaboration. Professionals must spend time learning about the underlying theories in related discipline areas. As a member of the collaborative team, each of us must be willing to take a risk, share beliefs, and remain open to the feelings and ideas of others. Through discussion, professionals from divergently different disciplines can work together to develop *common goals and strategies* to meet the needs of children and families.

I believe that the competency skills listed are learned early on in life and actually become part of one's personal character. Therefore, I think it would be difficult to teach novice professionals certain kinds of skills—such as respect for another professional's belief or discipline. This is a problem in most clinical professions; what if the young professional is not suited for interpersonal relationships? At best, one can strive to create a working environment that provides models of flexibility, respect, and support, but there must be a *personal core* of skills within the individual. While no single professional has all of the answers to today's educational problems, our collective networking can facilitate new ideas and techniques.

Analysis and Discussion

In considering the comments and insights provided by the various professionals, there appears to be a great deal of controversy about the critical factors that affect the collaborative process. Collaboration requires networking, sharing, and an exchange of information that clearly involves an ongoing communication process. Collaboration cannot be achieved "all at once"; instead, it suggests a long-term learning process that can be achieved by means of "trial and error practice." The professionals acknowledge that in the exchange process, each teacher contributes her professional knowledge as a function of her instructional and experiential learning. Each professional has a different point of origin; different ideas, different perspectives, and different theoretical schema. Perhaps, the term "opinion" is not as accurate as "perspective." It is conceivable though, from a parent's point of view, that when the professional appears to be inflexible and unwilling to incorporate information, the professional appears to be opinionated. Flexibility suggests a willingness and an openness to consider the viewpoints of other teachers and contributors. Obviously, the parent is a very important contributor to this process, although she or he is not professionally trained.

With so many different points of origin, given differences in training, philosophy, and life experience, it is not surprising that decision making becomes a complex process. Who is right? Who is accurate? Which procedure or technique should be used? Should therapy be recommended? Does the child have a disability? The discipline differences provide a source of knowledge and perspective that are important to understanding the nature and scope of the child's learning problem. Professional diversity can also provide a certain degree of difference and confusion. Is the difference in the information across professionals relevant? Is there a difference because the terminology is different? The collaborative process stimulates discussion and diversity in decision making. The differences in perspective, as well as the conflicts that arise as a function of that difference, must be resolved by the group through the development of interactional strategies.

It is interesting to note that all of the professionals felt strongly about the fact that interpersonal aspects and attitudes dramatically affected the interdependent relationships among the collaborators. Collaboration is an ongoing process that reaches a crescendo during a moment of "creative crisis." When professionals cannot agree, the human aspects of personality, self-esteem, and respect facilitate or inhibit the development of common goals and strategies to meet the needs of children and families. Collaboration provides a mechanism for each of us to learn about ourselves as complex individuals—the personal self and the professional self. The interface between these two sides of us determines our ability to contribute to the collaborative process. Collaboration presents an opportunity for us to contribute to the creative learning of children and families in education, and to learn about the inclusive professional that we must all become.

QUESTION 2: HOW DO YOU COLLABORATE WITH OTHER TEAM MEMBERS AND PROFESSIONALS IN SCHOOL? DOES COLLABORATION ALWAYS WORK?

Response: Regular Education Teacher Surveys

Collaboration usually occurs on an informal basis. There is a major scheduling problem that needs to be addressed if collaborative teaming is going to become a more formalized aspect of the educational process. Presently, an annual meeting, a monthly meeting, or an after-school workshop does not provide the quantity, quality, or the consistency of interaction necessary to develop inclusive classrooms. Inclusion requires that schools reorganize and think about educational instruction from new perspectives. Collaborative models can only work when all of the professionals contributing to child-based decision making are participating as equal partners. Collaboration does not work when one member of the group acts as a primary decision maker for all of the other professionals. Listening represents a critical skill in collaborative teaming.

Teachers must learn to separate their egos from their decisions. There is no room for power brokering on a collaborative team. The team works most effectively when everyone has an equal status and mutual respect. Attending inclusion meetings will not provide teachers with the mechanism to address the ongoing problems that will occur in inclusive classrooms. To achieve inclusion, collaborative teams must engage in ongoing decision making. Schools must make a commitment to inclusion by supporting collaborative teaming.

Finally, there is a significant problem in developing a common definition for collaboration. Collaborative decision making represents more than just information sharing. Presently, parents are not perceived as equal contributors, stakeholders, or decision makers. This is a significant barrier that must be addressed in every school. Teachers and parents must develop a working definition for collaborative teaming that *includes* parents as equal partners.

Response: School Psychologist

HELENE MERMELSTEIN, PSY.D.
Collaboration occurs generally on two levels, the formal one and the informal one.

At the formal level, the guidelines are more clearly defined. Someone has a problem and asks for a team meeting. A meeting is called by an administrator and she or he sends out a memo inviting all staff members to participate who have contact with that child. The collaboration generally has a *specific goal* or focus and a specific child is discussed. The leadership is very clear at these meetings and there is usually a time constraint since it is held during lunch. All team members have an opportunity to discuss, question, or add information. Decisions generally result from professional consensus.

Informally, collaboration occurs on an ongoing basis. For the psychologist, it is with teachers, aides, parents, specialists to a lesser degree, and administrators. It can consist of a designated meeting or talks in the classroom, staff lounge, or even in the hall if necessary. The success and the amount of collaboration depend on the personalities of the individuals involved. The psychologist's role depends a great deal on the collaborative process; therefore, it is important that she or he try to make it satisfactory to those involved, and successful.

I tend to collaborate informally with the classroom teachers I work with. As I am in and out of their classrooms, we may discuss issues while the children are not present or working elsewhere. When a specific issue comes up, teachers have requested meetings to discuss these issues. Generally issues deal with behaviors or concerns of specific children. Sometimes they deal with notes that parents have sent to the teachers.

While in the classroom, if I have a good working relationship with a specific teacher whom I know will want the input, we collaborate while the children are in the room. For example, while setting up a behavioral program for the whole class, I will work with the teacher to implement it in a hands-on manner.

Psychologists should also collaborate with each other. This lends itself to peer support, growth and development, and a strong sense of professionalism. School psychologists often do not have the opportunity to collaborate with other psychologists. Psychologists should have the opportunity to bounce ideas off one another, share cases, and add insight, information, and support.

When two or more individuals want to work together, I believe it works successfully. I have success with some of the teachers I work with because there are few *control* and *boundary* issues. If the teacher is consulting with me, she knows that she is an active participant in the process and that both of us cannot achieve anything without the support of the other. Sometimes the process does not work because consultees often want psychologists to provide them with quick solutions, easy answers or help them get the child out of their classroom.

Informally, when someone approaches me, the process is more of a collaborative one. Formally, my experience has been that the person asking for a meeting with an administrator often does not become part of the solution and, therefore, does not implement any of the suggestions made. For example (this recently happened), a teacher calls a meeting because she feels a child's behavior is becoming more bizarre in her classroom. She is uncomfortable with this child and is unaware how anxious this child makes her feel. She would prefer that the child be removed from the classroom, but does not say it. Team members corroborate her view of the child. His behavior is indeed more bizarre. However, the psychologist attempts to explain that he is a high functioning pervasive developmental disorder child (recently he went to a psychiatrist who confirmed this diagnosis). The psychologist attempts to give a profile of a child with this type of disability and explain how to help him when he becomes self-involved. The meeting ends and it is still unresolved for the teacher. She continues to feel uncomfortable with this child; she indicates that she has not been helped by the meeting.

On the other hand, I have been to meetings where people have taken notes and have continued the process informally by meeting with others on their own time. Collaboration can be an exciting experience because you are *problem solving*, or brainstorming, with people who have different areas of expertise. Collaborative decision making often results in solutions that you would not necessarily generate alone.

Response: Regular Education Teacher

DEBORAH LEVINE, M.S.

Collaboration needs to be done both informally and formally. Staffings should be set up periodically to consider those children who might be encountering a problem. The specialist, psychologist, classroom teacher, and assistant discuss and brainstorm during this session. Each member of the team helps to relay what happens in each modality: dance, art, and music. The individual needs of the student are then discussed. Follow-up meetings are held to evaluate the suggestions made and the student's progress. These sessions are so productive, I recommend conducting them for every child, even if there is no problem. Each child would benefit from a formal meeting such as this, whether it be twice or three times throughout the school year. This session time should be built into the scheduling of each teacher in the team.

Informal collaboration goes on all the time. Specialty teachers and parents need to visit the classroom to discuss any suggested child projects and progress with the regular education teacher. Written plans are also shared between the classroom teacher and specialists in an effort to integrate individual goals with the class work. I encourage feedback from other teachers and parents on how children feel about their work. My written plans are also shared with parents to keep consistent communication between what is going on in the classroom and the home. Any new classroom project involves a great deal of collaboration. This involves the teachers, administrators, parents, and, most important of all, the children. Children must learn to work together.

Collaboration is the ultimate goal for success in meeting the individual needs of each student. The team approach for problem solving, planning, and program implementation breaks professional isolation by linking the teachers, specialists, parents, and administrators. This is essential for accomplishing the student's specific goals. The teamwork provides all members with a support *network*. No one individual has all the skills needed to meet the social, emotional, and academic needs of each child.

Teams also act as a tool for problem solving. If the collaborative team uses specific problem-solving techniques, then solutions to complex issues should come about more easily and effectively. A quality outcome will occur from multiple perspectives rather than a unilateral approach. The teams need to involve the parents meaningfully, and the school needs to be accessible to the parents. The team needs to meet with the teachers and specialists regularly, share responsibilities and develop a working relationship. The team needs to share responsibilities. I feel that no one team member has all the answers. When a group of individuals works together toward common goals, complex programs can then be developed and implemented.

School personnel need to support and share the school's *philosophy* of educating the student. Realistically, however, scheduling presents a problem in terms of collaborative decision making. The teacher, specialist, and teacher assistant need time to bond to promote the school's philosophy and have the appropriate technical and communicative skills. In-service and training for the staff should be built into the schedule of the school year. Collaboration does not work unless it is built into the everyday schedule. The organizational meetings must be built into each teacher's schedule. Collaborative meetings must be viewed as part of the educational curriculum. The role of administration is critical in terms of recognizing staff, organizing the team, and selecting the most appropriate members to work together. It is important that consideration be given to personalities and existing relationships. Teams must develop interpersonal relationships in order for collaboration to be effective and for the team to achieve optimal results for each child.

Response: Dance Movement Therapist

DEBRA MCCALL, M.A., A.D.T.R.

I see collaboration ("how we interact" as "equal and interdependent") as functioning both formally and informally. The creation of IEPs as they are now undertaken consists of an enterprise in which each professional works *within* his or her respective discipline to formulate what is necessary and best for the student. Informal exchanges occur across disciplines to establish *consistency* of goals where necessary. For example, as a dance movement specialist, I usually consult with a teacher when considering children for individual dance movement therapy. Likewise, I informally consult with other specialists to ascertain whether our goals are mutually compatible.

Additionally, much informal collaboration occurs in day-to-day exchanges with teachers and fellow specialists in the hallway. Often, between sessions, I either inquire about or report to a teacher regarding behavior and performance of a student that is new, exciting, laudatory, troublesome, or of concern, etc. I often benefit from knowing information that the teacher has, such as a new sibling has arrived, or a grandparent has passed away, etc. These exchanges *humanize* the caring environment we provide for the student and also create *interdisciplinary* connections that serve to reinforce the team's goals. With such information, I can often provide experiential situations that indirectly attend to the issue at hand, thus allowing appropriate "ventilation" or "acting out" for the student. In such a manner, I reinforce the classroom goals.

Response: Special Education Teacher

LINDA CASILLO, M.S.ED.

Collaboration at SLCD is achieved through special staffings or team meeting time. A designated time is set aside, either before school, during lunch, or after school, to discuss one specific child. These formal meetings can be requested by any team member. All members will be notified of the meeting and will be given an opportunity to give and receive information regarding the specific child. Collaboration can take place when team members:

1. Establish a philosophy for:
   a. education of the children
   b. structure of the classroom
   c. method and approach for teaching.
2. Establish the goals for the child.
3. Establish the goals for the team. What do we want to accomplish?
4. Monitor the goals for the children.
5. Monitor the structure, method and approach for learning.

Collaboration should take place formally during scheduled meetings on an individual child. Collaboration consisting of the aforementioned goals can also be achieved informally if team members are willing to reach out toward each other to *share* information and give *feedback*. Team members should also feel comfortable enough to utilize each other's expertise and seek information without having a formal meeting. Formal meetings require flexible schedules for parents and teachers to share pertinent information on child progress and learning problems.

Unfortunately, if there is not a *commitment* to be part of a team, collaborative decision making can turn into a losing situation for the child. By this, I mean that the child's approach will not be seen in terms of the whole child. A dissatisfied team member (individual, parent) might disregard the team's decision and approach the situation from his or her *own perspective*.

I think Bill Koch's strategy used on the all-women's racing yacht *America* applies perfectly here. As stated in *To the Third Power*,

> No individual stars! One person cannot win a race, but one person's mistake can cause a loss. Each person must do his job the best he can and rely on his teammates to do their job the best they can. When the team succeeds, everyone is a star. On a team, if one person tries to be a star, he ends up with different goals than his teammates and ultimately his actions will hurt, not help, the team. Concentrate on attitude and teamwork! (p. 220)

Response: Regular Education Teacher

MAUREEN SHAPIRO, M.S.

Collaboration is achieved through our multidisciplinary team. The team consists of the speech pathologist, classroom teacher, assistant teacher, psychologist, occupational therapist, music therapist, creative art therapist, and adaptive physical education or dance movement therapist and administrators. Team meetings to discuss children or whole classes are scheduled regularly or on an as-needed basis. Annual review meetings are scheduled to discuss individual children's progress and future educational placement. IEPs are developed utilizing the team approach.

We have *team teaching* on the preschool level, where a special education teacher and a speech pathologist are the primary service providers. They work simultaneously to develop curriculum and address language difficulties within the classroom. Strategies are shared to the benefit of the children.

At the school-age level, teachers often meet collaboratively to address curriculum issues and appropriate intervention strategies. Often the school-age program plans holiday shows and trips, as well as a culminating graduation show, which is always thematic in nature.

I often collaborate with willing team members. When working with the speech–language pathologist, we plan and implement a curriculum regulated to the child's needs. According to Bush (1991) in her book *Collaborating with Teachers and Parents*, "Language skills and academic subjects are so interdependent, special educators should try to collaborate with teachers whenever possible, and base instruction on curriculum and classroom material to better accomplish IEP goals." We often work cooperatively and combine effective techniques. For example, we have recently been working on a multicultural unit that has been implemented in the classroom as well as in the therapy session. Bush suggests the use of classroom curricular materials in any remediation program.

When working with the class psychologist, behavior management techniques are established and implemented. Most of the team specialists are willing and eager participants in the effort to collaborate and integrate academic learning. Materials are often shared to help reinforce a particular skill. I also collaborate and develop curricula with other colleagues. We have implemented cooperative learning in the area of social studies and science. The teachers have worked together to establish a hands-on program which has been successful. Collaboration, when achieved through the cooperation of professionals, achieves benefit for the child. The difficulty lies in defining collaboration and then actually achieving *true collaboration*.

Analysis and Discussion

The professionals discuss the fact that collaborative teaming generates specific goals for members of the team. This suggests that there is an educational problem or concern, a set of behaviors that must be addressed, and instructional procedures that must be discussed with a specific resolution in mind. Collaboration can be achieved formally or informally by two, three, four, or five members of an interdisciplinary, multidisciplinary team. Formal meetings require specific adjustments in schedules and a commitment from school districts. Administrators need to set aside a meeting time for professionals to discuss educational programming. To achieve the goals of collaboration, schools must make a commitment to such formalized meeting times. This would mean that collaboration is just as valuable as direct child care or classroom teaching instruction. Collaboration is teacher intensive and labor intensive; it requires creative energy, cooperation, and specialty expertise. Formal meeting times also require an agenda with a goal of problem solving in a single sitting; sometimes this is not possible. Other professionals may be necessary. Additional research and discussion may be needed; collaborative decision making highlights the fact that there may not be a "quick fix" or solution to classroom or child-based problems. Formalized meetings allow a large number of professionals to get together to discuss and to share their discipline knowledge. This facilitates a common focus in decision making, a consistency in thinking, and the generalization of common goals that underlie a transdisciplinary curriculum. Ongoing discussion stimulates flexibility in thinking.

The collaborative team proceeds through an evolutionary process which fosters the growth of the individual and the group; this humanizes educational decision making for children and families. Collaborative interaction stimulates ongoing communication and supports the important development of interpersonal relationships among professional members. These relationships are then reinforced through constant informal interactions in the classroom, in the hallway, in the lunchroom, and in the therapy room. Informal collaboration usually involves two or three members of the multidisciplinary team. These meetings are highly individualized and suggest more of a "grassroots need," depending on the child and the context.

Informal meetings appear to be much more frequent and easier to negotiate than the much more formalized constructs. The informal meetings are just as important to educational decision making, but seem to be based on and attuned to the interpersonal relationships among professionals. If teachers cannot communicate with each other, share their feelings and ideas, and feel comfortable with each other, they will not seek each other out informally. The formal meetings require everyone's attendance, but the informal meetings are utilized by professionals to work out and work through daily issues and problems. Collaboration can be achieved at a macro (formal) and a micro (informal) level. The process is the same, and the interpersonal relationships are pivotal. Collaborative meetings facilitate the development of curriculum goals and intervention strategies. The interaction between teachers allows for the integration of academic learning between divergently different professionals. This cooperative process enriches classroom instruction and allows for a team teaching approach, which represents the cornerstone of the inclusion classroom.

In addition, teachers indicated that there are many times when collaboration does *not* work. There appears to be an interesting tension between interpersonal issues that relate to dynamics of control and the process of learning about collaborative decision making. Collaboration involves problem solving or brainstorming. Often the solution that is generated is different from the individual recommendations that are proposed by team members. Collective decision making involves a consensus, a collective viewpoint that reflects everyone's judgment. In learning about the collaborative process, each individual learns to contribute to part of the final decision. As one professional indicated, there are "no individual stars." Functioning as a member of a team is different from accomplishing the job oneself; placing the professional and personal ego aside requires a strong attachment to colleagues and a commitment to the collaborative process. Team decision making involves a synergistic approach—collective thinking. The team decision reflects on the individual, but the individual contributes to the decision of the team.

To generate collective decisions, professionals need to communicate with one another on an ongoing basis. They need to network, to share their ideas, and to link themselves to the school's philosophy of education. The mission of the school must be clearly communicated to all of the professionals who represent the mission and utilize a collective approach to educational decision making. Professionals need to make a commitment to the mission and to the process of collective thinking. They also need to feel comfortable within a professional network. They need to feel comfortable with themselves and with their reliance on others for support and information.

The collaborative approach allows individual members to generate collectively holistic decisions about children. Each professional sees the child from a different perspective and in a different context. These individual pieces provide a holistic mosaic—a more complete picture of the child's learning style and abilities. Professionals cannot generate appropriate decisions from an isolated vantage point. Collaborative decision making creates a profile of the whole child, which facilitates a more accurate understanding of the child's individual educational needs.

Collaboration involves learning about the decision-making process. Members of the team do not necessarily begin the process as expert collaborators; academic coursework does not generally foster the development of this knowledge. Members of the team learn about collaboration as they engage in the process of collaboration. Collaboration allows professionals to integrate their academic knowledge and clinical expertise. The caution here, however, involves the willingness of professionals to engage in an interdependent learning experience. As one of the teachers indicated, collaboration can only be achieved through cooperation—collective thinking; the difficulty is learning to achieve true collaboration. The question that still needs to be answered involves the definition of true collaboration between teachers and parents.

QUESTION 3: HOW DO YOU COLLABORATE WITH PARENTS?

Response: Regular Education Teacher Surveys

Presently, there is no formalized mechanism to collaborate with parents. The first problem relates to the fact that contact with parents is very limited and often involves a telephone conversation or a notebook. The school day is not organized to meet with working parents on a regular basis. The nature of the interaction with parents at this point in time involves providing information and advice. In meeting with parents of children with disabilities, there is a much greater emphasis on discussing child progress, behavioral and social needs, and educational problems. Rarely do we have the opportunity for collaborative decision making. Educational information is *unidirectional*, from school to home, from teacher to parent. With the development of collaborative teams, a bidirectional exchange of information will have to be achieved. Parents and teachers will have to respect each other as partners in decision making and equal contributors to the inclusion classroom.

Response: School Psychologist

HELENE MERMELSTEIN, PSY.D.

Initially, the school psychologist sends out a letter to parents introducing herself as the class psychologist. Then we either contact parents or parents contact us directly. Psychologists contact parents for many reasons such as these:

- Informing parents of psychological test results
- Providing parents with necessary information
- Behavioral issues
- Referral issues

Many times parents will either contact psychologists directly or address issues to the classroom teachers who then refer the parents to the classroom psychologist. There are times when administrators refer parents to psychologists as well.

Depending on the goal, collaboration takes different forms. It may be a one-time meeting, or it may become counseling weekly. When working on specific goals, psychologists need to get the input from the parent and work with the parent so that the parent is *part* of the process. In order for the psychologist to work with parents, it is paramount to establish an open, trusting relationship. Rapport is tantamount. Because the school psychologist is part of an organization, this may not always be achieved due to how the parent feels about the school. This is even more difficult if the psychologist is part of a team when working with the parent. Parents can often become overwhelmed when they are meeting with many professionals at the same time. The CSE is an example of this. Between the psychologist and the parent, it is important to have equal status because hierarchical power relationships might restrict communication. Confidentiality is also a necessity.

Response: Music Therapist

LAUREN STERLING, M.A., CMT

At this point, I have not had the experience of collaborating directly with parents. I have only met with one set of parents whose child I service individually. I have had some indirect communication through written correspondence with parents. If a problem or a crisis arises with a parent, I usually receive pertinent information from either the administration or the classroom teacher. With regard to the child that I see on an individual basis, I have attempted to communicate with the parents in order to have a greater understanding of the child's behavioral and emotional issues. Direct communication and interaction with parents during the school day is critical but difficult.

Response: Speech–Language Pathologist

ANGELINA DeNOIA, M.S., C.C.C.

Collaborating with parents can be difficult at times. Many parents are interested in *what* their child is being taught. A select few are interested in *how* their child is being taught and what he or she is actually learning. This presents an opportunity for collaboration. Through a running dialogue (phone calls, written correspondence, classroom observations, meetings, etc.), parents and teachers can exchange information. What strategies are used in the classroom that may be used during work sessions at home? How can a parent facilitate social interactions on the playground? How can a parent model or provide cues when necessary? Only through this constant exchange of information can there be carryover; and only through carryover can there be progress. What does collaboration mean to parents?

Response: Special Education Teacher

MAUREEN SHAPIRO, M.S.

There are multiple ways in which I collaborate with parents. At the beginning of each school year, a meeting is held to discuss classroom goals and *expectations* with an emphasis on academic learning from a language-based approach. Parents are encouraged to be *active participants* and *partners* in their child's academic development. Parental objectives and expectations, as well as perceptions, are always welcomed for discussion. Suggestions about particular strategic approaches are considered and evaluated. Last year, a mother had discussed with me the advantages of utilizing a particular reading program. I did research on it, discussed it with colleagues, and implemented the program. The program is currently being utilized as a method in the classroom. Many children are having successful reading experiences.

Individual meetings are also held to discuss IEPs, test scores, internal CSE recommendations, and future goals for each child. Parents, however, are often not involved in helping to formulate IEP goals, given the organization of most school district CSEs; this is a problem for parents. In addition, meetings and phone conversations are held throughout the school year to discuss individual needs. Feedback from parents is always elicited. I utilize parent teacher contact books to encourage communication and participation. Parents have an opportunity to observe classroom instruction and therapy on a daily basis on the school's closed-circuit video system. This helps parents learn about educational techniques and procedures. It also provides parents with knowledge about *how* their children learn in class and socially interact with peers. To reinforce classroom learning in the home environment, special projects are created. Contracts are set up related to these projects that enable the parent, child, and teacher to work together. Parents need to learn about education in order to be involved with it. Parents need an academic knowledge base just as teachers do. Teachers need to teach parents; parents need to teach teachers.

Analysis and Discussion

Professionals discuss the fact that parents must proceed through a "passage process" concerning the acceptance of a child with a disability. Parents need to learn to deal with the grief and anger related to what many parents describe as "the death of normalcy." Parents clearly have perceptions and expectations of who their children are and how their children should learn. Parents also have expectations about what their children should learn and when. These ideas, feelings, beliefs, and expectations must be discussed with individual members of the team and the team as a whole.

Parents must learn about the education process, the instructional procedures used within the classroom, the educational routines, and the different professional disciplines. In order for parents to learn about their children and about the educational process, they must be actively involved in decision making and parent training classes. Parents need to read about developmental disabilities, educational techniques, strategies, and therapeutic theories. Very often, these issues can be discussed and presented to parents in educational classes that facilitate parent-to-parent discussions, and teacher–parent dialogues.

The collaborative process that must occur between parents and teachers can be formal or informal. When formal meetings are scheduled, the team has an opportunity to work directly with parents to discuss and to solve specific educational problems that are child specific. The entire team provides an interdisciplinary perspective that allows the parent to function as an equal partner and contributor. Interactions can also occur informally when the parent meets with the teacher or the occupational therapist separately. These meetings allow for parent and teacher to focus more specifically on issues related to a specific domain area of learning.

Whether meetings are formal or informal, the interpersonal dynamics determine the working relationships. Parents need to feel that they are respected and valued as equal contributors and partners in the decision-making process. Education has historically not allowed parents to make decisions about placement, educational procedures, or therapeutic strategies. Parental input was never recognized as contributing to the educational growth and development of the child. The collaborative process reorganizes the working relationship by placing parents on an equal level and status with professional members; parents are acknowledged at the outset so power plays do not define the decision-making process. Decisions are shared and parents are encouraged to participate and to be actively involved with their children's education.

Parents and professionals acknowledge that the educational demand can be overwhelming. At times, parents need to learn about their children and teachers, just as teachers need to learn about parents and children. Relationships work when there is acknowledged cooperation, trust, acceptance, support, and mutual respect. The parent and the teacher together can contribute and create a dialogue of exchange that generalizes learning from the classroom to the home.

QUESTION 4: IS INCLUSION APPROPRIATE FOR ALL CHILDREN WITH DISABILITIES?

Response: Regular Education Teacher Surveys

The majority of responses indicate that we do not believe that inclusion is appropriate for all children with disabilities. Children with special needs must be viewed as individual learners. The decision to place a child with special needs in a general education classroom must be based on individual factors of learning. The most important aspect related to decision making concerns the issue of *benefit*. Presently, no child profile is being used by schools to determine which type of child will benefit from an inclusion experience. Unfortunately, very little empirical research has been conducted that looks at issues related to type of disability versus level of disability for children in inclusive settings. Most teachers expressed great concerns about classroom disruptions and managing children with emotional and behavioral disorders. Children with physical challenges are perceived as being more easily included than children with cognitive challenges. Several teachers indicated that children who are easily distracted and impulsive will not benefit from large classroom settings. Several other teachers indicated that there is concern about the impact on regular education students and classroom learning dynamics. Many teachers indicated that parents of regular education students must be committed to the mission of inclusion if schools are ever going to create successful inclusion classrooms and curricula. All teachers agreed that there are many barriers to achieving inclusive classrooms: teacher training, staff development, scheduling, space reorganization, adaptive equipment, additional supplies and materials, additional support staff, additional educational costs, parent support, teacher support, administrative support, parent education, and the development of a school policy. Finally, teachers expressed the concern that inclusion needs to be defined as a policy, as a procedure, as a classroom, and as a learning process.

Response: School Psychologist

HELENE MERMELSTEIN, PSY.D.

From my understanding, inclusion is based on the least restrictive alternative doctrine. Congress intended that the SEA/LEA make available a continuum of alternative placements to meet the individual needs of children with disabilities. These included instruction in regular classrooms with supplementary services, special classes, special schools, home instruction, and instruction in hospitals and institutions. Congress also intended that decisions about the extent to which pupils with disabilities can be educated with nondisabled children be made on the basis of the child's individual needs and capabilities (Jacobs & Hartshorne, 1991, p. 135).

I believe inclusion is an exciting and necessary alternative for some children with disabilities. This alternative must be part of the continuum of services offered. It cannot be the only alternative offered. If this becomes a general practice, in effect, one abandons the notion of *individual* needs. Needs assessment for the individual, I believe, is one of the most important processes when considering placement for handicapped children. Looking at the whole child, the team can make a realistic placement that can take into consideration not only the child's academic development, but also the child's social and emotional development.

Inclusion decisions cannot be based on the type of disability or even the severity alone. The committee must consider many variables. For example: What are the support systems in place? How well are the teachers trained in handling certain disabilities? Are there guidance services or social skills training available? Will there be a way to help mainstream youngsters accept and interact with youngsters with disabilities?

Not only do we have to look at the services and facilities of the regular school, but we must also look at what is appropriate for that individual child. For example: Will a child be even more isolated because peers reject him or her in the regular classroom? Or will a child who does not have the availability to interact with nonhandicapped youngsters later be hindered when he or she needs to interact in the world at large?

I believe that to view inclusion as the answer to special education is to rob the child with a disability of the opportunity to be treated individually rather than as just fitting into some educational label. The goal for children with disabilities is the same goal we have for nondisabled children; that is, to *help the individual to reach her or his potential*. We have much to do before we will reach that goal for both populations.

Response: Music Therapist

LAUREN STERLING, M.A., CMT

With regard to the type of disability, many factors must be taken into consideration concerning the inclusion of children. Because there is such a varying degree of handicaps, it would be difficult to comment on all of them. A child with a purely physical handicap would probably have difficulty functioning in a regular classroom unless the environment and the professionals were equipped to accommodate the child's individual needs. A child with a cognitive or emotional disability would also have difficulty functioning in a regular classroom environment unless major instructional modifications were implemented within the curriculum. Perhaps the issue of type of disability needs to be set aside since it may make more sense to discuss a child's level of severity rather than type of disability—if inclusion is being considered.

A child with a mild disability, whether it is physical, cognitive, or emotional, would probably have the most success in a mainstream environment. This is not to say that inclusion can be achieved without a great deal of contextual, professional, and curricula change. It is my professional belief that a child with a moderate or severe disability, from an educational and ethical point of view, should not be placed within an inclusion setting.

I believe that a child's level and type of disability both play a role in his or her ability to develop friendships with children without disabilities. From an idealistic point of view, I believe that relationships can definitely be formed between children with and without disabilities. I believe that both individuals can benefit and grow personally from this peer experience. On the other hand, there are going to be limitations that interfere with the child with a disability interacting with and developing a relationship with a child without one. Certainly, teachers can work to facilitate interactions between children with and without disabilities. In the last analysis, however, children cannot be "forced" to play with each other. Friendship involves a great deal more than classroom interaction; teachers cannot require that children play together after school.

It is also difficult to say how many children with disabilities should be placed in a regular classroom setting at one time. From my perspective, it would make sense for the ratio of children without disabilities to those with disabilities to be much greater; the fewer the number of children with disabilities within a regular classroom, the better. The type of disability and the level of functioning should determine that ratio within a regular classroom.

I understand that the inclusion classroom requires that children with disabilities be placed in classrooms with age-matched peers. If there is a marked difference in level of functioning between the child with a disability and the child without, it will be much more difficult to establish friendships and maintain the child with a disability within the instructional context of the regular classroom. Perhaps, the inclusion process should be initiated with very young children, since academic instruction would not play such a primary role within the preschool classroom. In addition, younger children are usually less inhibited about accepting social differences, and, therefore, it may be easier to facilitate the socialization process between children with and without disabilities.

I do not believe that inclusion can be achieved for *all* children with disabilities. Ideally, children with mild disabilities might benefit from being placed within a regular classroom. The regular classroom, however, requires a great deal of *modified* instruction and teacher training support. With this in mind, the child with a disability *may* learn to interact and to socialize with normal peers. This does not mean, however, that she is going to be able to advance academically within a regular academic setting that is not specifically geared to her learning problems and needs. There may be a trade-off here for children with disabilities that parents and educators may be willing to accept. Social interactions and positive role models may help foster the growth and self-confidence of a child with a disability. This does not ensure, however, that the social process will enhance academic learning and development.

Response: Special Education Teacher

LINDA CASILLO, M.S.ED.

As teachers, it is our responsibility to help children develop their own unique strengths and potentials. To achieve this goal, teachers and parents need to work together to create a nurturing educational environment that is sensitive to, but not restrictive of, children with special needs. Some children have more complex learning problems and, therefore, require individualized educational experiences in order to learn and develop. Currently, the educational trend is to have individualized teaching strategies implemented for children with disabilities within a regular education classroom. Can this truly be achieved? Some children with severe disabilities may not receive the maximum benefit from such a placement in an integrated setting. Children with severe disabilities need more specialized services that can only be provided in special schools or classrooms. "Simply placing handicapped children in the same educational settings with non-handicapped children does not accomplish all of the goals of mainstreaming" (Cooke, Ruskus, Apolloni, & Peck, 1981, p. 73). However, there are ways and means to make it possible for children with special needs to be educated in a regular classroom:

1. The teacher must structure the environment and adapt materials in order to determine the child's mode of learning. The teacher must have competencies in both early childhood education *and* special education.
2. Planning requires that children without disabilities serve as role models to stimulate developmental imitation in children with disabilities. Imitative learning is suggested when three or more children with disabilities are grouped with normal functioning children who might be slightly younger. Guralnick (1981) suggests that there be an absolute maximum of 33 percent handicapped children in regular classrooms. It is also important to consider integrating younger normal children with matched children with disabilities in order to decrease the developmental differences between peers. Children tend to more readily imitate those who are only slightly more advanced developmentally (Peck, Apolloni, Cooke, & Raver, 1978).
3. Parent involvement is a key factor in establishing inclusive classrooms. Specifically, parents can become the extended "hands" of the teacher.

The inclusive classroom requires a tremendous amount of modified instruction and collaboration between parents, teachers, children, and administrators. It is important to work through the emotional and educational barriers to the inclusive classroom before implementing any kind of program within a school district. Inclusion is a social experiment; parents and teachers need to realize that children are the subjects within this experimental process. Inclusion is based on the theory of social justice. The realities of the classroom, however, suggest that the notion of social justice may create severe learning problems if the pragmatic realities are not addressed first.

Response: Occupational Therapist

VERA GALLAGHER, O.T.R., B.C.P.

The child with cerebral palsy, dominated by primitive reflexes whose body may appear to be moving about aimlessly, but whose mind can focus on the realities of life, may be able to face the challenge of an inclusive classroom. The classroom needs to be equipped with the resources to make learning possible for this child; there may be a need for personnel, computers, wheelchairs, and major space accommodations within the classroom. Throughout the discussions related to inclusive programming, one cannot overlook the cost factors that are involved.

The development of friendships between a child with a physical disability and a child without may occur over time. The roles may begin as the child without a disability functions as the caretaker. As the relationship matures, it may be possible for more of a social exchange to develop as each child learns about the other. The cognitive, emotional, and social levels of the child with a physical disability will impact on instructional issues, as well as friendship issues within the classroom. A mild hemiparetic child may be able to socialize with peers on certain levels, but still may be stigmatized if competing athletically such as on a basketball court. The lunchroom, the gymnasium, the playground may still present barriers to social interaction when popularity and athletic competition become primary social factors.

The ratio of children with disabilities to those without in an inclusive setting is important to take into consideration. It may be necessary to set up an array of situations for the child with a disability with different ratios in mind; this would involve establishing more challenging contexts by factoring the number of children with disabilities into a specific activity. For the child who is not physically challenged, there are other difficulties in a regular classroom. Depending on the type and severity of the disability, the child may require major modifications in classroom instructional techniques. For regular education teachers, ongoing adjustments in teaching materials and procedures may be overwhelming. For children with behavior disorders and emotional impairments, adaptations in class size, personnel, and basic seating arrangements may be needed to prepare the regular teacher and children without disabilities for ongoing disruptions and outbursts.

Response: Special Education Teacher

MAUREEN SHAPIRO, M.S.

Placing the child with a disability in a regular classroom can be successful when a combination of factors are present. I believe that success can only be achieved when there is a true collaborative effort. The classroom teacher and the special education teacher should be the anchors of the team with assistance from the psychologist, therapists, and administrators. Parents must also take an active role. In addition, it should be assumed that all schoolwork needs to be at the student's current level of functioning. Therefore, classroom adaptations will be necessary to accommodate the child with a disability. I feel that the severity of the disability rather than the type of disability should determine whether inclusive programming is indicated. Obviously, classroom adaptations must be utilized to accommodate different types of disabilities. I feel that the greatest potential for success lies in the children with the mildest disabilities. It will also depend on the child's level of social competency. If the child's socialization skills are appropriate, the potential for success will be greater.

Friendships are difficult to establish between children with disabilities and those without. In our society, being different by choice is difficult; a child with a disability may not have the awareness, let alone the choice. Most people tend to associate with peers who are most like themselves. Children do have the wonderful ability to accept people for who and what they are, however, the older they get, the more discriminating they become. At some point, a disability can become a source of ridicule. This is not to say that friendships cannot develop; however, they will be limited in number and less common than peer friendships. The number of children with disabilities must be limited to a very small percentage because the goal of inclusive programming is to mainstream the child with a disability by placement in a classroom where the majority of the children are without disabilities.

The age of the child with a disability being placed in inclusive programming should be determined by the individual needs of that child. This includes the severity of the disability and the child's ability to adapt socially and academically. There will be a greater possibility for success if inclusion occurs at the youngest possible age of readiness. Inclusion, of course, is not possible for all children with disabilities. The severity of the disability can at times preclude the possibility of inclusion; the specific disability is not the only difficulty. The individual child's inherent ability to adapt can be a determining factor in the child's success. The level of social competency will also play a major role in the potential success of these efforts. A well-planned collaborative effort, with a willing team, is the only formula that can provide a fruitful outcome. This team must recognize that the curriculum can vary within the classroom, and that all the class members do not have to be working on the same material at the same time or in the exact same format. Curriculum planning is a major key to organizing classroom structure; this allows all the participants to grow at an individual rate.

Response: Speech–Language Pathologist

ANGELINA DeNOIA, M.A., C.C.C.

The very nature of special education indicates that the student requires specific modifications, whether that means instruction, environment, materials, or a combination of all three. By placing a child with special needs into the mainstream, he may not necessarily be afforded the attention and time he requires. In addition, when the teacher stops instruction to address that child's needs, the rest of the class must wait. The more fragmented the teacher's time becomes, the more distracted the teacher's concentration and focus become.

With regard to the student, there are arguments for both sides. A benefit of inclusion is that it may allow the children without disabilities to "model" for the child with special needs. However, what does it do for the *self-esteem* of the child? This child has been placed in a class with children of the same chronological age who are functioning at a much more advanced level. How does the child with special needs feel about himself?

Furthermore, how does the child with special needs fit in socially? Where is the feeling of social acceptance? When children do not share the same friends, experiences, interests, or hobbies, how do they communicate? What is the benefit of forcing children into situations that they may not necessarily fit into? Children deserve the right to be taught in an environment in which they can thrive and develop a sense of accomplishment. They must be able to achieve their goals academically and socially. Whether this can be achieved in an inclusion program or a self-contained program must be answered for each individual child.

Response: Speech–Language Pathologist

MARION TRAYNOR, M.S., C.C.C.

Inclusion has become very widespread. There are many benefits to using it as a service delivery alternative. For example, the child with a disability may receive better language models, have more opportunities for carryover, and have more opportunities for developing social skills. Additionally, modifying the classroom environment can also help children without disabilities and at-risk children. Although there appear to be many benefits to inclusive programming, I do not feel it is effective for *all* children. Judith Montgomery, the current president of the American Speech Language Hearing Association, said it best when she said, "I like the idea of all children learning together to the extent to which each is capable, and with the support that each one needs." (Montgomery, April 1995, p. 7). The reality is that not *all* children *are* capable of learning together, and inclusive programming does not provide enough support to meet *all* children's needs. I believe that each child has to be looked at individually to see how his or her needs can be best met.

We need to study inclusion's effectiveness before we decide that it is best for all handicapped children. Various criteria must be considered before placing a child with a disability in a regular education classroom. The regular education setting is not the least restrictive environment for all children. The least restrictive environment is the place where the child achieves the most success and retains a high *sense of self-esteem*. The regular classroom setting does not meet the needs of many children with severe communication problems, attending difficulties, and behavioral disorders. These children require a significant amount of individual attention. If the classroom teacher provided the child with a disability with all the assistance he or she needed, the teacher would have less time to instruct the other students in the class; this interferes with the regular education students' learning. Furthermore, the greater the number of students with disabilities in a classroom, the more planning, collaborating, and teacher training are needed. Each child with a disability requires different classroom modifications to best meet individual needs.

I feel that students with and without disabilities should have opportunities to socialize and develop friendships at an early age. When children are young, they can learn to accept the differences in each person and learn to appreciate those differences. However, I also feel many students with disabilities learn differently from their peers. They should be given the opportunity to learn in the environment that best meets their needs and still have opportunities for socialization. This brings me to the issue of pull-out services. In the field of speech pathology, as I am sure is the case in other disciplines, some skills are difficult to target in the regular education setting. The speech–language pathologist has many years of training and experience in these areas. The classroom teacher should not be expected to target these areas with the same expertise as the speech pathologist. The classroom teacher has many other responsibilities and cannot possibly learn enough strategies to teach these and other skills in a short period of time. Additionally, working on these areas is not necessarily *beneficial to all students* in the class and, as a result, may stigmatize the student with a disability. A foundation must be set before these skills should be targeted in the classroom. I feel a combination of push-in and pull-out services is best for most children. In conclusion, although there are many advantages to inclusion, there are also disadvantages. Inclusion is not effective if a child's specific needs are not met.

Analysis and Discussion

Teachers raised many issues concerning the meaning of inclusion and its implication for the placement of *all* children with disabilities within a regular classroom environment. Professionals were most concerned about the fact that the educational system needed to focus on the individual needs of the child in the classroom whether she had a disability or not. One of the most significant problems in general education is related to the fact that the diversity of child learners has not been adequately and appropriately acknowledged within regular education classrooms. As the diversity of learners has increased, the quality of education has decreased. One of the contributions to education from the field of special education has been the attention to individualized programming and the focus on specialization. If inclusion is to be achieved within the regular classroom, then diversity must be linked with individual programming. How can each child achieve his individual potential within the general education classroom? Inclusion involves dramatic change and educational reform. The classroom must be changed, the teacher must be changed, the supplies, materials, procedures, roles, responsibilities, and curricula—all must change. The underlying idealism of social justice is a lofty challenge for education. Can the ideal of inclusion be achieved for all children if the appropriate modifications cannot be achieved, given the realities of schools, parents, teachers, and communities? Is the ideal of inclusion appropriate as a goal for all children? Can general education accomplish everything for everyone?

One of the teachers indicated that there must be a trade-off and a compromise made given the realities of any school, organization, or environment. Are parents and teachers willing to accept the compromise of social interactions and normal role models in lieu of individualized learning and academic development? Inclusion does not ensure that the social environment will enhance academic development. Inclusion is an experiment that attempts to equalize the learning environment for all children. It attempts to provide a maximum benefit, given a social mix of child learners, but can all children benefit from the regular environment? Should the regular environment be viewed as beneficial to all children? Educators of children who are deaf argue adamantly against the regular classroom for that type of learner. Is the regular environment the *normal* environment for all children with disabilities? For members of the deaf community, deaf society and deaf schools represent the normal environment.

Another issue concerns the realism of social development involving peer partners and the role of friendship in classroom instructional learning. Can friendships be facilitated, initiated, and maintained by means of a classroom curriculum? Can meaningful relationships be established even though children are at very different developmental levels of functioning? If children do not seek each other out after school for work study, play dates, parties, and nonacademic partnerships, have the goals of friendship and socialization been achieved? If education teaches friendship in school, how can these classroom goals be generalized to the home environment? If the home is the natural environment, should we not pay attention to the role of friendship in contexts other than the classroom?

Many parents describe a painful process of social rejection which indicates the presence of many barriers for the child with a disability. Can popularity be mandated? The process of athletic selection and competition for teams must be reconsidered and changed if inclusion is going to be achieved in all areas of educational endeavor. How can educators ensure that disabled children will not be stigmatized or picked on by peers without disabilities? Should schools have a curriculum before they implement the program? Should teachers be trained before children with disabilities are included in regular classrooms? Should parents and teachers agree on an educational mission before an inclusion program is implemented?

Certainly, we cannot imagine all of the possible problems that will arise as inclusion moves forward. Ultimately, attitudes must be changed and commitments must be made to the mission of inclusion if collaborators are going to work through the long-term issues. Inclusion provides an opportunity for schools to transform the educational system and the process of child learning. It allows for parents, teachers, and administrators to study program effectiveness and alter program components that are not beneficial to all children. Inclusion involves a choice. Teachers, parents, administrators, schools, and communities—all must make an investment in the process. Parents cannot be forced to include their children, and teachers cannot be forced to work in inclusive classrooms. Perhaps that is the most important issue that needs to be discussed and addressed—choice. Perhaps that is the most important variable in the inclusion experiment—choice. The extent to which all of the collaborators choose inclusion, a commitment will be made to the mission and to its success. Inclusion requires—in fact, it demands—the commitment of all, since the creation is a classroom, a society of child learners.

The range of problems and issues that will arise as children with disabilities are included within the regular education classroom is overwhelming. Professionals cannot imagine all of the possible problems that will arise as inclusion moves forward. The child who cannot organize herself because she is overstimulated by auditory and visual input needs an environment that provides a balance of flexibility and structure. Given the present demands on regular education, can the needs of all children with disabilities be ensured within a regular classroom? As it is, regular education teachers complain about child diversity and meeting the needs of regular education children. Clearly, with the projected cuts to education, regular education classrooms are going to be getting larger and larger. Will the child with a disability get lost in the regular classroom? The regular education classroom must be equipped to handle the needs of children with disabilities. The benefits of such a setting may be lost without the proper resources. If professionals and parents can collaborate effectively, identify problems, and agree to a common mission, then there is a possibility that some children with disabilities may succeed in a regular classroom.

Finally, many attitudes interfere with the success of inclusion. Parents who have expectations that classrooms must be homogenous settings will clearly have serious problems with inclusion. Inclusion seems to be affected by many barriers and boundaries. How can a school district argue social justice if there is a better program in a private school or another community that the parents want their child to attend? Inclusion cannot be defined as a classroom within a specific school district. Public schools if they truly believe in the social justice of inclusion should look beyond their borders to nonpublic and private schools. If social justice is the issue, then educational reform must include *all children* and *all schools*. The final issue concerns the relationship between the classroom and the community. There must be a relationship between the philosophy of the classroom and the multicultural goals of the community. If the classroom functions as a separate entity from the community, it may limit social relationships and activities such as play dates, extracurricular interactions, and peer networking. Parents and teachers must work together to coordinate a belief system about the classroom and the home environment.

It may be more difficult for a child with a disability to function in an inclusive classroom. It may be more difficult for most children with disabilities to achieve their potential in an inclusive classroom. Parents need to decide what is in the best interest of their child. *Everything* may not be achievable for the child as a function of inclusion. What is the primary priority? The reality in most school districts throughout the United States is that inclusion cannot be achieved for all children. The inclusion programs that will be developed will probably be restricted programmatically by financial constraints and reimbursement issues. Financial trends will fluctuate and children with disabilities will unfortunately get caught in the "crossfire." The goal of education is to provide children with skills to be productive members of society. Perhaps when parents are empowered with *choice* to make decisions about their children, inclusion may have a better opportunity for success. Parental choice is a difficult issue for most public schools in American education. Inclusion cannot be achieved without parental choice, leading to a significant dilemma for public schools.

❧   *A Few Words from Toya Davis*   ❧

It is my personal belief that those who wish to implement inclusionary programming must start with the premise that inclusion is *not* for every child! If we begin with that premise, we have a greater probability of developing a successful inclusion program for some children.

As the parent of a child who was diagnosed with severe language and communication deficits, I have traveled that long and arduous road from having to place him in an early intervention preschool program before the age of three, having him attend an out-of-district self-contained kindergarten, then returning to his district but not his home school for first and second grades. At the end of second grade, his testing revealed that he was ready to be mainstreamed or included with the regular population, every mother of a special needs child's dream come true. But along with the euphoria comes anxiety; will my child fit in both academically and socially? Up until this stage, he had been a big fish in a little pond. Would he succeed, or would this new world he was entering chew him up and spit him out?

Training is a critical part needed to ensure that inclusion is successful; training includes classroom teachers, resource room personnel, teacher consultants, speech–language pathologists, teacher assistants, psychologists, librarians, music and art teachers, lunchroom personnel, custodial staff, etc. Parents also need training; parents of both normal learners and of children with special needs. If this piece is eliminated and everyone else is included, the program is doomed in most cases to failure. You need the support of parents to operate a meaningful inclusion program.

Parents of normal learners must be brought together with the parents of learners with special needs to discuss concerns each party may have about this new endeavor—inclusion. If this is not done, the agency/school will be faced with the "NIMBY" syndrome—not in my backyard. Unless this step is implemented, the first time an incident occurs between the two groups, hard feelings will develop and the battle lines will be drawn; instead of a cooperative effort, you will have a battleground.

Inclusionary efforts must be focused at the early preschool and elementary-aged population in grades kindergarten through second. In my opinion, that is when we have the greatest window of opportunity for success, and also ensures that the child's self-esteem remains intact. I also believe that if an organization is looking to implement an inclusionary program, it should start with that population which affords the greatest opportunity for success, the child with a mild impairment who also has high social skills.

Those professionals who may be teaching these types of classes must make a special effort to ensure that the children with special needs are not singled out or picked on, because children can be cruel to one another. If inclusion is to be a success in the real world, the classroom environment must be individualized, so all students learn and reach their learning potential.

Toya Davis

QUESTIONS FOR CLASSROOM DISCUSSION

1. Describe the kinds of barriers to inclusion detailed by various professionals.
2. What kinds of competency skills are necessary for successful collaboration?
3. What do schools need to do to encourage parents to become part of a collaborative team?
4. What are the important components of collaboration?
5. When does collaboration work and when does it not work?
6. Is inclusion appropriate for all children with disabilities? State your opinion and provide a rationale.

BIBLIOGRAPHY

Bricker, Diane D. (1989). *Early intervention for at-risk and handicapped infants, toddlers, and preschool children* (p. 227). Palo Alto, CA: Vort Corporation.

Bush, C. (1991). *Collaborating with teachers and parents.* Tucson, AZ: Communication Skill Builders.

Cooke, T., Ruskus, J., Apolloni, T., & Peck, C. (1981). Handicapped preschool children in the mainstream: Background, outcomes, and clinical suggestions. *Topics in Early Childhood Special Education, 1,* 73–83.

Coufal, K. (1993). Collaborative consultation for speech/language pathologists, *Topics in Language Disorders, 14*(1), 1–4.

Guralnick, M. J. (1981). Programmatic factors affecting child–child social interactions in mainstreamed preschool programs. *Exceptional Education Quarterly, 1*(4), 71–79.

Idol, L., Paolucci-Whitcomb, P., & Nevin, A. (1986). *Collaborative consultation.* Rockville Pike, MD: Aspen.

Jacobs, S., & Hartshorne, T. (1991). *Ethics and law for school psychologists* (p. 135). Brunden, VT: Clinical Psychology Publishing Company, Inc.

Koch, W. (1995). *To the third power.* St. Paul, MN: Tilbury House.

Larsen, P. C. (1995). *To the Third Power* (p. 220). Gardiner, ME: Tilbury House Publishers.

Meacham, M. L. & Peckham, P. D. (1978). School psychologists at three-quarters century: Congruence between training, practice, preferred role and competence. *Journal of School Psychology, 16,* 195–206.

Montgomery, J. (1995). Inclusion, observation, outcome. *ASHA, 7.*

Peck, C., Apolloni, T., Cooke, T., & Raver, S. (1978). Teaching retarded preschoolers to imitate the free play behavior of nonretarded classmates: Trained and generalized effects. *The Journal of Special Education, 12,* 195–207.

Schein, E. (1988). *Process consultation.* Reading, MA: Addison-Wesley Publishing.

School District Surveys

Anonymous surveys were circulated to 77 school districts on Long Island and New York City; 56 were returned. The data collected for the surveys were analyzed in three separate parts: direct responses to questions, barrier analyses, and anecdotal comments.

It was clear that discussion of inclusion triggered intense feelings among professionals. The primary concern expressed within the survey related to the fact that school districts were being required to create and to implement inclusive classrooms without the benefit of educational models and field testing.

PART I: SURVEY ABOUT INCLUSION

1. All children with disabilities should be placed in a regular education classroom without regard to the *type* of developmental disability.

   Disagree *100%*

2. All children with disabilities should be placed in a regular classroom without regard to *level* of disability.

   Disagree *100%*

3. Decisions concerning inclusive opportunities should be based on the individual needs of children with disabilities.

   Agree *100%*

4. Part of the decision-making process for the placement of a child with a disability in a regular classroom must involve the impact on learning and instruction for regular education students.

   Agree *93%*

5. Schools need to have access to successful inclusive models. There is not enough technological support and information on successful inclusive programs.

Agree *95%*

6. In determining whether a child with a disability can benefit from inclusive opportunities, the following developmental characteristics must be taken into consideration. Please rate each of these skills by noting their level of importance in your committee's decision-making process.

Use 1–5, 1 signifying least important, 5 signifying most important.

a. Social skills	*54%* *
b. Level of language functioning	*48%*
c. Prereadiness skills	*32%*
d. Self-awareness	*25%*
e. Impulse control	*77%*
f. Emotional development	*57%*
g. Cognitive ability	*30%*
h. Behavioral skills	*80%*

*Percentage signifies designation of importance as values 4–5.

7. Children with disabilities who are more severely impaired require more special education and less inclusion.

Agree *51%*

Disagree *25%*

*Other *24%*

*Explanation:

a. Depends on type of disability.
b. Depends on level of disability.
c. Depends on degree of disruption and instructional needs within the classroom.

8. Children with disabilities who are less severely impaired require less special education and more inclusion.

Agree *64%*

Disagree *17%*

*Other *19%*

*Explanation:

a. Depends on level of disability.
b. Depends on type of disability
c. Depends on degree of disruption and instructional needs within the classroom.

9. In order to ensure *successful* inclusion, state policy should begin the inclusion process early at the preschool level.

Agree *74%*

Disagree *16%*

*Other *10%*

*Explanation:
a. Presently, there are no successful inclusion models.
b. There is the assumption that inclusion will be successful for *all* children.

10. Successful inclusion requires integrated opportunities, program and teacher integration. Inclusion opportunities should be integrated into the child's day to meet his individual learning needs: physical, social, and instructional.

Agree *98%*

Disagree *2%*

PART II

1. The following factors represent barriers and problems for schools to develop inclusive classrooms. All checked variables were counted and calculated as percentages.

a.	Teacher training	*80%*
b.	Staff development for special educators	*68%*
c.	Scheduling	*59%*
d.	School space reorganization	*39%*
e.	Additional space and materials	*36%*
f.	Adaptive equipment	*39%*
g.	Additional instructional staff	*59%*
h.	Increased educational costs	*63%*
i.	Parent support	*46%*
j.	Teacher support	*59%*
k.	Staff development for regular educators	*73%*
l.	Staff development for administrative personnel	*59%*
m.	Parent support and understanding	*48%*
n.	Parent education	*48%*
o.	Development of a school policy	*39%*

PART III: COMMENTS AND RELATED ISSUES

1. As school districts, we need to stop using the word *inclusion*. It has too many "promises" and little evidence of educational results. Many parents of children with severe disabilities are often the most vocal about inclusion. Yet, these children need the most intensive assistance as early as possible in their educational experiences.

2. *Collaborative Decision Making.*   Inclusion will only be achieved successfully if the State Education Department supports collaborative decision making between teachers and parents. Parents must agree to inclusive classrooms and schools. Parents of children without handicaps cannot be forced or coerced into inclusive settings. The degree to which parents of children with and without handicaps are forced to accept inclusive classrooms is the degree to which inclusive education will fail statewide.

3. *Teachers.*   Presently, there is no teacher education training program statewide for regular education teachers who will be working with children with special needs. Inclusion will not be achieved successfully if regular education teachers do not have the background, knowledge, and skills to successfully meet the needs of children with and without disabilities within a classroom. Children cannot be included before teachers are trained. Teacher training must occur *before* children are included.

4. *All teachers are not the same.*   There is a frightening assumption in inclusive education that a special education teacher can be replaced by a regular education teacher. Academic training and professional experiences indicate that special education teachers and regular education teachers are different, and that the difference is critical to the appropriate instruction of children. There is a further assumption that in a regular education classroom, a paraprofessional can replace a special education teacher and manage the educational needs of a child with developmental disabilities.

   The assumption that teachers can replace each other and that teacher certifications are no longer important in the education of children becomes particularly problematic at the preschool level. In preschool, the model being proposed by the state education department replaces a certified teacher with a day care provider. Education is not day care; day care is not education. The nature of instruction will change and the quality of programming will change when a certified teacher is replaced by a day care provider.

   Early intervention represents a critical period for learning. If there is ever a time when the needs of a child with a disability must be addressed, it is during this formative preschool period. To substitute a special education teacher with a day care provider suggests a dangerous trend in education—a managed care approach. Why not substitute the cardiologist with the family practitioner? Why not substitute a nurse's aide for a physician? In the long run, a managed care approach to *education* will decrease the quality of education. If this continues, then we all accept and say that day care = education. We must ask ourselves, if the following statement is true: Can day care replace education?

5. *Curricula.*   Presently, no inclusive curriculum has been created and/or developed at the state or local level. It cannot be assumed that children with special needs placed in regular classrooms will learn in exactly the same way that normal children learn—but slower. Inclusion requires *adaptation* in instruction, curriculum, materials, supplies, resources, teacher training, and parent education. None of these things has been investigated or accomplished to date. These things cannot be done *after* children are included—they must be done before children are included in regular classes.

6. *Child profile.* There is no empirical research that defines whether or not a child will *benefit* from an inclusive classroom. Children with special needs who are placed in regular classrooms and disrupt the learning and instruction of other children will ultimately undermine the mission, the process, and the ultimate achievement of inclusive education on the school-age level. Child benefit must be identified *before* a child is included. School districts must develop a child profile so that the appropriate children receive inclusive instruction. This ensures that the child with special needs will benefit from the inclusive setting and will not be disruptive to regular peers. This ensures that regular education students accept and receive the child with special needs and that all children will benefit from the inclusive process. The present proposal "dumps children into regular classrooms" without regard to individual needs.

7. *Peer facilitation.* All of the research literature indicates that a key factor to inclusion success relates to child facilitation and training. Presently, there is no organized program and no curriculum that details child facilitation and inclusive goals within a regular classroom. Again, classroom goals, instructional procedures, and normal child facilitation procedures must be developed *before* children with disabilities are included.

8. *Parents of children without disabilities.* Inclusion requires that children with developmental disabilities be placed in regular education settings. This means that part of the inclusion process involves embedded programming for peers without disabilities. The state education department cannot develop an inclusion model without consideration of preschool children without disabilities. Part of the rate-setting methodology must involve the incorporation of normal children. In addition, parents of non-handicapped children will not *pay* to be in settings with children with disabilities.

All of my research during the past two years has indicated significant negative attitudes about inclusion from parents of children without disabilities. Parents of children without disabilities take the position that if they pay for preschool, nursery school, or child care, they do not want children with special needs within the classroom. SED's preschool model does not take this factor into consideration. The proposal places the *burden* of developing programming for normal peers on the "4410 preschool providers." If SED wants to successfully develop integrated programming, then it is incumbent upon SED to deal with the barriers that interfere with inclusive education. The most significant barrier involves parents of children without disabilities.

Finally, preschool education is not mandated in New York State; as a result parents of children without disabilities must pay for nursery school and child care services. Children without disabilities benefit the educational instruction of children with disabilities. *Inclusion cannot occur without normal peers.* This is a system set up for failure. If SED wants inclusive education for preschool children, it must *subsidize* education for children without disabilities. This factor will ultimately undermine inclusive education and programming on the preschool side.

9. The implications for the drastic changes on the preschool side will have broad-based negative implications for CSEs and school districts. A preschool child with

disabilities may receive an IEP which indicates 50 to 75 percent of inclusion. When the child becomes school age, the school district's CSE will then be required to provide the child with the same *level* of inclusive instruction. With the present definition of least restrictive environment, CPSEs will no longer be able to generate decisions based on individual needs; school district CSEs will be faced with the same dilemma. Inclusion decision making will not be based on the individual needs of the preschool child or his *ability* to benefit from inclusive instruction but rather on an artificial "market driven system—special education itinerant teacher program or related services *only*."

Epilogue

Two years ago, my colleague Dr. Christine Radziewicz and I discussed a textbook project about a subject very close to both of our hearts. Neither one of us could have imagined at the time the rapid changes in educational reform in New York State that would emphasize the controversy of this book. We feel that we have been through a process of learning that has transformed both of us. In writing this textbook, we have learned a great deal about the theoretical and the educational underpinnings of school-based decision making. The process of engaging parents, teachers, administrators, and children in an ongoing discourse about inclusion has given us both a sense of challenge and humility about the mission of schools in American society.

We started this book with an idea about inclusion. We have completed this book with a very different idea about the role of schools and the responsibilities of parents and teachers in decision making. Our collaboration and teaming with all of the stakeholders have given us a perspective about the future that is both awe inspiring and inspirational. We both believe that inclusion is an achievable ideal for children with developmental disabilities. It is, however, the reality of the schools to engage in a process that requires self-inquiry and self-investigation to develop a collaborative decision-making process. Inclusion is an opportunity for all and a benefit for some. It is this leap of faith that mandates a safety net for children progressing within the educational system. Every school must define the term *child benefit*. Every school must establish a process of collaborative decision making to ensure that all of the stakeholders are invested in the mission and the process. Every parent must be committed to the classroom and every teacher must be educated about the responsibilities related to child diversity. Inclusion creates a foundation for a new partnership in learning. Inclusion creates the opportunity for including parents in schools as well as children. Truly, parents and teachers must think about the nature of education in new and different ways if inclusion is to succeed. We have learned that the success of inclusion at each and every level is based on the collaborative process. Collaboration has transformed both of us and we truly share that mission with all of our colleagues in education.

Dr. Ellenmorris Tiegerman-Farber
Dr. Christine Radziewicz

233

I N D E X

Academic programs
  curriculum development and, 123–126
  goals of, 71, 123–125
  in inclusion classroom, 6, 97, 98, 173
  instructional modifications and, 6, 143
Adams, L., 76
Adeigbola, M., 36, 106, 133
Administrators
  collaboration and, 66
  collaborative decision-making process and, 85,
      104, 105, 107
  collaborative team and, 104–109, 171–172,
      183–184
  decision-making process and, 49
  gender issues, 168–169
  inclusion and, 48
  inclusion classroom and, 88, 106–107, 172
  parents and, 104, 108
  resources and, 58, 84
  role of, 90, 104, 117
  teachers and, 50, 59, 84–86, 108, 205, 208
Algozzine, B., 165
Alper, S. K., 165
Alpert, Millie, 149–152, 153
Alternative communication systems, 37
Ambrosio, Cathy, 61–62
American Deaf Association, 139
American Sign Language (ASL), 139–140
American Speech Language Hearing Association, 220
Americans with Disabilities Act, 15
Anderson, B., 149
Apolloni, T., 217
Argott, L., 36, 106, 133
ASL (American Sign Language), 139–140

Assessment
  administrators and, 105
  Assessment Profile, 45–54
  of child benefit, 40
  of communication skills, 46–52
  of inclusion, 30
  multidisciplinary team assessments, 44, 45–54
  outcome-based criteria and, 40, 81, 83, 86
  of placement options, 7
  psychological, 53
Association for Children with Down Syndrome, 27
Association of Supervisors and Curriculum
      Development, 15
Auditory training, 27
Autism
  behavior management skills and, 132–133,
      142–143, 145
  communication skills and, 144
  individualized instruction and, 145–146
  least restrictive environment and, 142–143
  Public Law 101-476 and, 3
  socialization skills and, 144–145
Ayres, C. B., 177

Barber, P., 164
Behavior management skills
  autism and, 132–133, 142–143, 145
  child benefit of inclusion and, 220
  classroom goals and, 93–94
  disability level and, 133
  inclusion classroom design and, 79, 80
  perceptual report card and, 178–179
  placement options and, 28
  regular education teachers' concerns about, 40, 49

Behr, S. K., 164
Behrmann, J., 12, 15, 17, 94, 130, 172, 176
Belluck, P., 10
Belous, R., 167
Benefit. *See* Child benefit of inclusion
Beninghof, A. M., 76
Bilingual instruction, 165–166
Billingsley, F., 60
Birch, J. W., 32
Brain injury, 3
Bricker, D. D., 199
Brockett, D., 130
Bronfenbrenner, U., 163
Brown, L., 130
Bunch, 120
Bunch, G., 176
Bursuck, W. D., 68
Burton, T., 133
Bush, C., 207, 208

Cardona-Morales, C., 166
Carlson, P., 86
Carr, 132
Carr, M. N., 8, 17
Carran, D. T., 136
Cartusciello-King, R., 97
Casillo, Linda, 199, 206–207, 217–218
Cerebral palsy, 36
Cessna, K., 76
Chalmers, L., 36, 59, 70, 77, 104
Chess, S., 68
Child benefit of inclusion
   autism and, 142–146
   behavior management skills and, 220
   of children with disabilities, 30, 40, 123,
      138–146, 214–224
   of children without disabilities, 18, 173,
      214, 221
   collaborative decision-making process and,
      138–146
   collaborative team and, 66
   definition of, 8, 29, 66, 231
   hearing impairments and, 138–142
   parents' perceptions of, 178
   partial mainstreaming and, 29
   regular education initiative and, 17
Child care programs, 147–148, 160

Child diversity
   of children with disabilities, 31–32, 133–134
   collaborative decision-making process and, 161
   curriculum development and, 126–127, 136
   inclusion classroom and, 130–134, 145, 170, 223
Children with disabilities. *See also* Disability level;
      Disability types; Peer relationships
   age versus stage of, 133–136, 216
   child benefit of inclusion for, 30, 40, 123,
      138–146, 214–224
   child diversity of, 31–32, 133–134
   expectations of, 80
   Individualized Education Program for, 123–124
   individualized instruction for, 6–8, 27, 71, 79,
      123
   normalization principle and, 4
   Public Law 94-142 and, 2
   ratio of children in regular education classroom,
      18, 131, 216, 218, 219
   social isolation of, 18, 75
   teacher attitudes toward, 72
   teacher in-service training and, 16
Children without disabilities. *See also* Peer
      relationships
   child benefit of inclusion for, 18, 173, 214, 221
   inclusion concept and, 12
   Individualized Education Program for, 123–124
   individualized instruction for, 71, 79, 123
   training about children with disabilities, 30, 48,
      71, 83, 144–145
Classroom goals
   collaborative team and, 91–95
   curriculum development and, 122–123
   diversity and, 126, 130
   inclusion classroom design and, 79, 80, 97
   Individualized Education Program and, 37, 41,
      75, 79, 92, 124
   teachers and, 70, 75
Classroom management
   in-service training for, 70
   regular education teachers' attitudes towards,
      49, 136
   teacher cooperation and, 59
Coequality
   of administrators, 105
   of parents, 88–91
   of teachers, 70–71

Collaborating with Teachers and Parents (Bush), 207
Collaboration
    competencies for, 194, 195–202
    decision-making process and, 66–68
    educational reform and, 67
    formalization of, 192
    inclusion and, 68
    as interactive process, 193
    parents' role in, 66, 184, 210–214
    parent-teacher relationship and, 195, 203
    professional collaboration, 96, 202–210
    teacher cooperation and, 136–137, 202–210
Collaborative decision-making process
    academic goals and, 123
    administrators and, 85, 104, 105, 107
    child benefit of inclusion and, 138–146
    child diversity and, 161
    classroom goals and, 75, 97
    communication skills and, 78
    communities and, 116, 119, 171
    diagram of, 69
    educational reform and, 160
    evaluation of, 120
    implications of, 118–119
    inclusion classroom and, 68–70, 134, 169
    levels of, 121, 134, 171–172
    parents and, 89–91, 97, 108, 161–163,
        170–171, 176, 185
    parent-teacher relationship and, 87–88, 91,
        94–95, 107, 169–170, 184, 230
    placement options and, 133–134
    problem identification, 117–118
    professional collaboration and, 209–210
    teachers and, 71, 85, 87–88, 108, 230
Collaborative teaching, 39. *See also* Coteaching;
    Team teaching
Collaborative teams. *See also* Collaborative
    decision-making process
    administrators and, 104–109, 171–172,
        183–184
    child benefit of inclusion and, 66
    child diversity and, 130
    classroom goals and, 91–95
    communication skills for, 67–68
    diversity issues and, 120–122
    inclusion and, 161
    inclusion classroom and, 68–70
    parents and, 88–104, 171–172, 176–177

    parent-teacher relationship and, 95–96, 99,
        102–103
    professional collaboration and, 205, 208–209
    teachers and, 70–88, 134–135, 171–172
Comer, J. P., 182
Committee on Preschool Special Education
    (CPSE), 4, 6, 26
Committee on Special Education (CSE)
    decision-making process of, 6–7, 26, 29, 41,
        42–43
    inclusion and, 66, 232
    least restrictive environment definition and, 6, 10
    mainstreaming and, 4
    as multidisciplinary team, 66
    parents' role, 99, 175, 176, 211, 213
    partial mainstreaming and, 28–29
Communication boards, 37–38, 144
Communication skills
    assessment of, 46–52
    autism and, 144
    child benefit of inclusion and, 40
    classroom goals for, 94
    collaborative decision-making process and, 78
    for collaborative team, 67–68
    cultural diversity and, 165–166
    disability level and, 18–19, 133
    hearing impairments and, 139–140, 142
    inclusion and, 37–38
    linguistic diversity and, 120–122, 165–166
    parents of children with disabilities and, 92
    placement options and, 6–8, 28
Communities
    collaborative decision-making process and, 116,
        119, 171
    cultural needs of, 108, 116, 119, 223
    expectations of, 117
    goals of, 106, 116, 223
    school district planning and, 55
Conflict resolution, 182, 197
Consultant teacher services, 29–30, 143
Cook, L., 67
Cooke, T., 217
Coparticipation
    of administrators, 105
    of parents, 89–91
    of teachers, 70–71
Core curriculum, 41, 59
Cornelius, G., 182

Cornell, C. J., 163
Correa, V. I., 165
Costs. *See also* Resources
    inclusion and, 35–36
    mainstreaming and, 9
    regular education initiative and, 17
    for school districts, 55, 58
    of special education, 2, 4, 17
Coteaching. *See also* Team teaching
    goals and, 78
    inclusion and, 39, 59, 70, 77–79
    teacher attitudes and, 135–136
    teacher in-service training and, 58
Coufal, K., 67, 70, 71, 91, 193
Council for Learning Disabilities, 123
CPSE (Committee on Preschool Special
        Education), 4, 6, 26
Crais, E., 67
Crowe, L. K., 136
CSE. *See* Committee on Special Education (CSE)
Cultural diversity
    classroom goals and, 122–123
    collaborative team and, 120–122
    communication skills and, 165–166
    communities needs and, 108, 116, 119, 223
    conflict resolution and, 182
    deaf community and, 138–142
    early intervention and, 147
    parents' role and, 160, 164–165, 179
    parent-teacher relationships and, 184
Curriculum development
    academic programs and, 123–126
    classroom goals and, 122–123
    curriculum modification and, 126–127
    inclusion and, 40–45, 230
    in inclusion classroom, 81–84, 122–125
    individualized instruction and, 40, 82, 83, 85
    parents and, 98–99
    for peer facilitation, 144–145
    peer instruction and, 83, 122, 125, 126
    teacher cooperation in, 59
    transdisciplinary curriculum, 71, 122, 123,
        126–127, 136

Dance movement therapy, 27, 198, 206
Davis, Toya, 224
Deaf community, 138–142, 222. *See also* Hearing
    impairments

Decision-making process. *See also* Collaborative
        decision-making process
    administrators and, 49
    collaboration and, 66–68
    of Committee on Special Education, 6–7, 26,
        29, 41, 42–43
    gender issues in, 169
    for mainstreaming, 44
    participants in, 31
    regular education teachers' role in, 49
DeMontfort Supple, M., 184
DeNoia, Angelina, 201, 212, 219–220
Denton, M., 74
Dettmer, P., 68
Developmental disabilities. *See also* Children with
        disabilities; Mild disabilities; Severe
        disabilities
    bilingual instruction and, 165–166
    consultant teacher services, 29
    disability level and, 17–22, 30–34, 41, 131–133,
        216, 219
    disability types and, 36–37, 41, 130, 172,
        216, 219
    diversity of, 31–32
    moderate disabilities, 17, 32, 34, 133
    of preschool children, 2
    teacher in-service training concerning, 70
Diaz, R. M., 166
DiCola, J., 149
Disability level
    curriculum development and, 41
    diversity and, 131–133
    inclusion and, 17–22, 30–34, 219
    peer relationships and, 133, 216
Disability types
    collaborative team and, 172
    curriculum development and, 41
    diversity and, 130
    inclusion and, 36–37, 219
    peer relationships and, 130, 216
Diversity. *See also* Child diversity; Cultural diversity
    curriculum development and, 40
    of developmental disabilities, 31–32
    disability levels and, 131–133
    disability types and, 130
    inclusion and, 38
    inclusion classroom and, 130–134
    individual needs of children and, 17

Diversity, *continued*
    linguistic diversity, 120–122, 165–166
    in parents, 160, 164–165
    preschool education needs and, 147–148
    special education teachers' expertise and, 136
    of teachers, 194, 230
Domain areas. *See* Academic programs
Dougherty, J. W., 136
Doyle, M., 36, 40, 41, 55, 133
Dyck, N., 68
Dyer, D. B., 107

EAHCA (Education for All Handicapped Children
    Act), 2–3, 175
Early intervention programs, 3, 13–14,
    146–149, 230
Ecological environment
    inclusion classroom as, 68, 79
    parents and family as, 163–164
Education, U. S. Department of, 11
Educational reform
    collaboration and, 67
    collaborative decision-making process and, 160
    communities' role in, 116
    early intervention and, 147, 149
    legislation and, 94, 106
    parents' role in, 108
    social problems and, 2, 147–149, 160, 161
    in special education, 18
    teachers' role in, 108
Education for All Handicapped Children Act
    (EAHCA), 2–3, 175
Edwards, P., 164, 165, 169
English as a second language (ESL), 165
Equipment, for inclusion classroom, 128–129
Ethnicity issues, 169. *See also* Cultural diversity
Evans, D., 36, 38, 39, 106, 133
Expectations
    of administrators, 86
    behavioral expectations, 93–94
    of children with disabilities, 80
    collaborative decision-making process and, 68, 69
    of communities, 117
    curriculum development and, 84
    goals and, 75
    inclusion classroom design and, 79
    outcome-based criteria and, 81, 83
    of parents, 84, 98, 164, 169–170, 178, 223

    teacher cooperation and, 71
    of teachers, 86

Family. *See* Parents
FAPE (Free and appropriate education), 3
Farlow, L., 93
Ferguson, J., 34, 128
First, P., 35–36, 129
Fletcher, T. V., 166
Flexibility
    collaboration competency and, 196–197, 202
    parent-teacher relationship and, 96
    professional collaboration and, 96, 205
    in teachers' schedules, 59, 79, 84, 88, 102,
        205, 208
Floating teachers, 59
Florida United Students with Exceptionalities
    (FUSE), 38–39
Foley, D. J., 74
Fox, J., 146
Fradd, S. H., 165, 169
Free and appropriate education (FAPE), 3
Friend, M., 67, 68, 75
Fuchs, D., 109
Fuchs, L. S., 109
FUSE (Florida United Students with
    Exceptionalities), 38–39

Gallagher, Vera, 218
Gallo, F., 167
Gender issues, 168–169
General education classroom. *See* Regular
    education classroom
General education teachers. *See* Regular education
    teachers
Gerrard, L., 133
Goals. *See also* Classroom goals
    of academic programs, 71, 123–125
    administrators and, 106
    collaborative team and, 68
    of communities, 106, 116, 223
    coteaching and, 78
    of inclusion classroom, 70, 74–77, 85
    outcome-based criteria and, 86
    socialization skills and, 75, 79–80, 93, 95
    teacher cooperation and, 74–77, 79
Group learning, and inclusion, 31
Guralnick, M. J., 217

Hambelton, D., 142
Hammittee, D. J., 79
Handicapped children. *See* Children with
  disabilities
Harris, D., 36, 106, 133
Hartshorne, T., 215
Hayden, L., 149
Hearing impairments, 36–37, 138–142, 173, 222
Hehir, T., 145
Heistad, D., 67
Helmstetter, E., 86
Henry Viscardi School, 26
Hines, R. A., 54, 59, 77, 79
Hinson, S., 79, 136
Hirschoren, A., 133
Hixson, P., 104, 105
Hoffman, L., 83
Holistic decisions, 209–210
Holland, Rachel, 15
Hollowood, T. M., 85
Home instruction, 26
Houldin, B., 142
Houston, D., 36, 106, 133
Hoyson, M., 149
Huefner, D. S., 106

IDEA (Individuals with Disabilities Education
  Act), 3–4, 11–12, 15, 147
Idol, L., 67, 68, 193
IEP. *See* Individualized Education Program (IEP)
Ihinger-Tallman, M., 168
Immigrants, 160, 164–165
Incidental learning, and disability level, 18
Inclusion. *See also* Child benefit of inclusion
  administrators and, 48
  assessment of, 30
  barriers to, 34, 153, 177, 214
  collaboration and, 68
  collaborative teams and, 161
  Committee on Special Education and, 66, 232
  communication skills and, 37–38
  concept of, 12–15
  consultant teacher services and, 29–30
  costs and, 35–36
  coteaching and, 39, 59, 70, 77–79
  curriculum development and, 40–45, 230
  deaf community and, 138–139
  definition of, 229

disability level and, 17–22, 30–34, 219
diversity and, 38
educational reform and, 94
historical review of, 10–12
individualized instruction and, 31, 136, 175
legislation supporting, 15
mainstreaming and, 4, 29, 31, 32–34
mild disabilities and, 13, 17, 38, 216, 219
mission statement for, 116
parent education/training and, 30, 89, 163,
  174, 176
parents of children with disabilities and, 19, 20,
  30, 102, 177
parents of children without disabilities and, 20,
  22, 97, 102, 176–177, 214
preschool children and, 13–14, 15, 146–149,
  216, 231–232
Public Law 101-476 and, 3
socialization skills and, 37
as social justice issue, 160, 173, 217–218,
  221–222, 223
teacher cooperation and, 38–39, 76
teacher in-service training for, 30, 48, 49–50,
  171, 197–198, 230
Inclusion classroom
  academic programs in, 6, 97, 98, 173
  administrators and, 88, 106–107, 172
  child diversity and, 130–134, 145, 170, 223
  collaborative decision-making process and,
    68–70, 134, 169
  curriculum development and, 81–84, 122–125
  design of, 34–36, 79–81, 97, 106–107,
    127–129, 134, 172
  diversity and, 130–134
  equipment for, 128–129
  goals of, 70, 74–77, 85
  parents and, 88–104, 174
  prototype for, 127–128
  ratio of children with disabilities in, 18, 131,
    216, 218, 219
  teachers and, 71–88
Individualized Education Program (IEP)
  for children with disabilities, 123–124
  for children without disabilities, 123–124
  classroom goals and, 37, 41, 75, 79, 92, 124
  curriculum development and, 83, 98, 122,
    126–127
  nonacademic activities and, 36

Individualized Education Program (IEP), *continued*
  parents and, 89, 122, 175, 212–213
  professional collaboration and, 206, 207
  Public Law 94-142 and, 2, 3
  samples of, 124, 125
  state requirements for, 3
  teacher cooperation and, 59, 79, 143
Individualized instruction
  autism and, 145–146
  for children with disabilities, 6–8, 27, 71, 79, 123
  for children without disabilities, 71, 79, 123
  curriculum development and, 40, 82, 83, 85
  inclusion and, 31, 136, 175
  inclusion classroom design and, 129
  resource room programs and, 28
  for severe disabilities, 6–7, 18
Individuals with Disabilities Education Act
      (IDEA), 3–4, 11–12, 15, 147
Innes, J., 139, 140, 141
Instructional mainstreaming, 32, 34, 35, 38, 58
Interdisciplinary networking, 59

Jacobs, S., 215
Jamieson, B., 149
Jayanthi, M., 75
Johnson, L. J., 79
Johnson, S., 146

Kauffman, J. M., 131
Kaufman, J., 123
Kelly, B., 74, 91
Kerns, G. M., 164
Kirchner, C., 173
Koch, W., 207
Koonce, D., 14, 37, 83
Kronberg, R., 36, 40, 41, 55, 133
Kurtines, W. M., 163

Laadt-Bruno, 89, 104
Lang, H., 141
Language therapy, 27, 143
Learning disabilities, 132
Least restrictive environment (LRE)
  autism and, 142–143
  court cases regarding, 15
  definition of, 6, 8–10, 18, 66, 131
  as goal, 75
  hearing impairments and, 138–139, 142

  individual needs of child and, 8, 9, 11, 18, 19, 131
  mainstreaming and, 6–10, 18
  Public Law 94-142 and, 2, 3, 60, 171
  regular education classroom as, 10, 18, 31,
      66, 131
  regular education initiative and, 11
  statement of, 54
Legislation. *See also specific laws*
  educational reform and, 94, 106
  inclusion and, 15
  parents and, 161, 176
  special education and, 2–4
Leister, C., 14, 37, 83, 88
Levine, Deborah, 196–198, 204–205
Levitan, S., 167
Lilley, 89
Linguistic diversity, 120–122, 165–166
LRE. *See* Least restrictive environment (LRE)
Lynch, E., 149

MacLachlan, P., 82
Mainstreaming
  decision making for, 44
  inclusion and, 4, 29, 31, 32–34
  individual needs of child and, 29
  least restrictive environment and, 6–10, 18
  normalization principle and, 4–6
  partial mainstreaming, 28–29, 45
  regular education initiative and, 11
  regular education teachers' attitudes toward, 50
  types of, 32–34, 35, 38, 58
Malen, B., 105
Mandato, Vincent, 185–187
Marston, D., 67
McCall, Debra, 198, 206
McCormick, C., 35–36, 129
McEvoy, M., 14, 146, 149
Meacham, M. L., 196
Melded families, 167–168
Mercury, M., 149
Mermelstein, Helene, 195–196, 203–204,
      210–211, 215
Mild disabilities
  definition of, 133
  inclusion and, 13, 17, 38, 216, 219
  least restrictive environment and, 10
  mainstreaming and, 32, 34
  placement options for, 7–8

regular education classroom and, 12
socialization skills and, 131–132
Miller, C. A., 107
Miranda, A. H., 167
Mission statement, 116, 134–135, 171
Model schools, 67, 68
Moderate disabilities, 17, 32, 34, 133
Montgomery, J., 220
Multicultural diversity. *See* Cultural diversity
Multidisciplinary team
assessments of, 44, 45–54
child benefit of inclusion and, 29, 40
Committee on Special Education as, 66
placement option assessment by, 7
Murray, J. N., 163
Music therapy, 27, 199–200, 212, 215–217

National Association of State Boards of
Education, 15
National Joint Committee on Learning Disabilities,
10, 21, 22, 31
Nevin, A., 67, 193
New York, 8–10, 175
New York State United Teachers, 137–138
Nisbet, S., 14, 37, 83
Nonacademic activities, 36, 45, 144
Nondisabled children. *See* Children without
disabilities
Normalization principle, 4–6, 138–139,
142–143, 222

Oberti, C., 88
Oberti, Rafael, 15
*Oberti vs. Board of Education of the Borough of
Clementon School District (New Jersey)*
(1992), 15
Occupational therapy, 26, 27, 218
Odom, S., 14, 146, 149
O'Sullivan, Lucy, 109–110
Outcome-based criteria, 40, 81, 83, 86

Palombaro, M. M., 85
Paolucci-Whitcomb, P., 67, 193
Parent education/training
collaboration and, 184
for inclusion, 30, 89, 163, 174, 176
teachers and, 48, 102
Parents. *See also* Parent education/training; Parents

of children with disabilities; Parents of
children without disabilities; Parent-teacher
relationship
administrators and, 104, 108
alternative family dynamics, 167–168
coequality and coparticipation of, 89–91
collaboration and, 66, 184, 210–214
collaborative decision-making process and, 89–91,
97, 108, 161–163, 170–171, 176, 185
collaborative team and, 88–104, 171–172,
176–177
Committee on Special Education and, 99, 175,
176, 211, 213
conflict resolution and, 182
curriculum development and, 98–99
decision-making process and, 49
diversity in, 160, 164–165
economic pressures of, 166–167
empowerment of, 175–176
ethnicity issues, 169
expectations of, 84, 98, 164, 169–170, 178, 223
family profile development, 177–178
gender issues and, 168–169
inclusion and, 13–14
inclusion classroom and, 88–104, 174, 217
Individualized Education Program and, 89, 122,
175, 212–213
linguistic differences in, 165–166
mainstreaming and, 9
mentors for, 173, 184
needs of, 170–177
parent meeting room, 183
perceptions of, 177, 178–181
perceptual report card and, 178–181
placement option decisions and, 7, 160–161
of preschool children, 147
Public Law 94-142 and, 2, 175
role of, 31–32, 87, 88–90, 160, 161–165, 179
school districts and, 27, 103
support groups for, 173
teacher cooperation and, 59
Parents of children with disabilities
advocacy of, 174–175
attitudes of, 50, 56–58, 92–93, 99, 100–101, 172
child benefit of inclusion and, 219
collaborative team and, 88–104
Committee on Special Education and, 29
emotional transition process of, 163–164, 213

Parents of children with disabilities, *continued*
    inclusion and, 19, 20, 30, 102, 177
    partial mainstreaming and, 28
    role of, 161
Parents of children without disabilities
    advocacy of, 175
    attitudes of, 172–173, 231
    inclusion and, 20, 22, 97, 102, 176–177, 214
    partial mainstreaming and, 28
    role of, 91, 97
Parent-teacher relationship
    collaboration and, 195, 203, 210–214
    collaborative decision-making process and,
        87–88, 91, 94–95, 107, 169–170, 184, 230
    collaborative team and, 95–96, 99, 102–103
    communication and, 161, 182, 183–184
    flexibility and, 96
    parent education/training and, 48, 102
    parent-teacher teaming, 95–96, 103, 160,
        169–170
Partial mainstreaming, 28–29, 45
Peck, C., 149, 217
Peck, C. A., 86
Peck, D., 11
Peckham, P. D., 196
Peer dyads, 38
Peer instruction
    curriculum development and, 83, 122, 125, 126
    diversity and, 31
    in inclusion classroom, 96, 134
    socialization skills and, 37
Peer relationships
    child benefit of inclusion and, 40, 216–217,
        218, 222
    classroom goals and, 92, 93, 94
    cultural diversity and, 165
    curriculum development and, 83, 122, 127
    disability levels and, 133, 216
    disability types and, 130, 216
    hearing impairments and, 140–142
    mainstreaming and, 34
    modification of, 96
    peer dyads, 38
    peer facilitation, 144–145, 231
    perceptions and expectations concerning, 80
    regular education teachers' attitudes toward, 136
    socialization skills and, 37
Peltier, G. L., 92

Perceptions
    of administrators, 86
    of children with disabilities, 80
    collaborative decision-making process and, 68, 69
    goals and, 75
    inclusion classroom design and, 79, 107
    of parents, 177, 178–181
    teacher cooperation and, 71
    of teachers, 86
Perceptual report card, 178–181
Personal growth, of teachers, 72–73
Peterson, K., 149
Physical mainstreaming, 32, 34, 35, 38, 58
Physical therapy, 26–27
Pianta, R. C., 166
Pierce, J., 34, 128
Pisarchick, S. E., 107
Placement options
    age versus stage of children with disabilities,
        133–134
    characteristics determining, 8, 9
    child benefit of inclusion and, 145, 214–224
    choice in, 14, 176, 223–224
    Committee on Special Education's decision-
        making process and, 6–7
    individual needs of child and, 8, 9, 18, 29,
        215, 221
    least restrictive environment and, 6, 9–10
    mainstreaming and, 4, 5, 28–29
    mild disabilities and, 7–8
    parents and, 7, 160–161
    regular education classroom as, 8, 9, 162
    severe disabilities and, 6–7
    transitional continuum of, 19
    types of, 26–30
Pogorzelski, G., 74, 91
Polansky, H. B., 17–18, 31, 133, 176
Polowe-Aldersley, S., 140, 145
Poverty, 166–167
Preschool children
    diversity of needs in, 147–148
    Education for All Handicapped Children Act
        and, 3
    inclusion and, 13–14, 15, 146–149, 216,
        231–232
    socialization skills and, 37
    special education programs for, 2, 3
Problem identification, 117–118

Professional collaboration, 96, 202–210
Program components, 4, 5
Psychological assessment, 53. *See also* School
    psychologists
Public funding, minimum education requirements
    for, 2, 3
Public Law 94-142 (1975)
  deaf community and, 139
  early intervention and, 146
  Education for All Handicapped Children Act
    and, 2–3
  least restrictive environment and, 2, 3, 60, 171
  parents and, 2, 175
  special education in school districts and, 27
Public Law 99-457 (1986), 2–3, 147
Public Law 101-476 (1991), 3
Pugach, M. C., 79
Pull-out services, 38, 39, 133, 221

Radziewicz, C., 68
Rasdall, J., 34, 128
Raver, S., 217
Reciprocity
  administrators and, 105–106
  parents and, 91
  teachers and, 71–74
Reeve, R. E., 166
Regional preschools, 147–149
Regular education classroom
  diversity and, 31–32, 223
  dynamics of, 39
  environment of, 34–36
  hearing impairments and, 141
  inclusion and, 13
  least restrictive environment definition and, 10,
    18, 31, 66, 131
  mainstreaming and, 4, 6
  mild disabilities and, 12
  as placement option, 8, 9, 162
  ratio of children with disabilities in, 18, 131,
    216, 218, 219
  severe disabilities and, 11, 17
  teacher cooperation and, 39
Regular education initiative (REI), 11, 17, 18, 19, 92
Regular education teachers. *See also* Teacher
    cooperation; Teacher in-service training
  academic curriculum goals and, 71
  attitudes of, 49–50, 72, 73, 135–136

behavior management skills concerns of, 40, 49
child benefit of inclusion, 214
children with disabilities and, 17
collaboration and, 66, 195, 196–198
collaborative team and, 134–135
hearing impairments and, 140
inclusion and, 13
instructional modification and, 29, 41, 143
parent collaboration and, 210
placement option decisions and, 7
professional collaboration of, 202–205, 207–208
role of, 31–32, 45, 48, 59, 136
REI (regular education initiative), 11, 17, 18,
  19, 92
Reich, C., 142
Reichart, D., 149
Report card, perceptual, 178–181
Resource room programs, 4, 5, 28, 39
Resources. *See also* Costs
  administrators and, 58, 84, 104–106
  collaborative team and, 172
  for educational reform, 116
  inclusion classroom and, 84, 104, 106
  minimum education requirements for public
    funding, 2, 3
  for school districts, 55, 58
Reynolds, M. C., 32
Richarz, S., 149
Rimland, B., 133
Roahrig, P. L., 105
Rock, E. E., 136
Rosenberg, M. S., 136
Ruskus, J., 217

Sacramento Unified School District v. Holland (U.S.
  Court of Appeals, 1994), 15
Safford, P. L., 107
Salend, S., 4
Salisbury, C. L., 85
Santos de Barona, M., 167
Sardo-Brown, D., 79, 136
Schein, E., 196
Schloss, C. N., 165
Schloss, P. J., 165
School districts
  inclusion and, 30–31, 48, 76
  inclusion classroom and, 85
  parents and, 27, 103

School districts, *continued*
  planning of, 55
  resources of, 55, 58
  special education teachers' role in, 55
  special education within, 27, 28–29
  teacher in-service training and, 50, 58–59
School for Language and Communication
    Development, 193
School psychologists, 195–196, 203–204,
    210–211, 215
Self-contained classrooms, 27–28
Self-esteem, 220
Severe disabilities
  child benefit of inclusion and, 220
  definition of, 8
  inclusion and, 17, 217
  individualized instruction for, 6–7, 18
  mainstreaming and, 32, 34
  placement options and, 133
  regular education placement and, 11, 17
  socialization skills and, 37
  special education schools and, 171
Shanker, A., 131
Shapiro, Maureen, 200–201, 207–208, 212–213,
    218–219
Shores, R., 146
Sign language, 37
Silliman, E., 83
Single-parent families, 167–168
Social interaction scale, 32, 33
Social isolation, 18, 75
Socialization skills
  autism and, 144–145
  child benefit of inclusion and, 40, 219
  class size and, 131
  curriculum development and, 83, 127
  disability level and, 18–19, 133
  as goal, 75, 79–80, 93, 95
  hearing impairments and, 140–142
  inclusion and, 37
  mild disabilities and, 131–132
  parents and, 92
  placement options and, 6–8, 28
  social interaction scale, 32, 33
Social justice
  collaborative decision-making process and, 139
  inclusion as issue of, 160, 173, 217–218,
    221–222, 223

Social mainstreaming, 32, 34, 35, 38, 58
Social problems, educational reform and, 2,
    147–149, 160, 161
Somoza, A., 138
Special education
  costs of, 2, 4, 17
  early intervention and, 146
  educational reform in, 18
  inclusion and, 15
  legislation on, 2–4
  in school districts, 27, 28–29
  social isolation and, 18, 75
  specialization of, 10
Special education schools, 26–27, 139, 171
Special education teachers. *See also* Teacher
    cooperation
  attitudes of, 51, 54–55, 71–73, 136–137
  child benefit of inclusion and, 217–219
  collaboration competency and, 199, 200–201
  collaborative team and, 134–135
  consultant teacher services and, 29, 143
  inclusion and, 13
  instructional modification and, 41, 143
  parent collaboration and, 212–213
  placement option decisions and, 7
  professional collaboration and, 206–207
  role of, 48, 54–55, 59, 70
  in self-contained classes, 27–28
  in special education schools, 26
Speech-language pathologists, 143, 201, 212,
    219–221
Stahlman, J. I., 40, 49, 50, 51, 72, 81, 107
Stainback, S., 130
Stainback, W., 130
State government, 2–3, 6
Sterling, Lauren, 199–200, 212, 215–217
Stinson, M., 141
Strain, P., 149
Support services, 4, 5, 26–27
Surveys, about inclusion, 192–193, 227–229
Svobodny, L., 149
Szapocznik, J., 163

Teacher cooperation
  child benefit of inclusion and, 218–219
  collaboration and, 136–137, 202–210
  consultant teacher services and, 29, 143
  diversity and, 134

goals and, 74–77, 79
inclusion and, 38–39, 76
Individualized Education Program and, 59, 79, 143
instructional differences and, 58–59
social mainstreaming and, 34
teacher in-service training for, 58–59, 79
team teaching and, 70–71, 77–79
Teacher in-service training
administrators and, 50, 84
for children with disabilities' needs, 16
for classroom management, 70
inclusion and, 30, 48, 49–50, 171, 197–198, 230
scheduling for, 205
for teacher cooperation, 58–59, 79
Teachers. *See also* Parent-teacher relationship; Regular education teachers; Special education teachers; Teacher in-service training
administrators and, 50, 59, 84–86, 108, 205, 208
attitudes of, 72, 119, 135–138
classroom goals and, 70, 75
coequality and coparticipation of, 70–71
collaborative decision-making process and, 71, 85, 87–88, 108, 230
collaborative team and, 70–88, 134–135, 171–172
consultant teacher services, 29–30
diversity of, 194, 230
goals of, 74–77
inclusion classroom design and, 79–81
perceptual report card and, 178–181
professional modifications of, 137–138
reciprocity of, 71–74
role of, 70–71, 90, 108
scheduling flexibility of, 59, 79, 84, 88, 102, 205, 208
team teaching and, 77–79

Teacher-to-pupil ratio, 27
Teaching assistants, in self-contained classes, 27
Team teaching
inclusion and, 36, 59, 70
professional collaboration and, 207, 209
teacher cooperation and, 70–71, 77–79
teacher in-service training and, 58
Thurston, L. P., 68
Tiegerman-Farber, E., 68, 97, 149, 173, 174, 176
Tingey, C., 146
Tipover effect, 18
To the Third Power (Koch), 207
Transdisciplinary curriculum, 71, 122, 123, 126–127, 136
Traumatic brain injury, 3
Traynor, Marion, 220–221
Turnbull, A. P., 164, 167
Turnbull, H. R., 167

Van Gunday, A. B., 80
Vocational programs, 27
Volk, D., 40, 49, 50, 51, 72, 81

Wandschneider, M., 149
Webb, N., 19, 30
Wehby, J., 146
Weismantel, M. J., 165
Westby, 89
Westby, C., 145
White, A. E., 73
White, L. L., 73
Wiese, M. R., 174, 184
Wikler, L., 168
Wilczenski, F. L., 79, 136
Wilkinson, L., 83

Yell, M., 91

BIOGRAPHY

DR. ELLENMORRIS TIEGERMAN-FARBER

Dr. Ellenmorris Tiegerman-Farber is an Associate Professor in the Department of Psychology at Adelphi University in Garden City. She teaches as an interdisciplinary academician. Dr. Tiegerman-Farber is a trained speech language pathologist who is also teacher-certified in special education. She has been in various academic institutions for the past 20 years, and has been on the faculty of Adelphi University since 1984. Dr. Tiegerman-Farber teaches courses in child development, disorders, language, and cognition; individual styles of learning; gifted and talented children; behavior and emotional disorders in children, and social psychology.

Dr. Ellenmorris Tiegerman-Farber is also the founder and executive director of a highly innovative school—the School for Language and Communication Development (SLCD)—located in North Bellmore, New York. SLCD is a non-profit educational institution providing services for infants, preschoolers, and school-age handicapped children by means of an inclusive educational model.

Dr. Tiegerman-Farber believes that teaching is a professional discipline, and as a result, the best teachers are mentored through challenging educational experiences. Clearly, modern American education is forging ahead with an inclusive model that integrates children with and without disabilities into general classrooms. Part of educational reform involves developing models that provide for interaction between parents and teachers. Dr. Tiegerman-Farber has advocated over the past 11 years for parents of children with disabilities as they proceed through various aspects of their children's programming.

Dr. Tiegerman-Farber has lectured extensively and spoken on radio discussing her ideas about children and families. She has written many books on early intervention and developmental disabilities in children: *Language Communication Disorders in Children* (1997), Macmillan Publishing; *Language and Communication Intervention in Preschool Children* (1995), Allyn & Bacon; and *Baby Signals* (1989), Walker Publishing. Dr. Tiegerman-Farber is married to Joseph Farber, an attorney, and they have six children.

246

DR. CHRISTINE RADZIEWICZ

Dr. Christine Radziewicz has worked in the areas of deaf education and speech language pathology for more than 20 years. She attended Gallaudet University on a federal grant and concentrated in the areas of audiology and deaf education. She taught in a school for the deaf and later trained sign language interpreters. In 1985 she received her doctoral degree in speech language pathology from Adelphi University and was a faculty member there for eight years. During that time she was a professor and clinical director of the Hy Weinberg Center for Communication Disorders. Many of her recent presentations, research, and publications have focused on the impact of hearing loss on the development of speech language and educational achievement. Most recently her research interest has concentrated on the realities of inclusion for children with and without special needs. In her present position of assistant director at the School for Language and Communication Development, she has developed an inclusion program for special-needs school-age students, kindergarten through third grade. This inclusive education program has incorporated a collaborative teaching approach, parental involvement, and curricula adaptations in order to overcome traditional barriers to inclusion.

Dr. Radziewicz has also authored several chapters in the texts *Language and Communication Intervention* (1994, 1995) Allyn and Bacon, and *Language and Communication Disorders in Children* (1993) Macmillan Publishing Co.